John H. Gerstner: The Early Writings

Volume 1

Compiled and Edited
by Don Kistler

Soli Deo Gloria Publications
. . . *for instruction in righteousness* . . .

Soli Deo Gloria
P.O. Box 451, Morgan, PA 15064
(412) 221-1901/FAX 221-1902

*

John H. Gerstner: The Early Writings is © 1997 by
Don Kistler and Soli Deo Gloria. All rights reserved.

*

ISBN 1-57358-072-4

*

The publisher acknowledges the kindness of Baker
Book House in allowing us to reprint several
chapters from *21 Programs for Young Adults.*

*

The article entitled "Who Is This Jesus?" was first
published in the February 1966 issue of MOODY
MONTHLY and is used by permission.

*

Thanks to Mary Semach for retyping
most of these articles.

Contents

Contents

Publisher's Preface

Soli Deo Gloria has had the great privilege of bringing into print many of John Gerstner's writings over the last ten years. We consider him one of the premier theologians of this century. R. C. Sproul, who studied under Dr. Gerstner during his seminary days, said that if he applied himself to study theology for the next 250 years, he wouldn't *begin* to know what Dr. Gerstner knew. That is high praise, indeed, from one of today's most prolific authors, and one of the finest communicators of biblical truth!

Many who are familiar with Dr. Gerstner know of him through his writings on Jonathan Edwards (*Jonathan Edwards, Evangelist; A Mini-Theology of Jonathan Edwards; The Rational Biblical Theology of Jonathan Edwards*), or from his more popular writings (*The ABC's of Assurance, Theology for Everyman, Repent or Perish, Reasons for Faith,* or *Reasons for Duty*). Perhaps they have read his collected primers (*Primitive Theology*) or his conversational systematic theology (*Theology in Dialogue*). They may have read his chapters on today's issues (*Justification by Faith ALONE* or *Sola Scriptura*). But before he was a nationally known author, he wrote regularly in Christian periodicals such as "*The United Presbyterian*," "*Christianity Today,*" and "*Moody Monthly*" while he pastored the Sunset Hills United Presbyterian Church in Pittsburgh, and before he was a professor of church history at Pittsburgh-Xenia Theological Seminary, where he mentored numerous men like Sproul and countless other pastors of churches around the country. In fact, it was largely at his prodding that Soli Deo Gloria went from being a part-time venture to a full-time publishing ministry.

The idea for this work came from the bibliography compiled by Jim Dennison at the back of the *festschrift* for Dr. Gerstner upon his retirement from Pittsburgh Seminary. The book was published by Presbyterian and Reformed Publishing Company in 1976 under the title *Soli Deo Gloria,* and it was that title that became the name which we chose for ourselves as publishers.

Most of these articles were taken (with only minor editorial changes for clarity) from the above-mentioned publications and others, some dating back to the mid-1940's. Some of these may seem outdated; we will leave that judgment to the individual. Some articles were later collected and published (*21 Programs for Young Adults*). Some have never been published before. Some of these chapters are transcriptions of lectures or written papers, so citations may be missing or faulty. Some are not dated at all; some we are able to date. Nonetheless, we are pleased to bring this collection into print, for, in our opinion, Dr. Gerstner is always worth reading!

There is sufficient material for a follow-up volume to this one. We pray the Lord of the harvest for more time and more typists to accomplish the task!

Here is Dr. Gestner the pastor as well as Dr. Gerstner the theologian. We love them both. Mrs. Gerstner quipped that she loved these writings most because they showed her husband as a pastor. She said, "I could understand him so much better then!"

Don Kistler
Soli Deo Gloria Publications

Dr. Gerstner's Testimony

I was born in 1914 of a mother who was a Methodist, in the sense that it was the Methodist church she stayed away from. My father was a Lutheran, in the sense that it was the Lutheran church from which he stayed away. Mother was casual, but father saw to it that I washed behind my ears. Neither had religious concerns for themselves or for me. Consequently they were surprised—pleasantly—when little Johnny got interested in the ministry.

That interest came through a girl I went with my senior year in high school. There was a minister in the United Presbyterian Church of North America (UPNA) I attended with her who, though he may have been thin in his theology, was quite determined to see that I, with ten dollars in my pocket got off to Westminster College (PA) in 1932. A high school teacher, the president of the college, and the Overlook Sanitarium (which gave me a job for room and board) helped me meet my expenses.

Before going to Westminster College I had one of the two most definitive experiences of my life. First, Philadelphia School of the Bible made me, for the first time, aware of the "crimson thread"—the theme of the blood of Christ—running through the Bible. The second definitive experience was when Professor John Orr, during my second year of college, said in a class that "regeneration precedes faith." When I came out of my Arminian trauma three weeks later, I was, and have remained to this day, a Reformed person, minister, and historical theologian.

I have reason to hope that the heavenly Father has had saving mercy on the otherwise hell-bound sinner before you.

Religion in the Home

Dr. W. R. Wilson, late Professor of Practical Theology at Pittsburgh-Xenia Theological Seminary, told a story illustrative of the fact that many people today are not very conversant with the techniques for religion in the home. He was preaching on one occasion concerning the necessity and value of the family altar. It seems that in the congregation was a carpenter who was much moved by the sermon. Indeed, he was moved into action and came afterward to Dr. Wilson to ask him how he should go about building a family altar: of what wood it should be made, the dimensions, and so forth! Of course, we do not need to have the ecclesiastical paraphernalia of the ritual, but we must make our homes places where God is honored and worshiped, where grace is said before meals, where family devotions are the central event of every day, where the Bible never needs dusting, and where the Sabbath day is the happiest of the week.

Religion Relates Family to God

Why is this so? Fundamentally, there must be religion in the home because it sets the individuals in that house in right relationship to God and to themselves. Observing religion in the home is the way of realizing the home's dependence upon, and responsibility to, the Lord. God has made His covenant of grace not merely with individuals, but has extended His concern to include, in a special manner, the children of believers. In Acts 2:39, for example, we read that the "promise is unto you, and to your children." In other words, the entire Christian family belongs to God in a unique sense.

1

Practical Religion Glorifies God

Strictly speaking, we should not think of the place of religion in the home—we should think of the place of the home in religion. It is religion that is the more comprehensive term. Home is a phase of religion; religion is not a phase of the home. It is our relationship to God that is all-important—our relationship to Him in every sphere of our activity: as individual responsible souls, as workers at our jobs, as citizens in our community, as members of our church, as parts of a family. There are duties and responsibilities appropriate to each of these spheres of living. Whatever you do, whether you eat, whether you drink, or whatsoever you do, do all to the glory of God. The question is always: How may we glorify God? The specific question is: How may we glorify God in our home? By practicing religion in the home we enable it to achieve its chief end, to glorify God and enjoy Him forever.

But Religion Does Not Ignore the Family

If we remember that the home is a phase of the kingdom of God, we shall not be tempted to neglect it in the interests of something else, not even the church. Pearl Buck has written a biography of her godly father in which she testifies that God had him, but infers that his family did not. It was said that he did not know the names of all the members of his family. Many who knew him feel that Mrs. Buck has not been fair to her father in her criticism. Whether this particular charge is or is not fair, it is undoubtedly true that it may be said of some people that God had them, but their family did not. This could not have happened if the message of the family altar had been remembered; the family itself is a part of God's kingdom.

Religion Rightens Family Relationships

Second, and we shall stress this point most because we feel it is most commonly neglected, religion in the home sets the members in proper relation to each other. This accomplishment is as essential as it is rare. We have seen many houses, scarcely any two of which were alike in structure. We never yet have seen any that has placed the roof in the basement or the cellar where the ceiling belongs. But the occupants of many sensibly arranged houses do stand in just such an absurd pattern. The head of the house, the father, is at the bottom, and the members, the children, at the top. Many a wife, whose scriptural role is to be subordinate in authority to her husband and superior in authority to her children, actually is the puppet of her offspring and the master of her lord. There are many other important things about a house besides the fundamental relationship of its parts. But we doubt the feasibility of debating the color of the walls, the number of rooms, or the plan of the garden, while the roof is still in the basement and the cellar where the ceiling belongs.

Father Is Head of the Home

The man's headship in the home must be re-established. The Word of God is explicit on this subject. Prevalence in our time of domestic administrations, based on Gallup polls conducted at family conferences, should not obscure the fact that such methods are wrong—indeed, sinful—except as a wise father may ask for them. There must be authority in the home if there is to be unity. And that authority is not the consensus of family opinion, but the traditional head of the house. Too long has this "head-of-the-house idea" been the butt of parlor jokes. It is a command as imperative as that we love God with all our heart, soul, mind, and strength. Husbands in a Christian family must fit themselves to lead, and wives must insist that they do lead. Most wives will do so, we confidently believe, when this duty is made clear to them.

Stupid Fathers "Left to Heaven"
    Speaking to a group of very alert young adults, I discussed this very point with some of the young ladies present, most of whom gave hearty endorsement to what has been said. They wondered about one thing: What was an intelligent wife to do with a stupid husband at the helm of the home? I answered that such a wife should try to influence her husband, but not coerce him. A wise husband will not merely accept the counsel of a good wife, but will seek it. But the young adults retorted, "What if he is not a wise husband, as is the case in point?" My answer was: "Leave him to heaven." That, they admitted, sounded reasonable, but would, they felt, prove difficult when it was so tempting to lay hands on him here and now!

Father's Authority Recognized
    If religion prevails in the home, parents will exercise, and be gladly yielded, authority over their children. Granted that there are "problem parents"; these are still sufficiently rare, in comparison to problem children, to permit the phrase to be striking rather than trite. Children in a Christian household will obey their parents in the Lord (and parents will not provoke their children to wrath). If a child thinks that he knows better than his father, let Dr. A. T. Robertson remind him that the one child in the history of the world who undoubtedly knew more than His parents was the most obedient Son who ever graced a home.

Christ's Recognition of Home Life
    Indeed, what more singular tribute is there to the worth of

the godly home than what our Lord gave by simply living in one! Thirty years! That is the price at which Christ valued home! And over all the earth, through all time, He pleads for all men and women that they should have what He declared to be so essential a background of quiet peace, in which growth of body, mind, and spirit can put forth its own powers; a background of honor, of affection, or personal tenderness such as can be found nowhere else in all the wide world but in the home.

What is the Basis for a Successful Marriage?

One of the most important prerequisites of a happy marriage is that you and your mate come from a happy home. In other words, if you wish to be successful in marriage, begin by being born from a successful marriage! A wise selection of your parents is the best guarantee of a wise selection of a mate. There have been a great many sociological tests run to determine the qualities that make for success or failure in marriage. Many different ones are reported by the various investigators. On one success factor, however, there is practical unanimity: the parents' marital happiness makes for the children's marital happiness. Burgess and Cottrell (a study of more than 500 couples), Terman (a study of 792 couples), Popenoe (a study of 2000 couples), and many others agree emphatically on this point.

Basic Principle: From Happy Home to Happy Home
Burgess and Cottrell, in *Predicting Success or Failure in Marriage*, have shown that where husbands have had constant conflict with their mothers only 14% had happy marriages. Where there was no conflict, 49% were happily married. Where the husband was happily related to his father he made a happy adjustment to his wife in 54% of the cases; an unhappy adjustment in 25% of the cases. Where the husband was in conflict with his father his own adjustment to his wife was poor in 43% of the cases and good in only 20%.

As the very percentages would suggest, this principle (from happy home to happy home) is not hard and fast. Some marriages of children from happy families are unfortunately unhappy. Some marriages of children from unhappy homes are fortunately happy. By and large, however, there is a solemn responsibility placed on every mother and father to ensure their children's happiness by realizing their own.

It should also be noted that the principle (from happy home to happy home) does not rest all the responsibility on the parents alone. Happy or unhappy homes may be the effect of the children as well as of the parents. Let children obey their parents in the Lord, and in everything about the home display their discipleship, and any home will be happier.

With these qualifications in mind, this principle remains a basic foundation of successful marriage: from happy home to happy home. If we have had a good home, we should be deeply grateful to God. If we have not had one, we should thank God for being aware of our liability, and strive, by His grace, to provide one for our children.

Second, there is the matter of selecting your mate. This allows for personal liberty in exercising a free choice. Unfortunately, of marriages contracted by those under twenty, we suppose that most (not all) of them are completely innocent of any deliberate premeditation or forethought. Judge Lindsay has advocated companionate marriage precisely because many young people have given less thought to their choice of mate than to the purchase of a hat. While we must renounce Lindsay's cure of the social disease of incompatibility, we should agree with his diagnosis of its cause.

Intelligent Choice of Mate

Love at first sight, together with its wartime variation, love at first flight, remains the cardinal domestic heresy. It probably has done as much to wreck homes as alcohol and gambling combined. No one is less likely to make a happy marriage than an adolescent in the spring. We know that at that time of year the sap begins to flow. So do the slush, gush, and mush. When "that feeling" comes over a person, let him (it usually is a he) write poetry, pick daffodils, study his lessons, or play baseball. But let him not go shopping for a bride.

Of course those for whom these last words are especially designed will not be reading them. Still, those of you who do read them must convey the message somehow. Tell them that if they think of marriage before the age of twenty, they should discipline themselves to give it a little more consideration than they will give to their next sundae, which they may be thinking about while you tell them this. Ask them to do all this for the happiness of the one they fancy they love. If they cannot listen, then give them your blessing to help them overcome the handicap under which they unwittingly begin.

Young people must be warned about the "romantic" marriage, and especially during wartime. A columnist once wrote that after the military war is over the domestic war will begin. Pastors, teachers, friends, but especially parents, must prevent this by educating young people to exercise this modern privilege of intelligently choosing a mate.

If youth asks, "What should we look for in a mate?" your answer should be: If you are selecting a wife, the thing to look for is Christian character; if it is a husband, the thing to look for is Christian character.

Higher Education Helpful

There are other prerequisites for successful marriage than those already discussed. We have time merely to mention some of these before commenting on the fundamental characteristic. A high level of formal education has been shown to be a decided domestic asset. (In other words, although Mary was a good wife to Benjamin Disraeli, modern studies reveal that she would have been even better if she had known which came first, the Roman or the Greek Empire). Also, some sex instruction during childhood and adolescence by parents or other responsible persons is productive of a wholesome attitude toward marriage. This, in turn, makes for happiness in marriage itself.

The greatest factor in a successful marriage remains yet to be stated. Where the parents are the head of the children, and the husband is the head of the wife, and Christ is the head of the husband, that marriage is inevitably successful. That home in which each member is related to the other according to the will of God, and all are subject to the Savior, is not merely successful—it is blessed.

This returns us to our first principle: a happy home produces a happy home. It is God who produces the original happy home and preserves and enhances the happiness of all others.

Religious Life Most Assuring

There is a very definite statistical correlation between religious life and success in marriage. For example, it has been shown that those who have had a religious wedding are more likely to have a successful marriage than those who have not. In one study it was observed that of those married by a clergyman, 46% were very happy, as against 19% who were married by other than a clergyman. Again, of those who went to Sunday school only until about ten years of age, 20% were later happily married as against 53% of those who attended up to twenty-five years of age. On the other hand, of the first group 47% were unhappily married as against 15% of the latter group. Other experiments have revealed that of those who did not attend church at all, 35% were very happy in their marriage as against 50% of those who did attend regularly. Of the first group 37% were unhappily married; 22% of the other. Figures lie sometimes; statistics are never completely reliable, and data of this sort are necessarily qualified, but certainly this is clearly proven: God in the home makes for happiness in the home. We preachers are tempted to say to the sociologists, "We told you so."

Marriage, true marriage, should be a vital phase of the kingdom of God. It is a sphere in which two souls function as one, epitomizing on earth that unity which characterizes the celestial harmony of the three persons who inhabit eternity. It is to be contracted intelligently, adhered to faithfully, and enjoyed richly. If its sacred nature is understood, its divine laws respected, and its lofty purpose realized, it will be, as it was meant to be, at once a preparation for, and a preview of, heaven.

If the rules for success in marriage were to be reduced to a formula, none better could be offered than the inspired words of the great apostle:

"Wives, submit yourselves unto your own husbands, as unto the Lord" (Ephesians 5:22).

"Husbands, love your wives, even as Christ also loved the church, and gave Himself for it" (Ephesians 5:25).

How to Get Along with People

The Bible teaches us: "If it be possible, as much as lieth in you, live peaceably with all men" (Romans 12:18). These words are not meant to be taken this way: "As much as *in* you lieth, live peaceably with all men." Rather, they should be construed thus: "As much as lieth in *you*, live peaceably with all men." They are to teach, insofar as we Christians are concerned, that there should be no cause for friction. We should get along with people, and, if we do not, it must not be our fault.

It is implied in this text that a peaceable situation may not prevail, even though we provide no occasion for a lack of harmony. Even our Lord's life could scarcely be considered peaceable. Although the Son of Peace Himself gave no just cause for criticism and hostility, these did at last lead Him to a cross, the punishment for criminal disturbers of the peace.

Ten Helpful Maxims

Our concern now is not with this negative aspect of the situation, but with a discussion of our own duty to live peaceably with all men as much as lieth in us. A merely suggestive answer to the problem (how to get along with people) we present in the form of a number of maxims.

1. Thou shalt not magnify the faults of others and all the while minimize thine own. Must your brother's sin always appear as a beam (a saw-log) and your own as a moat (a splinter)? If it is impossible for you to find any excuse whatsoever for your neighbor's minor defect, but, at the same time, you are capable

11

of discovering explanations for your own most grievous vices, you will not get along with people. A little boy once asked his mother, "Mother, why is it that whenever you do anything wrong it is because you are nervous, but if I do something wrong it is because I am naughty?" If it is possible, discover the nervous causes of your friend's misdemeanors and some naughtiness behind your own.

2. *Thou shalt not minimize the virtues of others and magnify thine own.* Have you ever had occasion to return an article to a store because, you say, it was not what you had ordered, or the price was not right, and so forth? Have you had the salesperson expose your "mistake" mercilessly and vindicate himself completely? How did you feel toward him? You need not answer that question.

We are reminded of one girl who illustrates a better way of dealing with customers. She was exceptionally dull, but she was placed in a responsible place in the complaint department of a store.

The manager was criticized for putting such an incapable person at such a trying task. He explained: "She is the most successful person we have ever had at that job. When people come in with complaints, she does not find fault with them. She sympathizes with them. She cannot understand how the store could ever have made such a mistake, and cannot get over how good the customer is about the entire matter. Before it is all over, the complainer begins to feel ashamed of himself and the complaint is withdrawn." This girl got along with people because she magnified their rights and minimized her own.

3. *Thou shalt not insinuate sordid motives to another's acts.* Men's acts should be viewed in the best possible light. The benefit of the doubt should always be given. It is a sound reminder that by their fruits, and not by their roots, you shall know them.

4. *Thou shalt not judge by appearances.* Before you proceed to
an unfair criticism that will help you to lose friends and influence people the wrong way, you should recall the celebrated
case of one who did just that—the "owleologist" in the barbershop presented in the amusing poem by James Thomas Fields
entitled "The Owl Critic." The man, feeling himself an expert in
the stuffing of owls, began to find all sorts of fault with the owl
in the barbershop. The head was too flat, the neck jammed
down, an owl could never roost in that position, the toe should
not turn out, and so forth.

> Just then with a wink and a sly normal lurch,
> The owl, very gravely, got down from his perch,
> Walked round, and regarded his faultfinding critic,
> (Who thought he was stuffed) with a glance analytic,
> And then fairly hooted,
> "I'm an owl: you're another. Sir Critic, Good day!"

5. *Thou shalt not lose a chance to laugh.* Christian people
have many occasions to condemn; it therefore becomes imperative for them that they should make the most of every opportunity to smile and be pleased. Papa, of *Papa Was a Preacher*
fame, was a strict disciplinarian, and a fighting angel in his
home and out, but he got along with people because, as his
daughter said in her book about him,

> Fierce for the right, he bore his part
> In strife with many a valiant foe;
> But laughter winged his polished dart,
> And kindness every blow.

6. *Thou shalt not indulge personal antipathies.* We quote
these relevant words:

> I do not like thee Dr. Fell,
> The reason why I cannot tell.
> But this one thing I know full well,
> I do not like thee Dr. Fell.

Need we remark that the speaker of these words did not get along with Dr. Fell?

7. *Thou shalt not try to "get even."* The odds are against it. It does not settle matters, but disturbs them further and makes peace elude us. Patrick was furious with a certain friend of his who had the bothersome habit of thumping his friends on the chest in a playful sort of way. Patrick had had about enough of it, and so he put a firecracker in his chest and said to a friend, "The next time Mike thumps me on the chest he will explode this firecracker, and will he be sorry!"

8. *Thou shalt not gossip.* People may like to hear what you are saying, but they will not like you for saying it. Bear in mind the classic definition of gossip: "The low form of the communion of saints."

9. *Thou shalt not hold a grudge.* Grudges are fatal, as the following anecdote will show you. Sandy's wife was dying. She said to her husband, "Sandy, I'm dying, and I want to ask you one last favor. Will you please let Aunt Jennie—I know you don't like her and aren't speaking to her—but will you let her ride with you to the funeral? This is my dying wish." Sandy was moved. He replied, "I'll do it for you, Margaret. But it will ruin my day."

10. *Thou shalt not expect to get along with all of the people all of the time.* One very congenial gentleman had the policy of agreeing with everyone all of the time. When Mr. Black said one thing, he agreed with him. And when Mr. White said the exact opposite, he agreed with him. And when Mr. Gray pointed out the inconsistency of agreeing with these opposite opinions, he

agreed with Mr. Gray also. But, strangely enough, this man did not get along with any of them. Let us face the fact that we shall not be able to live peaceably with all men. We must live peaceably, as much as in us lieth, and these simple maxims should lead us a way in that direction.

The Duty to Relax

An ancient legend tells of the apostle John hunting in the fields. When an ardent Christian friend saw him, he rather rebuked the Apostle for wasting his time in such frivolous activity. The kindly John then took the bow that he had in his hand and, pointing to it, said, "Do you see how taut this bow string is? That is because it is in use and must be ready. But when it is not in use it is not kept taut; rather, the tension is removed so that the power of the bow will be preserved. So it is with the Christian. He cannot always be kept taut; he must learn to relax if he would do his work well."

We must recognize that relaxation is a duty. Sometimes to do nothing is the one thing we must do. Our work is to rest; our duty, to be free of duty; our task, to end all tasks; and our only serious responsibility, to be free of all responsibility.

The Purpose of Vacations

Among this writer's friends is a very devoted Christian girl. She loves Christ and used to serve Him earnestly—too earnestly. Her driving conscience allowed her no respite from duty, no moments of blessed ease. An inner whip lacerated her tender soul at the first thought of relaxing her eternal vigilance. It so happened that this girl married a minister who, while not more conscientious than his wife—that would be impossible— was more wisely so. Gradually he has preached to her the "gospel of relaxation." But, he tells us, it was no easy thing to change his wife's outlook. Though now they laugh together about it all as a thing of the past, there were times when the going was grim.

The husband tells an amusing incident in the "deconscientization" of his wife. They were about to set out on their vacation after a year of strenuous pastoral effort. He was anticipating the rest eagerly. Before they left the house they had family devotions, and, much to the amazement of the young minister, he was hearing his wife ask God to make the vacation a very useful and profitable one. He stopped the prayer right there and said, "Ruth, this vacation is not supposed to be useful! It is to be playful. Nor is it going to be profitable in the sense you mean: we are going to waste our time. Now don't go praying any more for a 'useful and profitable' vacation, because neither I nor God will listen to you."

The Need for Change

We all need some rest; that is axiomatic. How much rest we need varies with our natures and the nature of our work. Sameness in any job has been demonstrated to be tiring. Poffenberger tested students doing the monotonous work of constant addition and some other students working on intelligence tests with their assortment of mental tasks. The first group of students declined in efficiency 20% while during the same period the latter group increased in efficiency 20%. Miles and Skilbeck increased the work product of a group 14% by giving two 15-minute periods of a different type of job.

However, the change, if too radical, becomes fatiguing. When, for example, a person must alternate between addition and subtraction, conflicting assignments, there is a decline in efficiency.

Of course, unfamiliarity with a task can make it exhausting. It has been observed that a boy, when he first begins to write, does so with his whole body, cocking his head, crossing his legs and uncrossing them, twisting his torso, screwing up his face. At the end of the first line he has done the equivalent of a day's work!

Value of Periodic Relaxation

Granted that some leisure time is necessary (the amount to be determined by the individual in the light of the aforementioned principles), how can it be put to best advantage? Almost every person has his own method. Jesse Jones, of whom we have read so much, is able to work 14 hours a day because of periodic relaxation.

Galloway, president of the Baltimore and Ohio railroad, is able to keep going at a hard pace because each hour he takes time to go over his collection of toy elephants. Edison's amazing capacity for work would have been impossible were it not that just about whenever and wherever he became sleepy he slept, if only for a brief interval.

Kant, the greatest modern philosopher, at exactly three o'clock each afternoon, walked up and down his street eight times, rain or shine. For indoor sport he devised a unique game: in order to ensure himself adequate exercise he would place his handkerchief at the opposite corner of his room from his study desk so that whenever he needed to blow his nose, a walk across the room and back would be rendered inevitable! Nurmi, famous distance runner, actually rested while he ran. He kept holding himself back, seeing to it that he did not run faster than a certain pace in order not to tire himself too soon.

In contrast to these more or less casual and amateurish techniques for resting, Jacobson has developed a very elaborate science for the relaxation of the muscles that requires, for example, six days to relax one leg.

Help for Frayed Nerves

Music has charms to mend frayed nerves. David's playing on the harp was medicine for the soul of Saul. In more modern times, Kirby has found that pure rest reduced the tonicity of the system somewhat and that something mildly stimulating, such as music, had a better effect on those engaged in more or less mental work.

Education, generally, is a good morale builder. Not only does a leisure-time study refresh greatly, but it also has the interesting by-product of making our major employment itself more pleasant and efficient. The uneducated working woman's efficiency in her employment tends to reach its peak when she is thirty, while the educated woman continues progressing long after that age. The life span of unskilled male workers in mills is shorter than that of skilled workers after forty years of age. Education helps, both off and on the job.

Finest Rest Is Spiritual

In the last analysis, the finest rest is spiritual. Without this, all other rest is futile. "Man's heart is restless until it finds its rest in Thee." Augustine knew that no amount of physical well-being or mental freshness could satisfy a man whose inner being was tossed to and fro with doubts and fears. How pertinent his advice is for our age, which is willing to spend six days relaxing a limb and hardly six minutes providing rest for the spirit. What does it profit a man if he limbers up his whole body and loses his peace of mind? "Come unto Me," the Master said, "and I will give you rest . . . Learn of Me, for I am meek and lowly in heart; and ye shall find rest unto your souls" (Matthew 11:28–29).

The Cost of Discipleship

We will use a simple acrostic of the word "cost" to indicate the cost which Christ requires of those who would come after Him. "C" represents "cut out your dearest temptations"; "O" is "offer up yourself as a sacrifice"; "S" is "sell all that you have"; and "T" is "totally commit yourself to Christ."

The "C" in Cost

"C" represents "cut out your dearest temptations." Our Lord said, "If thy right hand offend thee, cut it off and cast it from thee" (Matthew 5:30). The word "offend" means "is an obstacle to." Anything that is an obstacle to a person is to be removed. It need not be a vice at all. It may be a very legitimate thing. It may cause another person no trouble at all. But if it is an obstacle to you, no matter how permissible it may be in and of itself, you are to remove it. Remove it, no matter how much it hurts to do so.

Cutting off one's hand or plucking out one's eye is not thought of as anything but an excruciating operation. It is painful in itself, and the effects of it are a distinct handicap for life. All of this is no doubt intended by Christ to impress the disciple with the radical character of His demands. No matter how much a part of you a thing may have become, you are to remove it. Remove it regardless of the consequences. These consequences, however severe, will be temporal. A failure to remove this offense will have consequences that even eternity cannot exhaust. "It is profitable for thee that one of thy members should perish, and not that thy whole body should be cast into hell" (Matthew 5:30).

20

Consider the rich young ruler who came to Christ inquiring about eternal life (Luke 18:18–27). Ultimately, he went away sorrowing because he was not willing to part with his wealth, even to save his own soul. His wealth had become an offense to him. That wealth was legitimate in itself. It may even have been an indication of his diligence, competence, and frugality. It was certainly a sign of divine graciousness to this man. But there was no doubt in Jesus' mind that the young ruler's wealth had become a stumbling block to him. It stood squarely in the way of what the young man seemed to sense was of greatest importance, eternal life. Innocent as this wealth was in itself, it was fatal for him unless he would "cut it off" or "pluck it out." But the young ruler chose to go whole into hell rather than maimed through life.

The "O" in Cost

"O" is "offer yourself as a sacrifice." The Master was a "Man of sorrows and acquainted with grief." All His followers are required to be, in their own degree, the same. "Blessed are they that mourn, for they shall be comforted" (Matthew 5:4). But none will be comforted *by* Christ who do not suffer *for* Christ. All the other griefs of men come upon them more or less inadvertently, and not as matters of choice. But the suffering occasioned by following Christ is a consequence only of the choice to follow Him.

Christ did make it very plain that, if any man came after Him, there would be a cross for him to carry. It was a cross that would not come upon him unless he came after Christ. But if he came after Him, it was certain to come upon him. "The world hates Me," Jesus told His disciples, "and it will hate you also." The servant cannot be greater than his master. "In the world," He said, "ye shall have tribulation" (John 16:33). And

His greatest apostle, Paul, who suffered more for Christ's sake than any other, echoed the same words: "All that will live godly in Christ Jesus shall suffer persecution" (2 Timothy 3:12).

It is interesting that Christ spoke most of the sufferings of His disciples just before He was to leave them. Knowing that He would no longer be visibly present with them to console and encourage them, He promised them another Comforter who would be with them always. The Holy Spirit would strengthen them and enable them to endure hardness as good soldiers of Christ. He wanted them to be prepared for what they would be called to suffer for His sake, but at the same time He assured them that they would be given grace to endure these sufferings.

The "S" in Cost

"S" stands for "sell all that you have." Every Christian is required in his heart to "sell" all that he has. That is, no one may have anything that he dares to call exclusively his own. For all things are God's and nothing is ours. Everyone must recognize this fact and act accordingly. God does not require everyone, or even very many, actually to sell everything. But He does require everyone to recognize that he has nothing except that which he has received as a trust from God.

No man can be Christ's disciple who does not acknowledge that his money is not his own to do with as he pleases, but that it is entirely God's to do with as God pleases. Thus God has always required that a certain amount of our income, such as the tithe, be set aside for His uses. This does not mean that only a tenth belongs to Him; but by the giving of a tenth we indicate that everything we have belongs to God. When we have paid our income tax, we are thereby freed of obligation to the government. But when we have given our tithe, we thereby say that to God belongs all the rest and that we must use it in His service as faithful stewards.

In return for relinquishing the small hold we have on earthly things, Christ wants us to inherit the whole earth. "Blessed are the meek, for they shall inherit the earth" (Matthew 5:5). Not only has Christ given us all things needful for this life, but He has also promised us the world to come. All this is ours, and heaven too. "For whosoever hath, to him shall be given . . . but whosoever hath not, from him shall be taken away even that which he hath" (Matthew 13:12). But the best of all is not that we have this world and the next, but that we have God Himself. To have this world and not God would be to have nothing. To have God and nothing would be to have everything. As the medieval saint said, "He who has God and everything has no more than he who has God and nothing more." God is everything.

The "T" in Cost

"T" stands for "totally commit yourself to Christ." The most central theological idea preached by Christ was that of the kingdom of God. A vast literature has been produced in modern times concerning this rich teaching of Christ about the kingdom. There are, of course, some differences in this literature, but all agree that this much is included in the doctrine: The kingdom of God is a place where God rules supremely over the wills of men who are willingly submitted to Him. The idea of sovereignty is central. One who enters the kingdom of Christ abandons all personal rights. He never *had* any, of course. But wicked men are not willing that God should rule over them; they think that they have such rights. Those who enter the kingdom of God acknowledge that they do not.

Absolute obedience is the minimum requirement of the

kingdom of heaven. But strangely enough, no man comes into his own until he ceases to *be* his own. No man comes to himself until he becomes the slave of Christ. And so we find that in return for submission to Christ He promises freedom from the bondage of sin. "He that committeth sin is the bondservant of sin," said Paul. But John 8:36 says, "But if the Son shall make you free, you shall be free indeed." His is a burden, to be sure, but His burden is light. He imposes a yoke, indeed, but His yoke is easy. We must teach and obey all that He has commanded us, but He promises that He will be with us to the end of the age as we do so.

The Two Roads

Yes, there are two roads. One is broad and requires no change in us. It has room for all our sins and prejudices and slothfulness and lust. The other is narrow and exacting; it requires that we should:

Cut out our dearest temptations,
Offer ourselves as a sacrifice,
Sell all that we have, and
Totally commit ourselves to the absolute
        sovereignty of Christ.

But the broad road which the majority takes leads to destruction in the end, and brings no joy along the way. Strangely enough, the narrow road not only leads to life, but all who travel it find that Christ's promises are true and that His Word is life indeed. Not only is the outcome happy, but the path itself, with all its exactions and denials, is a glory road.

Is it True That Right and Justice Will Triumph in the End?

"There's a divinity that shapes our ends, roughhew them how we will." That is Shakespeare's version. A modern wit has given a slight but significant rearrangement: "There's a divinity that shapes our ends rough, hew them how we will."

The latter lines are indicative of a prevalent contemporary attitude towards history. Many think that the universe and purpose are strangers. Blind forces mold the fates of men with relentless certainty. Geography and economics, rather than free men and moral principles, explain the mystery of life, it is thought. Augustine in his *City of God* saw the panorama of events as ever tending to the establishment of the kingdom of God in spite of the formidable opposition of the prince of this world. But, where Augustine could see the operation of God or devil, Ratzel and Semple would find the operations of mountain ranges and plains, rivers and seas, tillable soil and desert.

Where man loses faith in God and providence, he invariably loses his grip on himself. When God's providence is denied, man's freedom usually suffers. So it happens that in an age greatly affected by the "bread and butter" interpretation of history, Spengler steps forth and draws the conclusion, in his *Decline of the West,* that man's free agency is an illusion. To this influential modern historian, history is not the product of free men, but men are the products of impersonal forces that make for growth and decay. Toynbee, however, has reacted against this in favor of "faith."

God's Sovereignty Absolute

Of all Christian groups, Calvinists have been most insistent on finding God in history. God's providence, we teach, extends over all His works, including the free activities of men. We are known particularly for the doctrine of the absolute sovereignty of God. But we have maintained alongside this doctrine, with equal emphasis, the complete and untrammeled freedom of men. Our critics have said that we could not believe in the providence of God and yet champion human freedom. A doctrine of divine sovereignty such as ours, they contend, would reduce man to a stock and a block. As an automaton, he would mechanically obey and fatalistically accept what came.

While they were saying this, the Calvinists were not only defending their freedom by argument, but were acting in the freest manner possible. Nowhere in the history of human affairs do we see men withstanding tyrants with greater independence and courage than our forebears did in France, in Holland, and in Scotland. These men said that they were free agents and, while some opposing theologians may have argued that they could not be, no royal monarch doubted it for a moment. Dean Inge once said that Luther was the cause of the Second World War because he taught that the church should be subject to the state. Inge has been criticized severely for saying that. But if he had said the same of the Calvinists (that they had sown the seeds of servility and bondage), he would not have been criticized—he would have been laughed out of court.

Man's Free Choice Possible

Strong insistence on divine sovereignty has made men free. Today we are getting a fresh demonstration of the reverse truth: denial of divine providence saps human freedom. Where

Ratzel and Allen have taught that there is no God in history, Spengler and Fisher have taught that there is no free agency. To sum up: where the universe is conceived as the product of blind chance, man has no chance; where there is no chance (but providence), man has every chance. To maintain that God directs the course of history is to answer in the affirmative our question, "Is it true that right and justice will win in the end?" Inasmuch as the Champion of right and justice reigns supreme, we must certainly believe that what He champions will prevail.

Nevertheless, right and justice will not win *until* the end. After His second coming Jesus Christ will judge the nations; then, and only then, will wrong be on the scaffold and truth on the throne. In the meantime, God gives us the responsibility and the opportunity voluntarily to bring about a reign of perfect justice which He Himself will establish ultimately by His own power.

Christ's Church Will Triumph

In the present age there is sufficient administration of justice to indicate its ultimate triumph, but not enough to establish it now. In spite of much opposition and many setbacks, there is more justice in Christian and Christ-influenced lands today than ever before. Here, as in other regards, the gates of hell are proved unable to prevail or stand against the church of Jesus Christ. While we bend every effort to make right and justice prevail here and now, we may feel the added stimulus of knowing that this cause will certainly triumph in the end, when He who bore the cross displays His scepter.

Religious Illiteracy

There are two outstanding and painfully obvious reasons why a return to a more faithful teaching ministry is imperative for the church. First, religious illiteracy among our professing Christians is staggering. Second, the inevitable result of religious illiteracy, namely religious indifference, is manifest in the same proportions.

Religious illiteracy is a sad fact, a dangerous fact, but a fact. Dr. Wilbur Smith, in his *Therefore, Stand*, relates these two typical instances:

> Some years ago the distinguished Professor Kittridge of Harvard was hearing a class in Macbeth, and during the class a student reading aloud came upon the word Golgotha. The professor asked his student what Golgotha meant, to which he replied, "I don't know, in fact, I never heard the word before." "Do you know what Calvary means?" "I have never heard the word." As may easily be believed by those who knew Kittridge, the learned and frequently sarcastic professor simply bowed his head and said, "The class is dismissed."

> A certain individual went to a post office in the city where I am writing, to mail a small package to a soldier, and the one weighing the package asked what was in the package. She replied, "A New Testament." "What is that?" he asked. "It is a part of the Bible." To this the clerk replied, "Do they call it the New Testament because someone just wrote it?"

This writer himself, as an erstwhile grader of Bible examinations in a Christian college, has been informed that Nathaniel was thrown into the lions' den, that Matthew was a republican, and that Dan and Beersheba were man and wife like Sodom and Gomorrah. This gross ignorance is so widespread in its extent, so ghastly in its nature, and so perilous in its portent that the church must begin again to teach her people—and thoroughly.

Religious Illiteracy Produces Religious Indifference

Furthermore, this is a day of relative religious indifference, although a higher percentage of the population than ever before are members of the Christian church. In 1890 there was but 22.5% of the population on the rolls; in 1942 there was 52.5%. Today the percentage is far higher. We have had a growth, but it has been a fig-tree growth—leaves without a corresponding amount of fruit. Over the past 25 years our churches have declined considerably in numbers of missionary aspirants, amount of giving, and other such significant indexes of spiritual tone. We have as good material today as we had in 1900, but what are we making of the souls God has entrusted to our spiritual care and perfecting?

Now if we are to remedy the present situation, it seems we must act in a *fundamental* manner. The axe must be put to the root of the tree. The logic of the *dilemma* is clear: religious indifference results from religious illiteracy, which in turn results from lack of instruction.

The logic of the *solution* seems equally clear: religious instruction will result in religious literacy (generally), which in turn will result in religious interest and activity (inevitably). (Note that we are assuming that the persons instructed are Christians.)

Religious Knowledge Intensifies Christianity

That a man's Christian life will be proportionate to his grasp of Christian truth may require proof. Many will say, "The most pious person I have ever met was a poor old lady scarcely able to read." Such cases, however, do not disprove, but rather demonstrate, our point. We must not forget that knowledge has not one, but two dimensions—both breadth and depth. Of the woman in question, her knowledge was undoubtedly scanty in its extensiveness, but profound in its intensiveness. She may only have grasped a few articles of faith, but these she understood deeply and experientially. So she really *knew* more than some student who had a broad general acquaintance with the whole field of systematic theology, but had assimilated very little of his knowledge. A container that is only two feet wide but ten feet deep will hold more water than one that is ten feet wide and only one foot deep. Our contention is that the *more real* the knowledge, the *more real* the Christianity. Show me a religious person and I will show you a person who has some knowledge of God in Christ, and one who could be made more saintly still by even more knowledge.

Fundamentals Included in a Teaching Ministry

There are various things which the church can do toward *teaching* "all nations . . . in the name of the Father, and of the Son, and of the Holy Ghost" (Matthew 28:19–20). First of all, it would be well for the minister in his preaching to adopt the advice of a popularizer of science who once said, "Never overestimate the knowledge of your audience; but never underestimate their capacity for knowledge." Second, officers of the church who are obliged to give assent to the creed of the church could reasonably be expected to know, before they assent, what the creed is. Third, should any Sabbath school teacher, the shortage of such not forgotten, be asked to teach who has not first been trained in *what* to teach? Fourth, is it right to admit a child to the communion table without first having established his faith and the practice of church attendance with reasonable thoroughness? And can such be done in six half-hour periods?

Examinations Required before Church Sessions

Fifth, new adult members are supposed to be examined by the board, according to one denomination. "In this examination special attention should be given to the doctrine of the Trinity—Father, Son, and Holy Spirit; the inspiration of the Scriptures of the Old and New Testaments; the atonement; the necessity of repentance and faith in Christ; the duty of separation from the world, of household religion, including family worship, of Christian giving and the evangelization of the world, of diligent attendance on the ordinances of divine worship, public, private, and family, and of conformity to the laws and usages of the Church." Can this be done with any adequacy unless these persons have been reasonably well instructed beforehand? We fear not.

Unless the church takes hold and does its best to stem the tide of religious illiteracy, the trend toward religious indifference will continue to grow, and at an alarming rate. Let us then be faithful to the command to "grow in grace, and in the knowledge of our Lord and Savior Jesus Christ" (2 Peter 3:18), that we be not as those of whom the apostle said, "For when for the time ye ought to be teachers, ye have need that one teach you again which be the first principles of the oracles of God; and are become such as have need of milk, and not of strong meat" (Hebrews 5:12).

How to Build a New Life

I've tried in vain a thousand ways,
My fears to quell, my hopes to raise;
My soul is night, my heart is steel,
I cannot see, I cannot feel;
For light, for light, I must appeal,
In simple trust to Jesus.

Let's appeal. What directive will Jesus give us that will quell our fears, raise our hopes, lighten our souls, and soften our hearts?

Here is the Master's plan for the new life that shall richer, fuller be. "Come unto Me, all ye that labor and are heavy laden, and I will give you rest. Take My yoke upon you, and learn of Me, for I am meek and lowly in heart, and ye shall find rest unto your souls. For My yoke is easy, and My burden is light" (Matthew 11:28–30).

It is well to detect in this gentle invitation the strong and unmistakable accents of regal dignity. "Come" is imperative, after all—not optional, really. Jesus speaks here as God and with the sovereign authority of Deity. This is the Creator addressing His creatures. We are not surprised, therefore, that He should say with calm confidence that His yoke is easy and His burden light. *Of course* His yoke is easy—it fits snugly, having been fashioned by a perfect Artisan who knew as perfectly the one for whom His work was designed! *Of course* the burden is light, because the same workman made both the burden and the back which bears it! He knows the weight of the one and the strength of the other.

By Accepting Christ's Yoke

Men are ever trying to be free of yokes and out from under the burdens of life. Young people, especially, are prone to have the "don't-fence-me-in" feeling. It is a pitiful thing how, while trying always to make life easier for ourselves, we manage, in spite of our intentions, to do just the reverse. Endeavoring to escape the burdens God has rightly and wisely placed upon us, we are crushed beneath the weight of our own freedom.

Here is the resultant paradox: When we accept the legitimately imposed yoke of Christ, we find it easy, while, on the other hand, when we cast it off we find ourselves laboring and heavy laden. We can understand how this can be in terms of the figure which our Lord here employs to convey His truth. A heavy yoke which fits the neck of an ox snugly would be easy to bear. A light yoke which did not fit would, because of the chafing and discomfort it would cause, be difficult to bear.

Let us take a more modern and urban illustration. When a man comes home in the evening he is supposed to like nothing more than to kick off his shoes, which he has had to wear around all day, and slide his feet into a pair of soft slippers. He needs something on his feet to be respectable, but as little as possible to be comfortable.

This writer had such a pair of slippers, and he was wont to use them for the same purpose. But this writer also had a dog. Now, to a dog a slipper is made not for the feet, but for the mouth; and not as something to be welcomed as a good friend, but something to be torn apart as a vicious enemy. Consequently, one of my slippers today has no padding in the sole, and the other is in a worse condition because it has half the padding left. I still wear the slippers (very rarely now because when some friends heard about our domestic tragedy, they forthwith formed a "We-Can-Take-a-Hint Society" and bought me a new pair). Nevertheless, I still occasionally wear the old slippers with the padding mostly out. But when I put them off prior to going out and slip into my shoes, my, how good those shoes feel! They may be much heavier, but how well they fit, and therefore how good they feel—how easy and how light!

Let us apply this Christian formula for the new life. Is it indeed true that Christ's yoke of self-denial is actually easy and the burden of His strenuous discipline really light? Let us see.

By Studying God's Expectations

Let us take a situation that many young people are confronted with at various times. You ask yourself whether you should go to the movies this evening. Well, if you are your own master, under no higher authority than yourself, the question is simple: Do I want to go? Do I have the means? If you both want to go and have the means, the whole matter is summarily settled. Apparently there is no yoke or burden to that type of life. Neither is there any satisfaction.

But you are a Christian; you are not your own master; you have been bought with a price and you belong to God. His will is your will. You ask whether you should go to a given movie, and many factors come crowding into the situation. Whether you want to go or not is far from finally determinative. Your desire may be but the wish of pampered tastes and require no satisfaction but discipline. Obviously, there is a yoke here that your worldly friend can disregard. You must ask not whether you *do* want to go, but whether you *should* want to go. And in answering that question, God, your family and your own true interests come into consideration. Is it the kind of picture that likely passes the divine Censor? Is it the kind, as far as you could ascertain, that is not only decent but profitable? (These

two questions alone would eliminate 75% of the possibilities.)
Further, I must be sure that my going does not work a
hardship on someone else. I must know that I not only have
the money in my pocket, but I must know that it is my money
and not the church's or a friend's. All this is of the nature of a
yoke, but the satisfaction of not just going to the movies, but
going to the movies to the glory of God, is far more enjoyable
than any movie itself could ever be.

By Disciplined Decisions

Take another concrete instance, and then we shall leave the
reader to apply the principle of the new life to the entirety of his
experience. One day, during a time of military conflict, a young
girl of college age came to this writer for some advice about a
problem troubling her. Right out of the blue she asked, "When
may I kiss to the glory of God?" One could see to look at her
that this could easily be a problem for her. The fine thing about
it all was that she was neither joking nor silly. Here was a
devoted Christian girl who wanted to honor her Master, and
wondered honestly about this all-too-promiscuously practiced
art. She was completely right in feeling that if and when she
kissed, it should be when—and only when—it was to the glory
of God.

I advised the rather rigorous policy of saving her kisses for
the man she someday intended to marry. At the same time, I
could see that following this principle might well mean that her
heart would, on some occasions, be broken, and some GI's
would be obliged to cross the waters without the memory of a
farewell smooch. She had a yoke that a "Victory" girl would
know nothing about, and she bore a burden that many a less-
devoted nominal Christian would not be bothered with; but her
yoke would be easy and her burden light, for she saw that,

though she would be obliged at times to displease some men, she would please her God (and, incidentally, the man she would marry).

The Relation of Whites to Blacks

Among Christians there appear to be two basic types of polity governing the relation of whites to blacks. One is to break down segregation by giving equality; the other is to give equality by breaking down segregation. Those favoring the first principle of action argue that if we give the black man justice and an opportunity to develop and establish himself favorably in the community, there will result spontaneous commingling emerging from mutual respect and admiration. If commingling is forced before the black has "arrived," the effort will be abortive and harmful to interracial friendship. The second group maintains that only by first breaking down the wall of partition shall we be able to vouchsafe the black man the benefits of equality.

Dr. A. M. Pierce, editor of the *Wesleyan Christian Advocate*, Atlanta, Georgia, is an exponent of the first polity. Speaking particularly with reference to the South, he says in his pamphlet, "Our Christian Obligation to the Negro":

> The writer does not believe that it would be wise to break down social barriers between the races in the South. The effort to do so would widen a breach that is gradually closing. If left alone, this question will eventually adjust itself. If the attention of the white race is centered upon an entirely fair deal toward the colored brethren in business, professional life, industry, domestic relations, education, courtesy, religion, civic affairs, . . . the question of social relations will take care of itself. As the Negro achieves worth, he will be treated with increasing consideration.

Segregation and Discrimination

As a representative of the other viewpoint, Dr. Mordecai Johnson of Howard University comes to mind. This writer heard an address of his. If my recollection of it is correct, then one of the main contentions of this black leader was that segregation spelled discrimination against the black man. As long as the black man was kept separate, he was kept subordinate.

This writer himself once had an experience which would tend to confirm Dr. Johnson's position and raise a question about the truth of Dr. Pierce's statement that "As the Negro achieves worth, he will be treated with increasing consideration." About a year ago we were discussing the race question with a Southerner. This white friend did not believe in the equal treatment of the black man. But he said that it was because he did not believe that the black man was equal to the white person as a matter of fact. As *he* had known him, he was not.

When I asked my friend if he approved of treating the black man as an equal when he proved himself to be such, he replied that he did. Then came the Philadelphia disturbance caused by elevating eight black persons to positions as motormen. I asked my friend if he approved of this promotion, assuming that these eight men were, as every report had it, equal in ability to the white motormen. He replied that he did not approve. And then it became evident that this man did not really intend to treat the black man as an equal, whether he proved himself equal in a given instance or not.

Worth Coupled with Respect

This last case does not disprove Dr. Pierce's thesis that a black man will be treated as an equal when he acts as an equal.

It only proves that one person would not then treat the black man as an equal. Although there undoubtedly would be others like him, these would not necessarily be the majority. We may assume that the majority of white people will acknowledge the black man's equality when they are persuaded that he deserves it. The element common to these two policies is that both favor racial intermingling. The difference is in the method of bringing this about. As in every great issue, we have our gradualists and our radicals. Despite this difference we may rejoice in the common purpose to bring to the black man his rights as brother man. That any other goal could be entertained when the Word of God teaches so emphatically the unity of the human race, its origin from a common Creator, and its union in the Savior of the world is inconceivable. That we could confess belief in the holy catholic church and then restrict our fellowship to those of like color is the grossest hypocrisy. That anyone could presume to racial superiority in a day of numerous painstaking and conclusive anthropological investigations annihilating the doctrine of the "pure race" bespeaks willful blindness. This is not to say that segregation, under any and all possible circumstances, is intrinsically evil.

Intermingling and Intermarriage

As for the method itself, I am inclined to believe that only the radical alternative is thoroughly Christian. Since the black man is our brother now, he should be treated as such—now. What God has joined together as brother and brother let not man put asunder as master and slave. If it is feared that such intermingling will tend to intermarriage, let it be remembered that thirty-three leading blacks once made the public statement that they had not the slightest desire for intermarriage. Further, in the North we have no noticeable trend to intermarriages.

Langston Hughes once attended a YMCA conference at Franklin and Marshall College when he was a young student. Among other subjects the black and white delegates discussed interracial relations. Various problems were examined, various solutions considered. A wholesome attitude prevailed and constructive suggestions were made. But Hughes felt that something should be done about all this—that some definite action should be taken embodying the principles that were approved. So he suggested that the YMCA conference adopt a petition that the college on whose campus it was meeting should receive blacks into its student body. When this plan was proposed, there was no little embarrassment, and even the YMCA leader was constrained to say, "There are some things in this world we must leave to Jesus, friends. Let us pray." What this man meant as a change of subject, let us remember is the most pertinent suggestion of all. Let us pray that God will have mercy on us white sinners!

Christians Seeking
Public Office

I have three things to say about Christians seeking public office: first, Christians should seek public office; second, Christians should seek public office in a Christian way; third, Christians should seek public office for a Christian purpose.

The Obligation

First, then, a Christian should seek public office. This he should do because he has a secular responsibility. He has a spiritual duty, but he also has a secular one. His spiritual duty is to preach the gospel, heralding redemption which can be found in no other name than Christ's, Caesar's not excepted. His secular duty is to make this a better world in which to preach this gospel.

There are those who would make our spiritual duty all-important, denying our secular obligations. Some, on the other hand, would affirm our secular task to the exclusion of the sacred. Gogarten, as a typical Barthian, says that for the church to show an interest in social activity evinces the presence of the devil in her midst. Modernists, diametrically opposed to all this, are, or were, exponents of the social gospel. For one group the gospel is nothing social; for the other the gospel is nothing but the social.

If a Barthian and a Modernist were watching a burning house, the Barthian would say to the Modernist, "The important thing is to save the people. Who cares what becomes of the house?" To this the Modernist would reply, "If the house had been made fireproof to begin with, the people would be safe."

The answer to these two extreme groups is to draw the circle and include both. Each errs in its negations. Let the socially minded remember that a man's relation to God is fundamental; let the evangelically minded remember that man's relation to man is vital. Christianity, like a building, requires foundation and superstructure. The foundation without the superstructure is useless; the superstructure without the foundation is impossible. To change the figure, a root that does not produce a tree is dead; a tree that does not grow from a root is artificial.

If we have the root of the matter in us, we must then allow it to bear fruit abundantly to the glory of the Father. We must redeem the time. We must bring every thought captive to Christ. Whatever we do, whether we eat or whether we drink, or whatsoever we do, let us do all to the glory of God. It is the grace of God itself which teaches us to deny ungodliness and worldly lusts, and live soberly (with proper concern for self), righteously (with proper concern for others), and godly (with proper concern for God) (Titus 2:12). As sons of the Reformation, we should remember the words of John Calvin: "Justification is by faith alone, but not by the faith that is alone."

The Method

Second, a Christian should seek public office in a Christian way. Here is where the pessimists smile. To many, seeking public office in a Christian way would be futile, even absurd. A man must choose, they say, between the love of God and the love of votes. It has been said of an outstanding American statesman of our time that while he cites choice portions of the Sermon on the Mount in his political campaigns, he relies on certain infamous city bosses to enable him to get the votes, by which to get the office, through which to put into practice these Christian principles, as a result of which such bosses would be put out of business. Serving Christ by courtesy of Hague and Kelly! This type of compromise many cynically suppose to be necessary if one would get political power. If it were true that we could not obtain public office in a Christian way, then the conclusion would be that we should not obtain office. The Christian seeking public office for Christian purposes must seek office in a Christian way.

But, it will be protested, does not the ultimate public welfare justify the Christian in resorting to temporary political expediency? The answer to that is a study of the nature of temptation. Temptation's attack always comes at the weakest point in our line of moral defense. Obviously, a Christian cannot deny his fundamental purpose and still remain a Christian; it is not so obvious, however, that he cannot deny Christ's method and still remain a Christian. There is the point of real temptation—namely to say that the end justifies the means. Christ refused this kind of temptation following His forty days in the wilderness. The Christian, like his Master, must resist subtle temptation to do evil that good may come, both in seeking and in administering public office.

The Objective

Third, the Christian should seek public office for Christian purposes. The Japanese preacher Kanamori, in his famous three-hour sermon, said that the state can kill the birds, but it cannot smash the eggs. Thus he noted the limitation of government-enforced morality. It was a check on wrongdoing, but not a cure for it. It could prevent some crimes, but it could not eradicate the evil nature from which they came. It could kill the birds, but it could not smash the eggs. While Kanamori cited this statement to indicate the weakness of government, we may cite it to indicate its strength. While it is not as great a thing to kill the birds as to smash the eggs, it is an important thing nonetheless. It is important because many people will not receive Christ into their hearts. People cannot be forced to accept the Savior, yet they must be forced to avoid some of the evil consequences in character and action of not receiving Him. To engraft a new and living branch is best. Where this is not possible, to prune the dead branches is desirable and necessary. If the heart is not changed by voluntary acceptance of Christ, it must be restrained involuntarily by the discipline of the law. What the church cannot do the state must in order that God's will may be done in earth, if not the same way as it is done in heaven.

It is the Christian who should and will carry out the purpose of public office properly and efficiently. Good government, after all, depends mostly on good men. In Disraeli's words, "We put too much faith in systems, and look too little to men." With some thoughtful and sound words by F. R. Barry we close these remarks:

> Why, we are asked, did the church do nothing to protest against the iniquities of the slave trade? The answer is: It did much more than protest; it abolished them—in the person of Wilberforce. How could the church sit still and remain inactive while the cry of the victims of mines and factories "came unto the ears of the Lord of Hosts"? The answer is that the church did hear their cry and delivered them—in the person of Lord Shaftesbury. And still today the claim can be fairly made that wherever you find constructive effort at work for social and personal regeneration, you will find that in nine cases out of ten there is Christian inspiration behind it.

No Dice

Haveman tells us that the United States is "the gamblingest nation that ever existed." It wasn't always that way. Time was when, in old New England, playing in any form was hardly permitted, much less playing for stakes. But it appears as if the new and worse extreme may continue. Gallup's poll reveals that many American people, especially New England people (53%), want legalized gambling.

A Gigantic Business

Gambling is really big business. One out of every two women gamble. The percentage is even higher among men. Furthermore, figures like these do not include people who play varieties of bingo at the movies and such places. That is because they do not pay extra to participate in the game, only the price of the show. The fact, however, is that many of these moviegoers would not be going this evening if it were not for the chance to win the jackpot. So they go to gamble and the movie is the consolation prize.

But, sticking to what everybody admits is gambling, it is still big business. Some say a $6 billion per-year business. Some say ten billion. Some say twenty billion. In any case, a big item even in these days of stratospheric national budgets. More, as one author points out, than the combined profits of all the hundred largest industries. Nor is Pittsburgh, to take one example, the least of the gambling cities in the gamblingest of nations. It specializes in numbers, but the annual total expenditure for all forms of betting is some one hundred million dollars.

What It Is

Now that we have started talking about gambling, it is about time we ask ourselves what it is that we are talking about. What is gambling? But, you say, everybody knows what gambling is. We think not. We believe that if people really knew what gambling is, gambling would no longer be. Because deliberately to arrange things so that huge wealth is offered for no good reason, and earned by nothing but luck, only needs to be stated to be condemned by all right-minded observers. Yet that is what gambling amounts to. It has been more briefly defined by Johnson as "the mode of transferring property without any intermediate good." A man would be put in jail for taking property that way, or put in an asylum for giving property that way, in anything other than gambling. That is the reason that the original meaning of the word "gambler" was "false gamester," or "one who played an unfair game." Old Aristotle lumped thieves and gamblers together. The Word of God condemns the practice roundly: "But you who forsake the Lord, who forget my holy mountain, who set a table for Fortune and fill cups of mixed wine for Destiny" (Isaiah 65:11).

The early Christian Church forbade it; even excommunicated for it. The Church Father Tertullian bluntly stated that a gambler was not a Christian, and a Christian would not be a gambler. In the opinion of most Christians through the ages, gambling comes under the heading of a violation of the eighth commandment: "Thou shalt not steal."

Its Effects

Gambling is not only bad in itself—it is worse in its effects. As the poet said:

This is the very curse of evil deed,
That of new evil it becomes the seed.

This could have been written especially for gambling. Here, for example, are a few statistics for England, 1895–1907. Please remember that these are only the ones that got on the record. Informed imagination could multiply these many times.

Results of gambling:

156 suicides or attempted suicides.
719 thefts or embezzlements.
442 bankruptcies.

Scotland tells the same story as its National League Against Betting and Gambling says: "The exploitation of the nation's nitwits by the unscrupulous gambling interests is a prominent factor in the nation's apostasy from religion, in the collapse of conscience, in the loss of moral values, in the growing dishonesty and lack of truthfulness and moral insensibility in the land" (quoted from Marx's *Gambling in America*).

Losing Our Heritage

What of the gamblingest nation in the world? Well, we are still great. Why? Because we have not yet completely lost the heritage which made us great. What was that? Honest work for an honest dollar, the dignity of human toil, respect for man, the fear of God. But the new craze for gambling is sapping our foundations. Like the scion of a wealthy family, we are betting our inheritance away. We are in the old cycle again: discipline produces wealth, but wealth tends to undermine the discipline which produced it. Gambling is undisciplined living. It is the enemy of society. It is the friend of the enemies of society. It is the keystone in the arch of the underworld. Drunkenness, robberies, prostitution, political corruption, dope addiction, murder—the whole empire rests on gambling. It is as if the devil had said, "Upon this rock, I will build my kingdom."

What You Can Do

What shall we do about gambling? May I suggest a few concrete proposals?

1. Think clearly. See what gambling is. Understand that in its very nature, be the stake high or low, it is a form of stealing.

2. Act consistently. Keep your skirts clean of this vice in every form. If a charity organization or a firehouse or whatever wants you to take a chance for their benefit, tell them you will do better than that. You will give them a contribution without a chance because you believe in their value to the community, and you do not believe in the value of gambling to the community. Again, if you think that you have some time for bridge, let people at the party know that you do not have time for gambling in connection with it. Public opinion is shaping up in favor of gambling. Why? Because you have not spoken and acted as if you really did know gambling is a bad word.

3. Do not let gambling be legalized. Kefauver has said that as long as it is not legalized there is still a chance of controlling it, but not afterwards. More important than what Kefauver says, is that Kefauver says it. That is, it is the Kefauvers of the country, those who are fighting against gambling and the rackets, who are opposed to legalization. And who wants legalization? The underworld, apparently to the man.

4. Inform yourself accurately. Here are a few books which you should read: Walter Arm, *Pay-off: The Inside Story of Big*

City Corruption, New York, Appleton-Century-Crofts, 1951. Herbert Asbury, *Sucker's Progress,* New York, Mead & Company, 1938. H. L. Marx, ed., *Gambling in America,* 1952. V. W. Peterson, *Gambling, Should it be Legalized?* Springfield, Ill. Thomas, 1951.

5. Get at the root of the problem and at the root of the solution. Someone has said, "You will never have an honest horse race until you have an honest human race." Once again, the heart of the problem is the problem of the heart. Read Dostoyevsky's *The Gambler,* and see that this is a habit-forming psychological narcotic.

The Answer—Christ

Enforcement, controls, probes, prisons, etc., will never drive out a desire. Important as these are, they can only curb this vice; they cannot uproot it. Or, as Kanamori used to say, "The state can kill the birds, but it cannot smash the eggs."

Who can smash the eggs of passion, the driving desire for the fast buck, the incurable hope of getting rich quick? Jesus Christ is the only One I know who has been able to make virtue more attractive than vice. He alone can make morals rise up and walk. He alone can make the gambler free indeed and at the same time truly rich. Not to meet Christ is the one chance which you can never let the gambler take!

Protestant–Roman Catholic Marriages

All we wish to do in this article is to quote the contract which all non–Roman Catholics who wish to marry Roman Catholics are supposed to sign, and provide a running Protestant commentary on it. We believe that if Protestant youth face the sheer facts of the case, they can, without exhortation, see for themselves what they should do.

I (the non–Roman Catholic party) therefore agree:

1. *That I will not interfere in the least with the free exercise of the Catholic party's religion.*

This, of course, appears to be a reasonable proposition. But there is more here than immediately meets the eye. First, the Roman Church is again in the role of claimant for religious toleration of her people, though she officially denies it in every way to non-Catholics. But we let that pass. Second, "in the least" is meant to imply that the Protestant will not even interfere by persuasion. He is not permitted to endeavor to convince the other party of the truth of Protestantism. Third, this permanently rules out the possibility of reaching a subsequent religious agreement unless on a Romanist basis. Otherwise, a lifelong religious separation must obtain. Fellowship on the deepest level of human experience, the religious, is utterly precluded.

2. *That I will adhere to the doctrine of the sacred indissolubility of the marriage bond, so that I cannot contract a second marriage while my consort is still alive, even though a civil divorce may have been obtained.*

50

We present a double protest on this article: first, Roman Catholic theory, as here stated, is too strict; and, second, Roman Catholic practice at this point is too lax. Let us elaborate. We say this teaching of the absolute "indissolubility" of marriage is too strict because the Bible makes it clear that adultery, at least, does dissolve the bond and entitle the offended party to legitimate remarriage. Our Lord is explicit on this subject: "Whoever divorces his wife, *except for unchastity*, and marries another commits adultery" (Matthew 19:9, cf. Matthew 5:32).

We say that Rome is too lax in her practice with respect to divorce, or, rather, annulment. By annulment is meant the declaration of a marriage to be null and void or non-existent. This is not a dissolution of the union, but a declaration that the union never was. Rome has utilized this power in a number of instances where it was tantamount to divorcing a couple.

This writer had a discussion with a priest recently in the presence of about twenty people. The question of divorce was being considered. I asked the priest if a Roman Catholic had legally married a non-Catholic out of the church and had lived with him for many years and had had twelve children by him, and then at the end of that time repented of having married out of the church and without its approval and wanted to have the marriage annulled, would that be possible? "Yes," was the answer. That means that a marriage of many years, sealed by the births of a dozen offspring, was never really marriage at all, because the Roman Church said it was not.

The case of Rear Admiral Lang was significant. Lang had married, divorced, and remarried. His first wife then died. While still married to his second wife, Lang fell in love with his Roman Catholic secretary and desired to marry her. Rome received Lang into the church and married him to his Roman Catholic secretary. How did the church dispose of the previously existing marriage? By divorce? No, marriage is indissoluble. By annulment. On what ground was the annulment of the second marriage made? On the ground that it had been contracted while the first wife was still living. So the second marriage was declared illegitimate even after the first wife had died. Rome therefore dissolved the "illegitimate" second marriage and made the third one "legitimate."

3. *That all the children, both boys and girls, that may be born of this union shall be baptized and educated solely in the faith of the Roman Catholic Church, even in the event of the death of my Catholic consort. In case of dispute, I furthermore hereby agree fully that the custody of all children shall be given to such guardians as assure the faithful execution of this covenant and promise, in the event that I cannot fulfill it myself.*

This means that your children shall, with your hearty co-operation, be taught such unbiblical doctrines as the following: 1. That the Roman Catholic Church is the only true church. 2. That outside the Roman Catholic Church there is normally no salvation. 3. That the Bible is not the Word of God to you except as previously infallibly interpreted by the hierarchy. 4. That salvation is not by grace alone, and we are not justified by faith. 5. That there is not one, but many mediators between God and man. 6. That forgiveness of sins can be made by the priest-confessor only. 7. That there is no priesthood of believers. 8. That one should "bow down and serve" images. 9. That the Pope, in official declarations to the whole church concerning morals, is absolutely infallible. 10. That the Virgin is able to turn Christ's heart toward us. 11. That Mary was immaculately conceived and sinless throughout life. 12. That the bread of the mass contains the actual substance of the body of Christ. 13. That baptism works in the mere administration, and, where it is not administered, regeneration is impossible and the unfortunate child is not saved. 14. That after death imperfect Catholics will go to purgatory to suffer the further punishment of their sins, alleviated, possibly, by the offering of masses for the dead. 15. That the Roman religion being alone true, all other forms of Christianity are false. 16. That because it is the duty of the state to act for the welfare of its citizens, it should in every way possible favor the true religion, that is, Catholicism, and suppress, as far as possible, all false religion such as Protestantism, and so forth.

According to the contract, you are to continue with this course of instruction even though your consort dies and is succeeded by a wife of your own faith.

Some Protestants will cling tenaciously to their Protestant associations, even though married to a Roman Catholic. Vigorously they assert that they will not compromise—they will live and die Protestants. But strangely enough, they show not the slightest concern that the principles for which they stand so staunchly themselves should be vouchsafed to their children. A person should be more concerned about his child than about himself.

4. *That I will lead a married life in conformity with the teachings of the Catholic Church regarding birth control realizing fully the attitude of the Catholic Church in this regard.*

It should be noted that the Roman Church believes in birth control. It is a particular method, namely, use of mechanical contraceptives, that it opposes. Its adherents are advised to use restraint plus a knowledge of supposedly infertile periods. In its advocacy of at least a degree of moral restraint, which mechanical devices do not require, we believe it is worthy of commendation.

5. *That no other marriage ceremony shall take place before or after this ceremony by the Catholic priest.*

This reflects the Roman belief that marriage is a sacrament, and can only be properly performed by the church, that is, the Roman Catholic Church, while, according to the Bible, marriage is a natural ordinance and may therefore be legalized even by a non-clergyman.

If someone says that all this is convincing only if he signs the contract, but not otherwise, let us add a few words. Even if this contract is not signed (in many cases it must be signed), this is nevertheless the position of the church to which your mate belongs. Nor will you be permitted to forget it. Often the mate will do the reminding, frequently the mate's priest and invariably the mate's family, and not infrequently the mate's and your children. Furthermore, it must be remembered that, if your Catholic consort is conscientious, he will feel morally obliged to have the terms of that contract in force whether signed or not. Also, if the Catholic party does not bring pressure, it will likely be because he or she is not a good Roman Catholic. While that may make for less domestic tension, it leads to general religious indifference, which is the worst of all situations, inasmuch as everyone should at least be conscientious about whatever he believes.

And here is another thought: Do you realize that the Roman Catholic Church itself approves heartily of my main purpose in this article? Do you know that they are praying along with me that my intention may succeed? No, they do not agree with my reasons for frowning on mixed marriages, but they most heartily agree with my frowning. In other words, it is the advice of both churches to their adherents not to marry across the lines with or without a contract. Our feelings are mutual.

A Formula for Prayer

The simplest Bible statement on prayer is that of our Lord in Matthew 7:7: "Ask, and it shall be given you."

We will deal with the two aspects of prayer as set forth here. The first is asking and the second is receiving. Our emphasis will be on asking because, in a sense, the receiving takes care of itself when once we learn how to ask.

First, then, our Lord's word "ask." This is a simple little monosyllable about which all of us think we know all there is to know. But in spite of the apparent simplicity of this familiar little word "ask," I doubt if the word really is well understood.

I take as my cue a hint from another minister that the best definition of the word is in a business phrase. We all know the familiar commercial expression, "supply and demand." According to that principle, a manufacturer tries to ascertain the demand for his particular article before he proceeds to produce an appropriate supply. He is a successful businessman who rightly judges the demand and adequately supplies it. So much is well known; however, it seems that the businessman also has another expression. He speaks of "efficient demand." By this expression he seems to mean the kind of demand which will lead the consumer actually to purchase the article. People have many wants and wishes, and even demands; but the only kind of demand that really interests the businessman is the kind of demand that leads a person actually to part with his money in order to satisfy it. This is what he calls "efficient demand."

Efficient Demand

And by "ask" our Lord also means "efficient demand." Let me illustrate. One day when I was a student in seminary, I saw a professor of mine and his eight-year-old son, Henry, and a puppy dog walking across campus. I had seen the professor and his son before, but never in the company of a puppy. So I remarked on the fact and received this explanation. About a month before, the son had asked his father for a dog. The father told his son that he could have a dog—as soon as he persuaded his father that he really wanted a dog. He said to his son, "If you ask for a dog, that means that every morning you walk the dog. It means that every evening you feed the dog. It means that when the dog becomes dirty, you wash the dog." Well, it took about a month for that boy to persuade his father that he really wanted a dog. And that is how it was that this day I saw the father and his son walking along with the new puppy for which the boy had asked. However, the boy did not keep the dog long. After a few weeks it was his father who was walking the dog in the morning and his mother who was feeding the dog at night. And as soon as it became apparent that his son had not really wanted a dog after all the father took the dog away.

Let me give another illustration. I once had a friend who was an invalid. His life was confined to his bed and his chair. He was, however, a very godly man and loved to listen to religious services on the radio and read his Bible. But his eyesight had so far failed that he was hardly able to see well enough to read his Bible any more. As I was speaking with him one day, I remembered some information received some time before. I had learned that the government had a special service for the blind. It provided a record player and records of classical literature and biblical readings. I mentioned this to my friend, who was interested. Both he and his wife seemed to be quite delighted at the prospects of hearing biblical recitations by master readers. So, after going through a little red tape, I was able to secure this government service. Not long after, there were a record player and some biblical records by my friend's chair in the living room.

Some time later, however, I noticed that the record player was no longer by his chair. Thinking it might have been moved to the bedroom, I commented on its absence. I was told that it had not been moved to the bedroom, but had actually been returned to the government because the good lady of the house felt that it did not go well with her furniture. Actually, it did not go at all well with her furniture. She had a very expensively and tastefully decorated room, and this record player was housed in a plain, sickish-green box that did not go well with anything in that room. Nevertheless, I was quite disappointed that the wife could have allowed her aesthetic tastes to deprive her husband of a source of great satisfaction to him. Also, incidentally, I could not help kicking myself for going to what little trouble was involved to secure the player when the people, at least the wife, did not really want it at all.

It is quite obvious what I am driving at in all this. In spite of this professor's very deliberate effort to ascertain certainly that his son really wanted a dog, the professor was fooled. The boy did not really want a dog at all. And in spite of the fact that I thought this family really wanted a record player, I was fooled. They did not really want a record player at all. These were apparent requests, apparent askings, that fooled me. Now this is the point—God, of course, cannot be fooled. He knows whether we are really asking or not. He knows whether our prayer is an "efficient demand" that would actually lead us to pay the price necessary to receive the answer to that prayer.

No Unanswered Prayers

I will now suggest something with which you may be disposed to disagree. My remark, however, is based on my best and most deliberate judgment. I think that we are utterly mistaken when we speak—and even sing—about the "problem of unanswered prayer." I do not think that there is such a thing as an unanswered prayer. There is no problem of an unanswered prayer. Our only problem is the problem of the unasked prayer. "Ye have not," says the Scriptures, "because ye ask not" (James 4:2).

Some of you may be saying to yourselves: when a preacher says that there is no such thing as an unanswered prayer, isn't he overlooking something? Hasn't he forgotten Gethsemane? Does he not remember the great prayer of our Lord which was not granted? No, I have not forgotten Gethsemane. But if you will look more closely at that experience of our Lord, you will notice that His prayer was not unanswered. For what did He actually pray? Did He indeed ask that this cup should pass from Him? If He did, His prayer was unanswered because the cup did not pass from Him. But I ask again, Did Christ really ask that the cup pass from Him? He definitely did not. Rather, His prayer was, "If it be possible, let this cup pass from Me" (Matthew 26:39). As soon as He realized that it was not possible, He said, "Nevertheless, not as I will, but as Thou wilt." That was His will: that God's will be done. That was what He wanted and what He asked for: that God's will be done. And God's will was that He drink the cup. It was Christ's will, therefore, that He drink the cup. His prayer was answered.

The promise of Christ is: "Ask, and ye shall receive." Anything that a Christian can really ask he shall receive. The promise is unconditional and absolute. Ask and it shall be given you. But you will notice that you never may ask for anything without stipulating, "If it be Thy will." That is, we simply do not know what things are good for us as God knows. And whatever we ask for, our intention is that it should be for our good. Since, however, we do not know as God knows what really is good for us, we will never ask for anything unless it is His will.

This is true of absolutely anything. If, for example, you are inclined to pray for a new car, you really only want a new car if it is good for you to have a new car. But that you do not know as well as God, who alone knows what is good for you. So the only way in which you would ever pray for a new car would be, "If it be Thy will—if it is good for me, then, and only then, let me have a new car." The same principle holds true for anything you can ever ask, including even food. In the Lord's Prayer, we ask for our daily bread; but you will notice that this petition follows another, namely, "Thy will be done." So only after asking that God's will be done do we ask for our daily bread. I repeat, we can never want or ask for anything unless "if it is God's will"; and, if we ask in accordance with His will, it shall most certainly be given to us.

On the other hand, we may ask for any virtue without saying, "If it be Thy will." We do not have to say, "If it be Thy will, let me have more love." "If it be Thy will, let me have more wisdom." "If it be Thy will, let me have more courage." "If it be Thy will, let me have more forbearance." "If it be Thy will, let me have more passion for souls." We do not have to prefix such a phrase for the simple reason that we know in advance that it is God's will that we have love, wisdom, and courage, for He says, "Be ye perfect, as your Father in heaven is perfect." So also, when we ask for the forgiveness of sins, if we truly and earnestly ask *in Christ's name*, we have the assurance from God's Word that our sins will be forgiven us (1 John 1:9), for this is God's will.

The Fine Art of Receiving

So much, then, for the fine art of asking. A few words about the fine art of receiving. As I said before, if we learn how to ask, the receiving almost takes care of itself. So it will suffice merely to give a few suggestions about this matter of receiving.

Before I make these suggestions, let me remind you once again that the promise is that, if we ask, we shall most certainly receive. The Scripture is full of wonderful proofs of this wonderful promise. One of our students at Pittsburgh-Xenia Seminary, in a faculty sermon one year, brought this matter home to us very vividly. He challenged us to make what he called "huge prayers." He said, by way of example, "Now let's take the prayer of Elisha." Elisha, as you know, was the successor of the great Elijah. For Elisha to have asked, the student pointed out, for even a half of the spirit of Elijah would have been a huge prayer. To have asked for a full portion would have been a very huge prayer, but Elisha actually asked for a double portion of the spirit of Elijah. "And," said the student, "what do you think happened? Well, count the miracles or wonders which Elijah did and what do you find? There were eight. And then count the wonders of Elisha and what do you find? There were sixteen!"

We come now to these few suggestions about the fine art of receiving. First, learn to use your imagination, you might almost say your sense of humor. Here is our trouble. When we kneel to pray and make our requests, we usually have a fixed idea in our own mind of the way in which God will send the answer. And, of course, if God does not send the answer in the particular form in which we expected, we are very likely not to recognize it.

Take, for example, the oft-quoted reference to the woman of whom it was said, "She prayed for patience, and the Lord sent her a green cook." Now let's study this terrible-tempered Mrs. Bang. She is obviously of a very irate disposition. She flies off the handle at the slightest provocation. She simply cannot control her temper. At the same time, she is a Christian woman. She is not at all complacent about this temper of hers. She knows she should control it, and she prays. Let's follow her into her closet. She is asking for strength. "Lord," she says, "give me patience." But she has a certain preconceived notion of the way in which the answer will come. She thinks that some miracle ought to take place—some strange and wonderful transformation that will cause her to rise from her knees a new woman, full of poise and patience. But it does not happen that way. As a matter of fact, the doorbell rings.

"Ah," she says, "at last that employment agency has sent me a new cook." She goes to the door and opens it and is not a little irritated to see the ungainly, disheveled-appearing woman who is standing there. Her patience is completely exhausted when the woman stumbles over the threshold and lands unceremoniously sprawled in the living room. Mrs. Bang is sure God has paid no attention to her prayer. The heavens are made of brass, and God simply has not heard her most earnest entreaties.

Meanwhile, God in heaven is smiling affectionately, for "She prayed for patience, and the Lord sent her a green cook." It was precisely because she prayed for patience that the Lord sent her this green cook. Mrs. Bang thought that patience would come by some sort of miracle, but God intended that patience should be learned by means of a green cook.

Some Answers Take Time

So remember, use your imagination, even your sense of humor, so that you may be alert to the myriad of ways in which a wonderfully wise God may choose to answer your request. Don't try to limit His infinite possibilities to your finite anticipations.

The second and last suggestion I would make is this: Remember, prayers, "huge prayers," often take a great deal of time to answer. I have a couple nephews who visited me once when they were aged six and four. At that time I had a cocker spaniel named Blondie. My nephews became very much attached to Blondie. As a matter of fact, they would not be satisfied until I promised them I would breed her and give them one of her puppies. That night they went to bed very happy. The next morning when they came downstairs, the first question was, "Where are the puppies?"

"Childish!" you say. Of course, it was childish. They were children. But when you ask huge prayers, when you ask for patience, love, and wisdom, you are asking for things which take time. If you expect these to develop overnight, you are being very childish.

The words we have been studying are the words of Christ. He taught us to pray. Having taught us to pray, does He have nothing more to do with our prayers? He still has everything to do with our prayers. He who taught us to pray "ever liveth to make intercession for us." The wonderful way in which our Redeemer, at the Father's right hand, still assists us in our prayers has never been more aptly depicted than by John Chrysostom. He told of a family in which the son was very fond of his father. The father had gone on a long journey and was about to return. The son wished to please his father by presenting him with something that the father liked very much. Knowing that he was especially fond of flowers, the boy went into the garden to gather a bouquet. It was some bouquet that he showed to his mother! There were weeds mixed with the flowers, all the stems were of different lengths, and there was a motley array of colors. His mother, however, was deeply touched at this indication of her son's love for his father. So she took the bouquet and sent her son out to play. Meanwhile, she removed the weeds, trimmed the stems to the same length, and arranged the flowers in a colorful ensemble. This was the bouquet the son presented to his father on his return.

In a similar manner, our Lord takes the bouquets that we offer, mingled as they are with weeds and arranged quite defectively, removes the weeds, arranges the flowers, and presents our prayers as a thing of beauty and efficacy to our Father in heaven.

Thus it is that, if we ask, it shall be given unto us.

Is Our Civilization Worth Keeping?

Before we can attempt an answer to the question, "Is our civilization worth keeping?" we must define the characteristics or tendencies of our modern culture. To do this in one article requires a brevity that just about precludes the possibility of absolute accuracy. The reader is asked to bear this in mind.

The most important thing to know about a civilization is its idea of God. Though multitudes of people act as if it were not so, still this question about God is actually more vital and significant than the fluctuations of the stock market.

Its Most Characteristic Attitude

The most characteristic attitude of our civilization, at least of the thinking members, toward God is doubt. You remember the cynical parable which defined the philosopher as a blind man on a dark night searching in an unilluminated cellar for a black cat that was not there. You also remember that the theologian, or the one who would know God, has been likened to this same blind man on a dark night searching in an unilluminated cellar for a black cat that was not there—and finding it. This is a typical university opinion with the exception of the "was not there" part. Most intellectuals are willing to concede that God may exist, that is, the black cat may be there, but they would deny that we can find him; that is, we are blind men in a dark cellar looking for a cat that is black.

While it may be true that the scholars are agnostic, the multitudes still believe. Is not an atheist regarded as somewhat odd? Do not the rank and file sing, "God bless America"? And do we not have "In God We Trust" on our money? Undoubtedly there is a prevalent conviction that God really exists. But, equally undoubtedly, it is God created in the public image, an indulgent modern father whom the true God resembles as little as He resembles Mars.

The Characteristic Described

Just as the prevalent academic agnosticism concerning the existence of God could be represented by the parable concerning a cat, so the prevalent public agnosticism concerning the nature of God can be represented by another parable about a cat. In *Alice in Wonderland*, is it not the Cheshire cat that begins to grin, and the grin grows and grows until there is nothing left of the cat but the grin? Our civilization heard something about the love of God, and it has conveniently let this idea grow and grow to such extremes that it has obliterated God! It is this heresy which explains the appearance in our day of the ungodly Christian: the person who, while living in ways usually deemed immoral, amiably accepts God and blandly regards himself, and is regarded by others, as a believer. Thus when someone was asked on a Sunday morning why the sergeant was swearing, this perfectly reasonable answer could be given: "Because he can't find his hymn book." Our age has come to call His name Jesus for, they fancy, He shall save them *in* their sins rather than *from* them.

The Outcome of Godlessness

What usually becomes of man when he will not have God in his thinking? God gives him up to a reprobate mind. When the son asks for his inheritance and desires to leave the father's house, the father must let him go—and let him eat swine's food. It has been said of psychology that it first lost its soul, and then it lost its mind. This is sober fact—the modern study of man began by denying his possession of a surviving spiritual entity called a soul, and then it proceeded to deny that behind his thoughts was a thinker. A French philosopher said, "The mind secretes thought the way the liver secretes bile."

A German philosopher said, *Man ist was er isst.* ("A man is what he eats.") Thus man, having lost his soul, lost his mind (reducing it to a mere function of the body), and this saying came into vogue: Tear down a church (the reminder of man's loss of soul) and you must build in its stead a mental hospital (the reminder of man's loss of mind).

Present Stage of Decline

Man, having lost his God and himself, should display a godlessness in his culture. And so he does. We cannot examine his total activity, but that is not necessary. A single quotation from Sorokin about art, which we will all recognize to be applicable to music, literature, and the rest of human endeavor, must suffice to indicate the present stage of decline: "To sum up, contemporary art is primarily a museum of social and cultural pathology. It centers in the police morgue, the criminal's hideout, and the sex organs, operating mainly on the level of the social sewers. If we are forced to accept it as a faithful representation of human society, then man and his culture certainly forfeit our respect and admiration."

Our Civilization Still Worth Keeping

In spite of all we have said, we believe that our civilization is worth keeping. It is not only worth keeping, but the Christian, as citizen, has the duty to strive to improve that civilization and uplift it.

Why is this so? Our civilization is worth keeping, first of all, because God, in His common grace, has allowed it to bear many fruits which we owe to Him. Our fine advances in scientific and medical research, for instance, the developments in education and in techniques of the arts, higher standards of living for the common man, improved sanitation and health standards—these, and many others, are the gifts of God's grace. Even though man does not use these gifts to glorify the God who gave them, and, in fact, often uses them *against* God, yet these gifts are there, inherent in the creation God made as well as in the powers of mind by which God has granted man the ability to discover the earth's riches.

God has given these gifts to us as tokens of His mercy and long-suffering favor. He has been pleased to bestow them on a people who often do not acknowledge Him in their hearts, nor thank Him as they ought for His blessings on their labors. Through these gifts, God in His mercy still calls to an apostate generation: "Turn ye, turn ye from your evil ways; for why will ye die?" (Ezekiel 33:11).

But It Is a "Cut-Flower Civilization"

But although these blessings of God's grace make our civilization worth keeping, the fact remains that our civilization carries within itself the seeds of its own eventual destruction and decay. Having turned from God, we are enjoying His favors, but without acknowledging them. You have heard the term, a "cut-flower civilization." And such are we, who, having denied the only living God—having cut ourselves off from the Root of Life—are like a cut flower that blossoms for a while in beauty, but soon dies because it has been separated from the source of its life. Increasingly, as we ignore or reject God, our civilization will show the effects of spiritual death and depravity in all areas of life. The good things the Lord has given us will be used to hinder man rather than bless Him. The fruits of science, for example, will destroy man rather than uplift and better his life. The benefits of extended public education will only serve to lead him further and further into a spiritual wilderness instead of returning him to the Father's home.

The Great Gift of Freedom

Greatest of all the favors that we today enjoy in our civilization is the gift of freedom. That gift was itself the product of Christian thought. It developed, as a seed, out of the religious culture of an earlier age. Today that earlier religious culture has been wiped away. But the seed has grown and blossomed and borne rich fruit. In the still nominally Christian cultures of today, a man is free to do what he believes is right before God and his fellow man, within the bounds of justice and order. He will not be imprisoned or sent to face a firing squad because he follows his convictions. He has personal freedom, political freedom, religious freedom. And this freedom is extended to the citizen, to the woman, to the black, to men regardless of race or creed. The human spirit, in the still nominally Christian countries, is not fettered in chains.

For this most precious of all gifts of our civilization, we have God to thank. But unless we, as a people, return in gratitude to that God and thank Him for the gifts He has given us, the day will come—and it may be soon—when the cup of our iniquity will be full, when judgment will fall upon us as it has also fallen upon other countries and nations that once were strong and glorious.

Pray God that our people and our nation may so repent before Him, and renew themselves, that our civilization in His eyes may be worth keeping for many years to come.

Faith Without Works Is Dead, Part One

1. *The Bible Directly Teaches This*

The Bible directly teaches the truth that faith without works is dead. The words of my theme are themselves, as you know, taken directly from the Epistle of James (James 2:17, 20, 26). And this truth is as directly stated in Romans, the great epistle on justification by faith alone. "Do we," asks Paul, "then make void the law through faith? God forbid: yea, we establish the law" (Romans 3:31). I shall explain later on how that is so. At this time it is sufficient to note that Paul never for a moment supposed that he was teaching any doctrine contrary to an insistence on the highest conceivable morality.

In Paul's Words
Paul asks further in the sixth chapter, "What shall we say then? Shall we continue in sin, that grace may abound? God forbid. How shall we that are dead to sin, live any longer therein?" (Romans 6:1–2). In 1 Corinthians 9:27 we find Paul saying, "But I keep under my body, and bring it into subjection; lest that by any means, when I have preached to others, I myself should be a castaway." These words are not the voice of a libertine who fancied that, because justification was by faith alone, apart from works, this gave him a license to sin. On the contrary, he taught that if he ceased the most diligent Christian discipline, he, though an apostle and preacher of the grace of God, would perish in hell. In the same epistle, he speaks as plainly, "Know ye not that the unrighteous shall not inherit the

kingdom of God? Be not deceived: neither fornicators, nor idolaters, nor adulterers, nor effeminate, nor abusers of themselves with mankind, nor thieves, nor covetous, nor drunkards, nor revilers, nor extortioners, shall inherit the kingdom of God" (1 Corinthians 6:9–10). Even the apostle James, whose letter has been called the Epistle of the Royal Law, did not preach the law with greater emphasis and insistence than the author of Romans and Corinthians.

In John's Words

The First Epistle of John likewise stresses the necessity of the most holy living. "If we say that we have fellowship with Him, and walk in darkness, we lie, and do not the truth" (1 John 1:6). Continuing in the second chapter, John says, "And hereby we do know that we know Him, if we keep His commandments. He that saith, 'I know Him,' and keepeth not His commandments is a liar, and the truth is not in him. But whoso keepeth His Word, in him verily is the love of God perfected: hereby know we that we are in Him. He that saith he abideth in Him ought himself also so to walk, even as He walked" (1 John 2:3–6).

In Jesus' Words

But Jesus Himself was the most emphatic of all. "If a man love Me," He said, "he will keep My words" (John 14:23). "Let your light," He commanded, "so shine before men, that they may see your good works and glorify your Father which is in heaven" (Matthew 5:16). "Herein is My Father glorified, that ye bear much fruit; so shall ye be My disciples" (John 15:8). "By their fruits," He said, "ye shall know them" (Matthew 7:20).

We have a record of only one instance in the life of Jesus when He cursed anything, and that was a *thing*, and not a human being. He came not to condemn the world, but that the world through Him might be saved (John 3:17). When He comes again He will come to condemn the unbelieving world; but His first mission was an offer of pardon. Nevertheless, Jesus did curse something, and that was the fig tree. But it was not because there was sin in a tree. Rather, there was something about that tree that was meant to teach men a lesson. What was it? It was a tree that had leaves, but no fruit. For this reason Christ cursed it as a warning that He would likewise, in the day of judgment, curse men who made profession, but bore no evidence of faith—men who said they loved Christ, but did not keep His commandments.

We could cite innumerable instances of the biblical insistence on holy living. For from beginning to end, the Bible insists that without holiness no man shall see the Lord (Hebrews 12:14). Only the pure in heart shall see God (Matthew 5:8). Faith without works is dead.

2. The Doctrine of Justification by Faith Implies It

Faith is necessary to justification. But it must be true faith. And a man must have it, not merely say he has it. No promises are made to mere profession, but only to possession. That Paul never for a moment thinks of faith as mere nominal assent to some proposition, but a real union in trust with Jesus Christ, is everywhere evident. For example, in the tenth chapter of Romans he says that we must confess with our mouth and believe in our heart that Jesus Christ is Lord (Romans 10:9). Confession with the mouth is an evidence of faith, but it is not conclusive proof unless it is coupled with belief in the heart.

Paul Teaches This

"What shall we say then? Shall we continue in sin, that

grace may abound?" This is the very objection against justification by faith that is still made today by the Romanists and by most everyone else who objects to this doctrine. How does Paul answer this objection? He answers it by saying that the question is preposterous. It is a psychological impossibility for anyone who truly believes in Christ to continue in sin. "How shall we, that are dead to sin [dead to sin because alive to Christ] live any longer therein?" The question is absurd on the surface of it. Paul does not stoop to further refutation. If a person truly repents of his sin and comes to Christ, he simply cannot go on sinning as he had previously done. If he does go on sinning as he had previously done, he simply has not meant it when he said that he believed in Christ.

James Teaches This

If it is true, on the one hand, that Paul teaches that faith without works is dead, it is true, on the other, that James teaches that justification is by faith. Let us show how this is so in the very passage where James says that justification is by works (James 2:17ff.). He begins by asking, "Was not Abraham our father justified by works, when he had offered Isaac his son upon the altar?" (2:21). This seems on the surface like a flat contradiction of the Pauline doctrine. But suspend your judgment for a moment till we look at the whole passage and you will see that James is here using the word "justify" in another sense. He continues, "Seest thou how faith wrought with his works, and by works was faith made perfect?" (2:22). In the context James is discussing the false and unsaving faith of merely nominal Christians in contrast with the faith of true believers. He points out that such nominal faith was exhibited even by the devils, who believe and even tremble. But true faith is exemplified in father Abraham. James is showing how the trueness of Abraham's faith is proved. Was it by the mere fact that Abraham professed to believe? No, it was proved ("justified") by what he did. His offering up of his son at God's command demonstrated classically that Abraham really trusted in God and did not merely say that he did. Such willingness to slay his dear son of promise established beyond doubt that Abraham believed. So, as James puts it, his "faith wrought with his works, and by works was faith made perfect."

In the next verse James comes to his conclusion: "And the Scripture was fulfilled which saith, 'Abraham believed God, and it was imputed unto him for righteousness' " (2:23). In other words, Abraham's willingness to sacrifice Isaac having proved that he believed God, it was his belief, not his works, that was counted to him for righteousness. It was not the sacrificing of Isaac that saved Abraham; it was the faith that was revealed in his willingness to sacrifice Isaac that saved him. This is the doctrine of justification by faith alone without works (without any contribution coming from the works, they being merely a proof of the presence of the faith), as purely stated by James as any sentence we have in the apostle Paul.

Indeed, the argument of James is based on the very same Old Testament statement cited by Paul: "Abraham believed God, and it was imputed unto him for righteousness." There is perfect harmony here. Both teach that justification (in the sense of a "being made righteous" before God) is by faith alone, and both teach that the reality of this faith can be shown by works only. James agrees with Paul that justification is by faith alone; and Paul agrees with James that faith without works is dead.

3. The Divine Purpose in Salvation Involves It

It is not only that the Bible explicitly states that faith without works is dead, and states it everywhere; it is not only that the central biblical doctrine of justification by faith without the works of the law implies this truth; but it is evident in that the very divine purpose in the salvation of the elect was the producing of a holy people. If this is the case, it is perfectly evident that the way in which God saves His people would not be hostile to the very good works for which He saved them. If God aimed at the producing of good works and then chose a method that would guarantee to render them unnecessary, this would be a flat denial of the intelligence of the all-wise God.

Salvation Is Unto Sanctification

That this is the purpose of God the Bible tells us very clearly. In Romans 8:29 we read: "For whom He foreknew, He also did predestinate to be conformed to the image of His Son." This shows that the eternal election of God was for the purpose of conforming His people to His Son. He predestined them to be "conformed to the image of His Son." And "whom He justified, them He also glorified" (Romans 8:30). There is no separation of sanctification and justification in the divine order of salvation. Justification is followed by sanctification, as the day follows the night. So also in 2 Thessalonians 2:13 we read: "God hath from the beginning chosen you to salvation through sanctification of the Spirit and belief of the truth." God's choosing, therefore, was "through sanctification of the Spirit."

In other words, where God chooses there is sanctification, and where there is sanctification God has chosen. If there is no sanctification, there is no divine choice. As Jesus Himself says, "You have not chosen Me, but I have chosen you . . . that you should go and bring forth fruit" (John 15:16). Why are men chosen? For the purpose of bearing fruit. Those who do not bear fruit are cut off and thrown into the fire, He tells us in John 15:6. Likewise Titus 2:13–14: "Looking for . . . the glorious appearing of the great God and our Savior Jesus Christ, who gave Himself for us, that He might redeem us from all iniquity, and purify unto Himself a peculiar people, zealous of good works." This means that the distinguishing characteristic of the true people of God is a zeal for good works. That is the very purpose for which Christ redeemed them from sin: that they should walk in "newness of life" and not fulfill the lusts of the flesh (Romans 6:4).

Salvation Is Unto Good Works

But perhaps the divine purpose in election and salvation is most plainly stated in Ephesians, where we read in 1:4: "He hath chosen us in Him before the foundation of the world, that we should be holy and without blame before Him in love"; and in 1:12: "That we should be to the praise of His glory." Especially in Ephesians 2:6–10 is this purpose most clearly announced, where we read that God has made us "sit together in heavenly places in Christ Jesus, that in the ages to come He might show the exceeding riches of His grace in His kindness toward us through Christ Jesus. For by grace are ye saved through faith, and that not of yourselves: it is the gift of God—not of works, lest any man should boast. For we are His workmanship, created in Christ Jesus unto good works, which God hath before ordained that we should walk in them."

Faith Without Works Is Dead, Part Two

There are many today, as in all ages of the church, who have tried to use the great doctrine of gracious salvation as an excuse for sin. Such persons will resent this doctrine that faith without works is dead. Many objections are raised against it because this doctrine cuts so ruthlessly into the lusts of men, professing Christians included.

"Objection" Found in 1 Corinthians 3:12–15

Some will say, consider 1 Corinthians 3:12–15. Here we are taught that some men, on their foundation of faith in Christ, build works of wood, hay, and stubble; yet all these works are burned away in the judgment, but they themselves are saved "so as by fire." Does this not teach that a person may be a true Christian who has never done a single good work, who all his days, few or many, has continued in his carnality as he had lived in it before his conversion?

All we need say against any such objection is to bring up the overwhelming testimony of Scripture, some of which we have already cited. If throughout the Bible faith without works is dead, is Paul going to teach in one verse that it may yet be alive without works? If the covetous, drunkards, and others shall not inherit the kingdom according to 1 Corinthians 6:9–10, are they going to be able to inherit it according to 1 Corinthians 3? If Christ says it is not possible to love Him and not keep His commandments, is His inspired Apostle going to say that it is possible? Certainly not, and especially so when Paul has written that the very predestination of God was for the purpose of conformity to Christ.

Whatever the interpretation of this admittedly difficult passage of the Bible, certainly it cannot be construed so as to subvert the whole foundation of the sacred revelation. To do so would be to make God a liar. The context in 1 Corinthians actually refers not so much to individual Christian living as it does to ministers and their works as pastors. It seems to refer to the fact that some evangelical ministers, though they build on Christ, do not build so wisely as other evangelical ministers who also build on Christ. The works of one shall stand and the works of the other shall fall, but the men themselves, as true lovers and servants of Christ, shall be saved while the fire of judgment destroys their work. It is not important that you accept the interpretation of this passage given here. What is important is that you be not led astray by a palpably false and, indeed, pernicious misconstruction of the passage.

"Objection" Concerning the Thief on the Cross

Another objection concerns the thief on the cross and all who, like him, are saved at the moment of death, before they have had opportunity to do any good works and thereby prove their faith. Faith without works was not dead in the case of this thief, it is said.

We answer: First, faith does immediately begin to produce good works and cannot exist a moment without that tendency. The thief on the cross, for example, did pray, and that already is a sign of true faith. He also rebuked the evil accusations of his fellow criminal, and this was a virtuous bearing witness to the truth. He likewise worshipped Jesus—a supreme act of faith. These things we know. What other good works he may have done before his moments on earth were over and he was with his Lord in paradise we need not know.

Second, works are recognized by God in the intention. God would have known that the thief on the cross—had he had opportunity—would have further confessed his sins, received baptism, joined the church, and lived a new life.

Third, the works are not really necessary for God—who knows the heart—but they are necessary for us, who can only know the heart indirectly through the things that come from it. God knew Abraham's heart before his great trial; it was Abraham who needed to know it. The test was not for God's sake, but for His servant's. So it is with the thief and all others who are saved in the last moments of life. No greater opportunity for works is necessary, because they are never necessary for God, nor are they necessary for men when they are about to go into the very presence of God.

Objection: "Another Gospel"

There are some who think that the doctrine that "faith without works is dead" subverts the whole foundation of gracious salvation. They think that this doctrine is "another gospel" (Galatians 1:6–7). Indeed, some have so said. They contend, "If salvation is by grace apart from works, how dare you make works necessary?" The answer is plain. The Scripture does not make works necessary as the foundation of salvation, but as the demonstration of faith. Works do not contribute a thing to our salvation, which is all of grace apart from works. Salvation is all of faith that no man may boast. Works and works alone, however, are the fruits by which we know true faith. As James teaches us, "faith wrought with his works, and by works was faith made perfect" (reached its goal or its expression, James 2:22). The Bible is equally insistent on two things: first, salvation is purely by grace through faith; second, the only true and saving faith is a faith that is full of good works, a persevering faith. What God has joined together let no man put asunder. According to the Bible, three propositions are true: 1. Works without faith are dead. 2. Faith without works is dead. 3. Salvation is by a working (or living) faith.

A Word of Warning

Let us give you a word of warning concerning a subtle error of our day. Perhaps an illustration will make it plainer and enable you to examine yourselves the more carefully to see that the grace of God is not in vain in you. The story is told of a man who once testified that, after becoming a Christian, he stole a light bulb from the company for which he worked. Each night as he looked to heaven in prayer, the sight of the bulb would disturb his conscience. Finally he returned it. This was his testimony: "If I had never returned the bulb, I would have gone to heaven anyway, but I would not have been happy along the way."

The man in this story may have meant well, but he did not speak well. He said, whatever he *meant* to say, that he could have been a thief on his way to heaven. But the Scriptures say that thieves shall not inherit the kingdom of God. Notice that the man did not say merely that he was overtaken in a fault, that he confessed it, and was restored. He said that, though he had been overtaken in a fault, never confessed it, and had never been restored, yet he would have been on his way to heaven, though unhappy along the way. How dreadfully mistaken! While the Bible says that Christians overtaken in a fault may be restored, it says that thieves shall not enter the kingdom of God. And a man who takes a bulb and never returns it is a thief. Faith without works is dead.

Examine yourselves, dear friends. Are you thieves? Have

you ever stolen something that you insist on not returning? It may have been something far subtler and less tangible than a bulb. Maybe you, by a lying tongue or an innuendo, have stolen someone else's good name. Maybe you are in the practice, even now, of regularly robbing God of His portion of money, time, prayer, or whatever it may be. Examine yourselves whether you are covetous, for the covetous shall not inherit the kingdom of God. True faith works by good works, and covetousness is not a good work. You may be overtaken, surprised by an act of covetousness of which you may humbly repent, and for which you are graciously forgiven by a merciful God. But are you in the habit of coveting? Is it established practice with you? Is it a way of life? If so, your faith is not genuine. Are you pure? But it is not enough to be pure merely outwardly, for God tries the heart, and adultery is in the intentions.

Salvation is by grace through faith alone. But be sure that your faith is not dead.

You're in the Army Now

Matthew 21:1–11 records the triumphant entry of Jesus Christ into Jerusalem. On this day He was heralded as the King. This acclaim He accepted, for He *is* a King. This King has subjects; indeed, they call themselves "servants (or slaves) of Jesus Christ" (Philippians 1:1). They acknowledge Jesus to be their only and absolute Sovereign. And only such does He acknowledge as members of His kingdom who recognize His sovereignty. "If any man will come after Me, let him deny himself (i.e., pull himself up by the roots; completely divest himself of himself, so that Christ may be his Master), and take up his cross, and follow Me" (Matthew 16:24). "If ye love Me," He said, "keep My commandments" (John 14:15). He drafts no one into His army. He shanghais no one. No one is conscripted. Only those are admitted who voluntarily enlist. On the other hand, those who wish to enlist are accepted only on condition of complete surrender to His will. One either takes Christ or he leaves Him.

Obedience First of All

The idea of the kingship of Jesus is almost completely lacking today. Our age seems to be allergic to terms like "authority," "commands," and "obedience." We prefer, rather exclusively, to talk about "winning," "persuading," "interesting," and "challenging." Let your children do, we say, not what they *ought* to do, but what they *want* to do. Read the Bible, not because it is *required* reading, but because it is *interesting* reading. Be honest, not because it is a *duty*, but because it *pays*. Come to church, not because you *have to*, but because you *like to*. Be a Christian, not because it is God's *will*, but because it is a wonderful *experience.*

A person nourished on this diet of self-expression experiences a rude awakening when he enters the army and the sergeant states the hour at which he is to arise, what he must do when he arises, how he is to do it, and what will happen if he does not do it. One day on a distant field he is told, "Tomorrow we will take that hill. Some of you will not live to see the victory; but we will take that hill." Then the one who has been nurtured on the marrow of self-expression, possibly in the church of Christ itself, bitterly says:

> *Ours is not to reason why,*
> *Ours is just to do and die.*

Of course, it is not for every private to "reason why." Of course, it is for him "to do and die." There is no other way. What army could ever win a battle if it consulted all its members before the attack? Confidence in those whose responsibility it is to "reason why," and obedience on the part of those whose responsibility is the doing and dying, is a necessary combination in any successful army—including the Christian army. "Onward, Christian soldiers, marching as to war, with the *crown* of Jesus going on before" would be better phraseology. It is Christ as King, not as Savior, who commands His victorious militia. And every member of that army must be obedient, just as its Commander before him was obedient "even unto death" (Philippians 2:8, ASV).

The Infallible Commander

Regard for authority is a great moral lesson that the church can learn from the army and war. It is another point at which the children of this world are wiser than the children of light (Luke 16:8). Certainly no man or woman who has served in the nation's army should feel that discipline is a matter of lesser importance in the army of Christ. Yet I have met some who, rather than being grateful for the severity of army discipline, have rebelled against it and, continuing their place in the Christian army, fancy that they are finished with discipline forever. Far from it!

The Christian army has a Commander who is infinitely more exacting! His regulations require constant observance; and there are no "leaves" and no areas free of the Commanding Officer's supervision. Christian friend, you are in the army now! It is worthy of note that the class of men who, as a class, come in for most consistent praise in the New Testament are the Roman captains. There are Cornelius and a number of others in the Acts and Gospels, but especially that unnamed centurion of whom Jesus Himself said, "I have not found so great faith, no, not in Israel" (Matthew 8:10). And this centurion's faith was displayed by his implicit recognition of the authority of Jesus Christ!

In spite of all this similarity, it remains to be said that there is also a great difference between this world's army and that of Christ. Our sergeants make mistakes; Christ never. Our captains sometimes exercise their authority to our detriment; Christ never. The rulers of this world desire authority for the opportunity it gives them to "throw their weight around"; Christ never. He says, "Take My yoke upon you . . . for My yoke is easy, and My burden is light" (Matthew 11:29–30). His is a slavery that spells freedom. Those who lose their lives for His sake testify that they find their lives at that very moment. It is those who try to avoid His yoke who labor and are heavy laden. It is those who try to break His bands and cast His cords from them who rage and are distraught. "Come unto Me," He says, "and I will give you rest." William Wordsworth's "Ode to Duty" expresses Christ's truth well:

Stern Daughter of the Voice of God!
O Duty! if that name thou love
Who art a light to guide, a rod
To check the erring, and reprove;
Thou who art victory and law
When empty terrors overawe;
From vain temptations dost set free
And calm'st the weary strife of frail humanity!

Stern Lawgiver! yet thou dost wear
The Godhead's most benignant grace;
Nor know we anything so fair
As is the smile upon Thy face:
Flowers laugh before Thee on their beds,
And fragrance in Thy footing treads;
Thou dost preserve the Stars from wrong;
And the most ancient Heavens, through Thee,
Are fresh and strong.

But while Wordsworth's poem expresses Christ's truth well, there is a simple hymn that expresses it better, less eloquently, perhaps, but more pointedly:

There is no other way to be happy in Jesus,
But to trust and obey.

Can Anyone Drink and Harm Only Himself?

We are all aware of the caustic charge that the Puritans of old England opposed bear baiting, "not because it gave pain to the bear, but because it gave pleasure to the spectators." It is very commonly assumed by "wets" that "drys" have opposed the use of alcohol because the wets enjoyed it. Actually, drinking is to be condemned not because it gives pleasure to some, but because, ultimately, it brings grief to all.

O'Reilly stepped up to the bar shouting to his colleagues, "When O'Reilly drinks, everybody drinks." Everybody drank. Then O'Reilly deliberately set his glass down and said, slapping a quarter on the bar, "When O'Reilly pays, everybody pays." How true it is that when the drinker pays, everybody pays, as we shall see.

Can anyone drink and harm only himself? Apparently the late Mayor LaGuardia did not think so when, concerning the formation of the Alcoholic Therapy Bureau in his city, he said, "We are not altogether altruistic about this. Don't forget that 80% of the cases in the magistrates' courts are alcoholics. This means a terrific cost to New York."

Can anyone drink and harm only himself? Leon A. Greensburg, Ph.D., did not think so when he said, "Before the day of the automobile, hazards of drunkenness were more largely personal. Now highway traffic makes . . . the drinking driver . . . a menace to safety. . . . The drinking driver who isn't manifestly drunk may yet be an awfully dangerous man."

The following joke is a bit too grimly realistic to be very funny. Two drunkards were riding in an automobile. One said to his friend, "I see that we're getting nearer town limits." "How do you know that?" asked the other. "We are hitting more people," was the answer.

Can anyone drink and harm only himself? Perhaps, if he were Robinson Crusoe. But if not, then the conclusion of the Yale School of Alcoholic Studies says "No": "It is almost impossible to comprehend or exaggerate the *tremendous loss to society, economically, socially, and morally*, involved in this demoralization, not only of these 600,000 persons who might have lived normal lives (the excessive drinkers), but of the millions of others, children, related members of families, and associates, whom this more than *half million* 'excessive' drinkers have affected almost as *disease carriers*." Furthermore, one out of every 20 drinkers will become excessive alcoholics, and there seems to be no way of knowing who these will be.

Can anyone drink and harm only himself? Not if the person in question ever has any children. But if he ever does, the fact must be faced that he will hand his offspring an initial handicap with which to begin their new life. Dr. C. F. Hodge's carefully controlled experiment with two pairs of dogs furnished valuable information: Bum and Tipsy were fed alcohol with their food; Nig and Topsy had no alcohol; otherwise the pairs, alike in blood and breeding, were treated the same. There was found to be a wide difference in the puppies of the two pairs; only 17.4% (that is, 4 out of 23) of the puppies of Bum and Tipsy were normal and able to live, while 91.1% (41 out of 45) of the puppies of Nig and Topsy were normal and lived.

It is not convincing to compare families of puppies with families of children, but it is interesting to note that this study by Dr. Hodge of an alcoholic dog family corresponded in percentage of normals to a study Dr. Lemme made in Switzerland of alcoholic human families, which showed 17.5% normals. Bianchi of the Royal University of Naples has said, "An alco-

holic mother gives to the world either a prostitute or a delinquent, when she does not give an epileptic, an idiot, or a lu-
natic."

Can anyone drink and harm only himself? Not unless he
was born without sexual appetites. But if that is not the case,
the following statements are significant: "Alcohol increases the
tendency to sex offenses. Many sad cases are reported of both
young men and young girls whose first seduction resulted
from uncontrollable excitement and loss of resistance brought
on by the first drink, and as a result they have contracted the
dread disease the first night of intoxication. Alcohol has a weak-
ening effect on the control of sex impulses, particularly in
women. Of patients who seek treatment for the disease, from
76% to 90% seem to have contracted it after taking alcohol."

Can anyone drink and harm only himself? Not if the person
has a mother who loves her son. If he does, then his mother
must suffer. If she does not, will someone explain why the
Congressional Record shows ever-increasing numbers of petitions from mothers asking the passage of bills forbidding the
sale of intoxicating liquors in or near military camps?

Can anyone drink and harm only himself? Indeed, if there is
no Jesus Christ. But if there is, what will Saul Kane reply to the
Christian missionary's words:

> "Saul Kane," she said, "when next you drink,
> Do me the gentleness to think
> That every drop of drink accursed
> Makes Christ within you die of thirst,
> That every dirty word you say
> Is one more flint upon His way,
> Another thorn about His head,
> Another mock by where He tread,
> Another nail, another cross.
> All that you are is that Christ's loss."

Can anyone drink and harm only himself? By this random survey of the social and spiritual effects of drinking is the answer not shown to be negative? The strong words of Evangeline Booth are unembellished fact: "Drink has shed more blood, hung more crepe on the door handles, sold out more homes, forced more people into bankruptcy, armed more villainy, killed more children, snapped more wedding rings, murdered more innocents, blinded more reason, disarmed more manhood, destroyed more womanhood, broken more hearts, blasted more lives, dug more graves than any other poisoned scourge ever let loose upon the world."

If these words are factual, and they are, then wisdom and common sense say, "No one can drink and harm only himself."

A Bird's-Eye View
of Church History

The Bible teaches but one story—the story of redemption. We will observe the response of people to that story. It is as you might expect: some respond favorably and some unfavorably. Some welcome their Savior while others resent the implication that they need a Savior. The former class, the believers, constitute what we call the church.

It is the story of this church that we wish briefly to sketch. As soon as there was one sinner who responded to the gracious overtures of God, there was the church. Adam, Abel, Seth, Noah, and the other early Genesis heroes evidenced their faith in God by the sacrifices they offered. The church existed there. But the church was not organized until Abraham was called out of Ur of the Chaldees to become the father of the faithful, and these faithful were now to be set apart from the rest of the world by a sign, circumcision, and a place, the land of Palestine. Further organization was accomplished under Moses.

The Church Existed before Christ

In Old Testament days the church was an institution different from the church as we know it today. It differed in various respects. First, church and state were one rather than separate. Second, the church was restricted almost completely to one national group rather than being universal. Third, the church was preparing for and anticipating the first coming of Christ rather than rejoicing in it as an accomplished fact and now looking forward to His return "to judge the quick and the dead" (1 Peter 4:5). Fourth, the church was in a state of childhood and discipline rather than maturity and freedom. Fifth, the emphasis, consequently, was on the external form which symbolized Christ rather than upon Christ Himself, manifest. Sixth, knowledge of God was through a special group, the prophets; and access to God in worship through another special group, the priests. Today the Word of God is completely revealed, and access is free to all by the last properly ordained priest, who is Christ Himself, "who ever liveth to make intercession for us" (Hebrews 7:25).

But in both dispensations it was one church, that is, a body of believers, though administered under the very different circumstances and modes which we have described. The Christian church, therefore, is the continuation of the Jewish church, just as the oak is the fruition of the acorn, or as the butterfly emerges from the chrysalis.

Christianity Is a Continuation of Judaism

If, however, the Christian church is the Jewish church reorganized along its modern lines, what is present-day Judaism? For that matter, what was the status of the majority of the Jews of Jesus' time who did not receive Him? Do they not claim to be the continuation of the Old Testament church? They do; especially the Orthodox Jews do. What then? The answer is, they are and they are not. They are the lineal descendants of the Old Testament priests and prophets; they maintain Old Testament ceremonies; they observe the Old Testament law. And yet they are not the Old Testament church. The Christian church is the true continuation of the Old Testament church, although it is not generally of the same nationality, does not maintain the Old Testament ceremonies, and has done away with most of the Old Testament ritual laws.

How then can we substantiate our claim to be of Abraham's seed and the continuation of the Old Testament church? The answer is, we are the same in spirit. The Old Testament looked forward to Christ, and we believe in Him; the Jewish church was saved not by works but by grace, and so are we; the Jewish church saw in the sacrifices and rituals so many pointers to Christ, and so do we; and while the Old Testament continued them because Christ had not yet come, we have discontinued them because He has come.

To Deny Christ Is to Deny Judaism

For a Jewish friend, therefore, to deny Christ is to deny not only Christianity, but also Old Testament Judaism. It is to reveal that he who is a lineal descendant of Abraham is not of his spiritual seed. Here is an interesting illustration of the principle of Christ: "For unto every one that hath shall be given, and he shall have abundance; but from him that hath not shall be taken away even that which he hath" (Matthew 25:29). To the Jew who has not Christ, even the Old Testament itself is his no more; the Christian, having Christ, has the Old Testament also.

This truth needs special emphasis because we are often beguiled into judging by appearances. It would *appear* that the Jew is the heir of the Jewish church. Especially would it appear so when it is remembered that the vast *majority* of Jews in Christ's day, and still today, do not believe in Christianity and did not and will not join the Christian church. Majorities, however, do not determine truth. It was that handful of original apostles and disciples, all of them Jews, who constituted the Jewish church, and not the majority who did not believe.

The Reformation, the Last Epoch of the Christian Church

The last great epoch of the Christian church was the Reformation. At that time something occurred rather similar, in one respect, to the great reorganization at the time of Christ.

The Jewish church just before Christ and the Christian church before Luther had one thing in common: they both had degenerated. True, they had done great things for God, had produced great prophets and saints, had kept the testimony of the Word alive. Yet they had declined through the gradual infection of false doctrine, the toleration of immorality, the development of a hierarchy of religious leaders who were not orthodox in teaching and were less so in example. Christ appeared, and the true remnant followed Him. And as the church of which the apostles were the head was the true Jewish church now made universal, so the church of which the reformers were the head was the true Christian church made pure. And just as the Jewish majority that did not accept Christianity ceased to be the true Jewish church, so the majority that did not accept the Reformation of Christianity ceased to be the true Christian church. But in each case the true church was made out of the remnant of the previous one.

The Real History of the Church

When people ask me, "When did Protestantism originate?" my answer is, "With Adam." It was the Roman church which originated in the 16th century A.D. But we do not read it so in history books. According to most of them, Catholicism began with the first pope and Protestantism began with Luther. Books say such things, however, because they almost necessarily judge by majorities and externals, and not by underlying principles and attitudes.

There, then, is the vital history of the church. Founded in Adam, organized with Abraham and Moses, reorganized, spiritualized, and universalized by our Lord, and purified by the Reformation. What will be the next epoch?

The Scriptural Case for Desertion as a Ground for Divorce, Part One

These articles will be devoted to the two crucial exegetical questions concerning desertion as a ground for divorce: First, "Does Christ's Teaching *Preclude* Divorce for Desertion?" Second, "Does Paul's Teaching *Allow* Divorce for Desertion?" We shall endeavor to prove that Christ's "except for adultery" teaching does not rule out desertion by implication, and that Paul positively teaches what Christ does not deny, namely, divorce for desertion.

Does Christ's Teaching Preclude Divorce for Desertion?

We assume that Christ allows divorce for adultery. Matthew 5:32 reads: "Every one who divorces his wife, except on the ground of unchastity, makes her an adulteress; and whoever marries a divorced woman commits adultery." Matthew 19:9 reads: "Whoever divorces his wife, except for unchastity, and marries another, commits adultery" (RSV).

It is well known that the Roman, Orthodox, and the old Anglican Churches have not interpreted these words to allow divorce (with right to remarry). Father Joyce's work, *Christian Marriage*, affords a statement of the Romish interpretation. F. L. Cirlot of the Episcopal Church has recently written a cogent argument for a return of the church to its former position.

It is interesting to notice that Cirlot does not appeal to traditional Romish arguments but, for the most part, attacks the textual authenticity of the "exceptive clause" itself. Fortunately, we need not discuss this intricate problem because the United Presbyterian Church is not calling in question the scripturalness of adultery as a ground for divorce. For the interested student, however, there is an able argument for Matthew's (where the exceptive clause is found) originality in Charles, *Divorce and the Roman Doctrine of Nullity*, Chapters I and II.

Textual Criticism Does Not Alter Argument

It will not be out of order to note in passing that no less a scholar than Streeter finds the critical argument for the priority of either Mark (where the exceptive clause is omitted) or Matthew inconclusive: "The Marcan version is almost invariably the shorter, but the brevity is caused by an omission of features in the Q version which are obviously original." The Q version is not an expansion of the Marcan—assuming anything about textual criticism, whether there ever was an original source called "Q" or not. It should be noted that a foremost New Testament critic finds no reason to believe that Mark's briefer statements are original and that Matthew expanded them. It is as reasonable to think that Mark abbreviated an original fuller account—as a matter of fact Streeter distinctly favors the idea. In other words, Cirlot and others have no certain right to assume that Matthew has added the exceptive clause to Mark's original account. We may with equal justification, so far as the text is concerned, assume that Mark simply omitted to state the exceptive clauses.

Christ Limits Ground for Divorce to Adultery

We assume that Christ specifically limits the active ground for divorce to adultery. There are those who, like Zwingli, have regarded the "one" exception as a mere instance of which there are others. Likewise some have maintained that Christ's teaching is "idealistic" and not conformable to the hard facts of life. We do not feel it necessary to criticize these positions inasmuch as they are not under question at this time. As of this moment the denomination officially rules out the "idealistic" interpretation inasmuch as it restricts divorce to the one ground, so far as Christ's teaching is concerned.

Paul Admits Desertion as Ground for Divorce

We maintain that Christ's restriction of the *active* ground for divorce to adultery is not inconsistent with Paul's admitting of desertion as the one *passive* ground for divorce. For the moment we are *assuming* that Paul does teach desertion to be a ground. We shall try later to *prove* that he does. Now we are merely saying that if Paul does teach so this does not contradict Christ's one exception. The reason we claim this is because, as we say, Christ is speaking of the *active* and Paul of the *passive* ground for divorce. This is what we mean by the distinction. Christ is saying that when a marriage partner commits adultery, the innocent partner may actively sue for divorce. The innocent party is taking the initiative in securing divorce. Now Paul is saying that when a marriage partner deserts the relationship he has broken the marriage and the innocent party may simply recognize the fact. The guilty party is taking the initiative in securing divorce because, practically speaking, separation is divorce. In the first case, the innocent party is active and, in the second case, passive. As the Lutheran theologian, Gerhard, stated it: "Christ speaks of him who turns from his wife; Paul to him from whom the wife has turned. Christ speaks of voluntary separation; Paul, of separation against the will of one."

Therefore, since there is no contradiction between a desertion doctrine in 1 Corinthians 7 and Christ's statements, the only question is whether Paul actually does teach the desertion doctrine. We have so far simply shown that he *may* have done so. In the succeeding article we shall attempt to show that he *did* so.

The Scriptural Case for Desertion as a Ground for Divorce, Part Two

We assume, first, that Paul was inspired of God and that his statements are, like Christ's, infallible. As a matter of fact, they are Christ's statements. In the Gospels we have the Incarnate Christ speaking directly; in the Epistles we have the resurrected Christ speaking indirectly through inspired human agents. This is the teaching of the United Presbyterian Church [now the PCUSA]:

> We believe that the Scriptures of the Old and New Testaments are the Word of God and are inspired throughout, in language as well as thought . . . and that they are an infallible rule of faith and practice and the supreme source of authority in spiritual truth (*Confessional Statement*, Article III).

1 Corinthians 7:10–16, the Scripture Passage Under Discussion

We maintain that in the "desertion" passage (1 Cor. 7:10–16) Paul is not disclaiming inspiration. To be sure he says, "To the rest I say, not the Lord, that . . ." A few commentators have fancied that Paul was here speaking as a private person, expressing an opinion rather than as an agent of divine revelation. The overwhelming consensus of opinion among students, both for and against desertion as a ground for divorce, repudiates this interpretation. It is generally agreed that Paul is here contrasting his revelation with that which the incarnate Christ gave. Notice that in verse 10 Paul is describing what "not I but the Lord" said. Here in verse 12, when he comes to deal with the believer-unbeliever marriage, he is authoritatively commentating on a subject untouched by the incarnate Christ's teaching in the Gospels. Hence he says, "I say, not the Lord." So far from denying revelation, he is unfolding supplemental revelation.

Paul here teaches, I maintain, that willful or malicious irremedial desertion is a ground for divorce. This brings us to the crucial part of our discussion. In support of the above position I shall adduce four reasons:

Paul's language favors divorce for desertion.
Paul's thought requires divorce for desertion.
Argument from analogy supports divorce for desertion.
Parallel in Christ's teaching suggests divorce for desertion.

Paul's Language Favors Divorce for Desertion
Let me present this crucial passage emphasizing the significant words. Here I am using the Revised Standard Version:

> To the married I give charge, not I but the Lord, that the wife should not *separate* [*choristenai*] from her husband (but if she does, let her remain single [*agamos*] or else be reconciled [*katalageto*] to her husband)—and that the husband should not divorce [*aphienai*] his wife. To the rest I say, not the Lord, that if any brother has a wife who is an unbeliever, and she consents to live with him, he should not divorce [*aphieto*] her. If any woman has a husband who is an unbeliever and he consents to live with her, she should not divorce [*aphieto*] him. For the unbelieving husband is consecrated through his wife, and the unbelieving wife is consecrated through her husband.

> Otherwise, your children would be unclean, but as it is
> they are holy. But if the unbelieving partner desires to sep-
> arate [*choridzetai*], let it be so; in such a case the brother
> or sister is not bound [*dedoulotai*]. For God has called us
> to peace. Wife, how do you know whether you will save
> your husband? Husband, how do you know whether you
> will save your wife? (1 Corinthians 7:10–16).

A word to the layman as we begin this word study. It is
not necessary to know Greek to evaluate the argument. Let any
reader simply refer to the above text where the Greek word is
transliterated alongside its English translation.

Does "Desertion Divorce" Carry Right to Remarry?

Another preliminary point of great importance is this: divorce in Paul's time carried with it the right to remarry. Even
opponents of my position such as Hovey, the Baptist, and
Cirlot, the Episcopalian, have admitted this. There was no
merely "legal separation" in those days. Separation from "bed
and board," without right to take another spouse, is a later
practice. Therefore, if we can show that Paul's separation was
tantamount to divorce, we have at the same time shown that it
entitles the deserted to remarriage.

Now we examine this word "separate" [*choristenai*]. In
verse 10 Paul says that "the wife should not separate from her
husband (but if she does, let her remain single or else be reconciled to her husband)—and that the husband should not divorce his wife." Quite obviously, apart from the parenthetical
expression, the basic doctrine is thus: "the wife should not
separate . . . the husband should not divorce." These are parallel
expressions, equivalent statements. Paul is saying that it is
wrong for either party to dissolve the relationship—neither
should divorce. Paul is really saying: "The wife should not divorce . . . the husband should not divorce." Only he is viewing

the wife as divorcing passively (that is, by separating, *choristhenai*); he is viewing the husband as divorcing actively (that is, by putting away, *aphienai*).

In other words, *choristenai*, "to separate," like *aphienai*, "to put away," means divorce. Definitely. Indeed, some have argued it is always the technical word for divorce, but we have never seen this proven. Nevertheless it is sometimes, although not exclusively, used for divorce. Compare, for proof, Charles's *The Teaching of the New Testament on Divorce* (pp. 114–15).

Separation-Divorce Leaves Marital Bond Sundered

Second, the separating wife is told to remain "single" (*agamos*—without husband). Thus, the separation-divorce leaves the marital bond sundered. The wife is single, without a husband. This compares quite exactly with the preceding context where Paul says in another connection of the automatic dissolution of the marital relationship by another sin: "Do you not know that he who joins himself to a prostitute becomes one body with her? For, as it is written, 'The two shall become one.' " Forgiveness, of course, can reconcile, but the very necessity of reconciliation implies the devastating effects of desertion which renders "husbandless," or adultery which unites to the prostitute.

The third word study will concern "be reconciled" (*katalageto*, verse 11). Opponents say this militates against our position because you cannot "reconcile" divorced couples. It requires more than that. However, Lowry aptly remarks: "But *katalassai*, as used in the New Testament and the profane authors, is fitted to suggest a reunion achieved with difficulty, rather than one achieved with ease and simplicity." Furthermore, it should be remembered that although this willfull desertion may entitle the deserted to remarriage, one need not exercise the prerogative. He may and should prefer reconciliation. Similarly, adultery entitles the offended party to divorce and remarriage, but he need not exercise the prerogative and may and normally should forgive and be reconciled.

It is admitted that this argument from language is inconclusive. It falls short of absolute proof. But it does yield, we believe, a strong probability. Critics will have to admit that it would have been difficult for Paul to find more suitable language to express the idea of divorce on the ground of willful desertion.

Paul's Thought Requires Divorce for Desertion

In the first place, I note that when Paul contemplated the wife as deserting he said, "Let her not marry." This implies that in the eyes of contemporary society and law she was divorced and might therefore remarry. Paul is saying that, while such procedure might be legal, it is not Christian inasmuch as she is the guilty, not the innocent party. Therefore he says, "Let her (not "them") not remarry."

Of far greater significance, however, are Paul's well-nigh conclusive words: "But if the unbelieving partner desires to separate, let it be so; in such a case the brother or sister is not bound" (verse 15). No longer "bound" seems inevitably to refer to the dissolution of the marital bond. At this point I feel the case is irrefutable. Perhaps the strongest indication of the correctness of our interpretation that "not bound" means "free from" the marital relationship is seen in the futility of the opponents in trying to interpret the word "bound." Most of them render the meaning thus: "The innocent party is not bound to try to regain the erring partner." Such a rendering seems futile, inasmuch as it should be obvious that a Christian would not feel obliged forever to try to re-establish a marriage sundered by a willful and malicious desertion. Furthermore, it is a sort of play on the word "bound" thus to construe it.

Argument from Analogy Supports Divorce for Desertion

This point leads into the argument from analogy. That is, willful, irremedial desertion is analogous to the death of the guilty party inasmuch as he has sundered himself completely from the marital relationship. As Charles Hodge understands Paul: "He teaches, first, that such marriages (believer-unbeliever) are lawful and, therefore, ought not to be dissolved. But, second, that if the unbelieving partner departs, i.e., repudiates the marriage, the believing partner is not bound; i.e., is no longer bound by the marriage compact. This seems to be the plain meaning. If the unbelieving partner is willing to continue in the marriage relation, the believing party is bound; bound, that is, to be faithful to the marriage compact. If the unbeliever is not willing to remain, the believer in that case is not bound; i.e., bound by the marriage compact. In other words, the marriage is thereby dissolved. This passage is parallel to Romans 7:2. The Apostle there says that a wife 'is bound by the law to her husband, so long as he liveth; but if the husband be dead, she is loosed from the law of her husband.' So here he says, 'A wife is bound to her husband if he is willing to remain with her; but if he deserts her, she is free from him." That is, willful desertion annuls the marriage bond."

The Parallel in Christ's Teaching Suggests Divorce for Desertion

In Mark, Jesus says, "And if she divorces her husband and marries another, she commits adultery." This is a strange saying because in those days only profligate women, such as Herodias, "divorced" their husbands. According to standard practice and doctrine, respectable Jewish women could be given, but could not give, a "bill of divorcement." Still our Lord speaks of the woman divorcing her husband. While it is likely that he was introducing a new regulation, it is not likely that it was soon understood as such. The first thing that would come to mind would have been the current way by which a woman divorced her husband—by leaving him or by desertion. If this is so, then Christ is here condemning the practice and Paul is saying the same thing, namely that if she leaves she should at least remain unmarried. But what we are here driving at is that in any case divorce and desertion seem to be equivalent terms.

With scant attention to what seem to be the two most cogent objections to our view this article will conclude. First, opponents contend that the Church Fathers did not recognize the two grounds for divorce. Apart from the fact that uninspired opinion, even of the early church, is never definitive, there is evidence that the case is considerably overdrawn. But most conclusive for our present consideration is this: the vast majority of those who appeal to the early church maintain that the Fathers knew nothing of *any* ground for divorce. If this were so, then the United Presbyterian Church, recognizing adultery as a ground, is at this moment on record as saying the Fathers erred. To find further error would not therefore surprise us.

The second objection is the practical one: "How long must the desertion last before it entitles the deserted to divorce and remarriage?" This is a thorny question, of course. Presbyterians have tended to say ten years; Lutherans say a shorter period.

There is much more that could be said, but in the interests of brevity and relative simplicity we rest the scriptural case at this point.

Justification by Faith Alone
Part One

The Spark that Lit the Reformation

Christendom has experienced many divisions during its history of almost 2,000 years. The two major ones were:

The separation between what is now called the Eastern Orthodox church and the western Roman Catholic church, which reached its final stages in A.D. 1054.

A division associated with the Reformation in the 16th century which gave birth to the Protestant movement.

Historically, the spark which lit the Protestant conflagration was struck by the hammer blow that Luther delivered when he nailed the 95 theses to the door of the Castle Church at Wittenburg. This act was not without precedent. This was the way a scholar announced his willingness to debate with other scholars on any given issue. There was no thought at this time of rebellion against Rome. In the theses themselves there was nothing anti-papal. They were protests against the abusive use of indulgences.

The immediate provocation of Luther's act revolved around a Dominican monk—one John Tetzel—who came from Rome into Germany to preach and to sell indulgences. Pope Leo X wanted to complete the building of the church of St. Peter in Rome. With this purpose in mind, he issued a bull granting an indulgence to anyone who would contribute voluntary offerings toward this cause. While it is true that the bull declared each gift "had to be accompanied by sincere repentance and confession of sin," the issuance of indulgences was being abused. They were being sold, and that shamelessly. The appeal was not so much to sincere repentance and confessions of sin as to escape from punishment in purgatory that one could obtain by the purchase of indulgences. Indeed, it was proclaimed that one's "loved ones" who were in purgatory could be delivered from punishment by the purchase of indulgences. Here is an extract from Tetzel's sermon:

> Listen to the voices of your loved ones: 'pity us! We are in dire torment from which you can redeem us for a pittance. Do you not wish to? Will you let us lie here in flames? Will you delay our promised glory?' Will you not then, for a quarter of a florin, receive these letters of indulgence through which you are able to lead a divine and immortal soul into the fatherland of Paradise? (Bainton, *Here I Stand,* p. 78).

In all fairness to the Catholic fathers, it is only right to point out that at the Council of Trent in 1563—after the Reformation had been fully established—they spoke out against the irregularity of granting indulgences by issuing the following decree:

> But desiring that the abusives which have become connected with them and by reason of which this excellent name of indulgences is blasphemed by the heretics, be amended and corrected, it ordains, in a general way by the present decree, that all evil traffic in them which has been a most prolific source of abuses among the Christian people, be absolutely abolished (Schroeder, *Canons and Decrees of the Council of Trent,* p. 253).

But Luther's protest went beyond his objection to the selling of indulgences. He insisted that it was a violation of the Gospel of God's grace to teach that one can buy release from punishment for sin by the purchase of indulgences and thus earn heaven by one's own sufferings either in this life or in purgatory. He saw that the teaching of Rome concerning indulgences involved the question of how the soul was to be justified before God. It was against this teaching that he protested with all his power. Little by little he saw that such teaching did great violence to the grace of God, by which alone man can be redeemed.

It will be well for us to be reminded of the teaching of the Catholic church on both purgatory and indulgences. According to a *Catechism of Christian Doctrines*:

> Those are punished for a time in purgatory who die in the state of grace but are guilty of venial sin, or have not fully satisfied for the temporal punishment due to their sins. There will be no purgatory after the general judgment. Since we do not know how long individual souls are detained in purgatory, there is need for persevering prayer for the repose of the souls of all who die after reaching the use of reason, except those who are canonized or beatified by the church. The souls in purgatory are certain of entering heaven as soon as God's justice has been fully satisfied (p. 143).

A recent *Handbook of the Catholic Faith* states:

> We do not know precisely of what this purification of purgatory consists. A part of the punishment will surely be the delay in beholding the beatific vision. Although it is not a doctrine of the church, it is taught by some that they also suffer physical pain by some agency similar to the fire of hell. On the other hand, there are those who say we must not give "a dreary interpretation to purgatory" as those who are there are of "the number of the elect" and are sure of heaven.

Indulgences have to do specifically with purgatory, but

Protestants ofttimes misunderstand the teaching of the Catholic church about both of these. In fact, many Protestants believe that an indulgence permits a Catholic to "indulge in sin" and that this privilege of sinning without punishment can be bought with a price. This is not true. Catholics absolutely repudiate any such teaching and, as we have seen, the Council of Trent "abolished all grants of indulgence which were conditioned upon a pecuniary contribution toward a specific object" (*The Catholic Encyclopedia*).

An indulgence, according to the official teaching of the Catholic church, is not a pardon of sin, still less is it a permission to commit sin. It is rather a release from temporal punishment which is granted by the church to those whose sins have already been forgiven. While grace has been restored to the one who has committed venial sin, usually there remain certain unpaid debts of temporal punishment. These can be eliminated in only two ways: first, through penance followed by confession; and, second, through suffering in purgatory.

The Roman Catholic church teaches that the time required in purgatory to pay for venial sins is shortened by the devotion of the faithful. "The faithful on earth, through the communion of saints, can relieve the sufferings of the souls in purgatory by prayer, fasting, and other good works, by indulgences, and by having masses offered for them" (*Catechism of Christian Doctrine*, p. 134).

From whence do these indulgences come, and on what ground can they be granted? The teaching of the church is that through the centuries a "spiritual treasury" has gradually been stored up by means of the "infinite satisfaction of Jesus Christ, and the superabundant satisfaction of the blessed Virgin Mary, and of the saints . . . which they gained during their lifetime but did not need" (*Catechism of Christian Doctrine*, pp. 337–38). These can be extended by the church to those who meet the specified conditions.

These indulgences can be gained only by the first person who receives them, and depend upon the saying of certain prayers, the doing of certain works of charity, or other good deeds. Indulgences can be gained for one's self as well as for loved ones. It must be remembered that no one knows, not even the pope, how long a soul has to remain in purgatory. God alone knows.

As far as we know, Luther heard of Tetzel for the first time at Grimma in 1516. He learned through his friend, Staupitz, that there was a seller of indulgences at Wurzen named Tetzel who was making a great noise. Some of his extravagant expressions were quoted, and Luther exclaimed with indignation, "If God permit, I will make a hole in his drum." There was no immediate confrontation with Tetzel, however, because Luther's elector, Frederick the Wise, and the Princes of Saxony—all of whom were indignant at this disgraceful traffic—had forbidden Tetzel to enter their provinces.

It will help our understanding of the times if we keep in mind that at this period Luther still respected the church and the pope. In fact, he wrote:

> I was at that time a monk, and a most furious papist, so intoxicated, yea, so drowned in the Roman doctrines, that I would have willingly aided, if I could, in killing anyone who should have had the audacity to refuse the slightest obedience to the pope.

However, we should also keep in mind that, at the same time, his heart was ready to catch fire for anything that he recognized as truth, and against everything he believed to be error. He said, "I was a young doctor, fresh from the forge, pardoned and rejoicing in the Word of the Lord."

We can better understand what he meant when he wrote of

"rejoicing in the Word of the Lord" when we realize that in the fall of 1515, two years before he nailed the theses on the door, he was immersed in the study and teaching of Paul's Epistle to the Romans. Also, from 1516–1517, he was lecturing on the Epistle to the Galatians. Roland Bainton says, "These studies proved to be for Luther the Damascus Road."

It was then that he began to see the light of the glorious Gospel of God's free grace. His new insights already contained the marrow of his mature theology. Incipient ideas were present in the lectures he gave in Romans, Galatians, and the Psalms from 1512 to 1516. The focal point around which all other doctrinal petals clustered was the affirmation of the forgiveness of sins through the utterly unmerited grace of God, made possible by the cross of Christ. His understanding of the purity and the power of God's unmerited favor was greatly enhanced. What a shock it was to him, then, to have the experiences that he had in the confessional at Wittenburg when his people came to him to make confession. He observed that the sins they were confessing were more gross and excessive than formerly: adultery, licentiousness, usury, ill-gotten gains—such were the crimes acknowledged to him. As a pastor, his heart ached for his people for whom he would have to give an account in the day of the Lord Jesus. He reprimanded, corrected, and instructed.

But what was his astonishment when these individuals informed him they would not abandon their sins! Greatly shocked, the pious monk declared that, since they would not promise to change their lives, he could not absolve them. Then, to his further amazement, they produced letters of indulgence from Tetzel which they got by going some five miles across the town line outside of the Province of Saxony where the huckster was holding forth. These letters absolved them from all sins. Luther replied that he had nothing to do with these papers and added: "Except ye repent, ye shall all likewise perish."

Greatly alarmed, the inhabitants of Wittenburg hastily returned to Tetzel. They told him that an Augustinian monk had treated his letters with contempt. At this report, the Dominican bellowed his anger. He stormed from the pulpit, implying insults and curses, and to strike the people with greater terror he had a fire in the marketplace lighted several times, declaring he had received an order from the pope to burn all heretics who presumed to oppose his most holy indulgences. It should solemnize us Protestants to realize that, if he had had his way and burned Luther, there probably would have been no Reformation, and no Protestantism.

Luther mounted his pulpit and, at the expense of incurring the wrath of his own Prince, he delivered his soul. He knew that Frederick the Wise had obtained special indulgences from the pope for the Castle Church at Wittenburg. Some of the blows he was aiming at Tetzel might fall on his Prince. It mattered not! His conscience was bound by the Word of God. He struck at the heart of the matter by saying:

> No one can prove by Scripture that the righteousness of God requires a penalty of satisfaction from the sinner. The only duty it imposes is a true repentance, a sincere conversion, a resolution to bear the cross of Christ and to perform good works. It is a great error to pretend to make satisfaction for one's sins to God's righteousness; God pardons them gratuitously by His inestimable grace.

Attacking the pretenses under which indulgences were continued, Luther stormed:

> They would do much better to contribute for love of God to the building of St. Peter's than to buy indulgences with this intention. . . . But, say you, shall we then never pur-

> chase any? I have already told you, and I repeat it, my advice is that no one should buy them. Leave them for drowsy Christians: but you should walk apart and for yourselves! We must turn the faithful aside from indulgences, and exhort them to the works which they neglect.

Then Luther demonstrated the boldness, the courage, and even the fiery temper which make him the great reformer that he was, for, glancing at his adversaries, he concluded:

> And should any cry out that I am a heretic, I care but little for their clamor. They are gloomy and have sick brains, men who have never tasted the Bible, never read the Christian doctrine, never comprehended their own doctors, and who lie rotting in the rags and tatters of their own vain opinions. . . . May God grant both them and us a sound understanding! Amen!

With these words, the doctor left the pulpit, leaving his hearers in great emotion at such daring language, and making a profound impression. Tetzel replied to it. Luther answered him, but nothing changed. Tetzel continued his traffic and his impious discourses.

Would Luther resign himself to these crying abuses? Would he keep silence? Again, had he done so, probably there would have been no Reformation and no Protestantism. But we should remember that it was not the church that Luther was attacking, nor was it the pope. Far from thinking of a revolution which would overthrow the primacy of Rome, Luther believed he had the pope and Catholicism for his allies against these "bare-faced indulgence mongers."

Then came that eventful day, October 31, 1517, when Luther walked boldly toward the church and posted upon the door the 95 theses against the doctrine of indulgences. The next day was All Saints Day which brought great crowds of pilgrims to the Castle Church. Here are some of the propositions:

"1. When our Lord and Master Jesus Christ says 'Repent,' He means that the whole life of believers upon earth should be constant and a perpetual repentance.

"6. The pope cannot remit any condemnation, but only declare and confirm the remission of God. If he does otherwise, the condemnation remains entirely the same.

"8. The laws of ecclesiastical penance ought to be imposed solely on the living and have no regard for the dead.

"21. The commissaries of indulgences are in error when they say that by the papal indulgence a man is delivered from every punishment and is saved.

"27. They preach mere human follies who maintain that as soon as the money rattles in the strong box, the soul flies out of purgatory.

"36. Every Christian who truly repents of his sin enjoys an entire remission both of the penalty and of the guilt, without any need of indulgences.

"42. We should teach Christians that the pope had no thought or desire of comparing in any respect the act of buying indulgences with any work of mercy.

"43. We should teach Christians that he who gives to the poor, or lends to the needy, does better than he who purchases an indulgence.

"50. We should teach Christians that if the pope knew of the extortions of the preachers of indulgences, he would rather the mother church at St. Peter were burned and reduced to ashes, than see it built up with the skin, the flesh, and the bones of his flock.

"51. We should teach Christians that the pope (as it is his duty) would distribute his own money to the poor whom the indulgence sellers are now stripping of their last farthing, even were he compelled to sell the mother church of St. Peter.

"62. The true and precious treasure of the church is the holy Gospel of the glory and grace of God.

"65. The treasures of the Gospel are nets which, in former times, the rich and those in easier circumstances were caught.

"66. But the treasures of the indulgence are nets with which they now catch the riches of the people.

"76. The indulgence of the pope cannot take away the smallest daily sin, as far as regards the guilt or the offense."

The hammer had fallen! The first spark flew! The conflagration was on, although neither Luther, nor anyone else, knew how great a conflagration it would be!

I would particularly call your attention to a fact of primary importance, namely that in these theses the evangelical doctrine of a free and gratuitous remission of sins was *for the first time publicly professed*. By this truth, light had begun to enter Luther's mind; by it also the light would be diffused over the church. The clear knowledge of this truth was what preceding Reformers such as Huss and Wycliffe had lacked. They sought to reform the life of the church; Luther reformed its teaching. This was by far the greater accomplishment. It is always folly to believe that a genuine Christian experience can be known apart from the truth of the Gospel. It is always true that what we believe really determines what we truly are. We should ever be suspicious of an untheological devotion. Luther saw—oh so clearly—that the real issue of his day (as it is of ours also) was how sinful man could be "accepted of God." His own incisive comment was: "In proclaiming justification by faith, I have laid the axe to the root of the tree."

He attacked doctrinal error in Rome's advocates; Huss and Wycliffe only attacked their lives. "Everything depends upon the Word," Luther cried, "which the pope has taken from us, and falsified."

In our times, too, we have forgotten this main doctrine of justification by faith and our neglect of this basic truth is senseless, shameful and dangerous. Now I grant that the 20th century is not the 16th century; but it matters not in what century a man lives. He is ever in need of the truth of that Gospel that enables God to justify him, declare him free from the guilt of sin, and accept him in righteousness. No man who is destitute of this knowledge can know the freedom and joy that comes only from God. Therefore the truth of justification by grace through faith needs to be proclaimed as urgently today as in the days of Luther.

During the ensuing year, Luther was required to present himself to the pope's representatives who called upon him to retract his teachings. He met his most severe trial when he was called to Augsburg on October 7, 1518, to appear before his judge, Thomas DeVio, surnamed Cajetan. Cajetan called for a complete submission to the pope and a retraction of all of his teachings. A long wrangling debate followed in which Luther had little opportunity to speak. He requested that he might put his protest in writing. This was finally granted. He dealt principally with the two accusations that Cajetan had made against his teaching:

First, that "the treasury of indulgences does not consist of the sufferings and merits of our Lord Jesus Christ, and of the 'saints;' "

Second, that "the man who receives the holy sacrament must have faith in the grace that is presented to him."

Luther replied that there are no super-saints who had done more good works than was expected of them, and therefore were able to supply a "superabundance of merits" that helped provide a "treasury" from which indulgences could be drawn for those who were deficient in merits. The Scriptures bear witness, Luther wrote, "that God rewards us far more richly than we deserve." Then he quoted the psalmist, who exclaimed in Psalm 143:2, "Enter not into judgment with thy servant, O Lord; in Thy sight shall no man living be justified." "Thus the saints are not saved by their merits, but solely by God's mercy," Luther declared. "I maintain this, and in it I stand fast. The words of holy Scripture which declare that the saints have not merit enough must be set above the words of men which affirm that they have an excess. The pope is not above the Word of God, but below it."

But Luther did not stop here. He showed that if indulgences cannot be granted on the basis of a superabundance of the merits of "saints," they cannot any the more be the merits of Christ. He proved that indulgences are barren and fruitless, since their only effect is to exempt men from performing good works, such as prayer and almsgiving. "No," exclaimed he, "the merits of Jesus Christ are not a treasury of indulgences exempting men from good works, but a treasury of grace which quickens. The merits of Christ are applied to the believer without indulgences, without the keys, by the Holy Ghost alone, and not by the pope. If anyone has a opinion better founded than mine, let him make it known to me and then will I retract."

Then he answered the second charge, namely, that he taught that one who receives the holy sacrament must have faith in the grace that is presented to him. "I affirm," said he, "that no man can be justified before God if he has not faith; so that it is necessary for a man to believe with a perfect assurance that he has obtained grace. To doubt this grace is to reject it. The faith of the righteous is his righteousness and his life."

In the practice of the Roman church, both indulgences and the sacraments brought money into the church. As D'Aubigne says:

> Indulgences were more or less an extraordinary branch of Roman commerce; the sacraments were a staple commodity. The revenue they produced was of no small amount. To assert that faith was necessary before they could confer a real benefit on the soul of a Christian, took away all their charms in the eyes of the people; for it is not the pope who gives faith; it is beyond his province; it proceeds from God alone. To declare its necessity was therefore depriving Rome both of the speculation and the profit.

Luther's attack upon these two lucrative practices of the church brought forth some angry retorts from Cajetan. But he was no match for Luther. Finally in an attempt to cow the insignificant Augustinian monk, he shouted, "The pope has power and authority over all things"; to which Luther quickly responded, "Except Scripture!"

But now we take a leap from the 16th to the 20th century. What is the situation today with respect to the teaching of the Catholic church on indulgences? In its March 24, 1967, cover story on Martin Luther and the Reformation, *Time* magazine quotes an unnamed Roman Catholic theologian from America as saying, "Luther was right on indulgences."

The *Christian Century* (April 26, 1967), in commenting upon this fact, stated that "though most progressive Catholics share this opinion, the Vatican itself apparently is not yet ready to concede the point. . . . The indulgence system has since been cleansed of its crasser commercial elements, but its 'works righteousness' focus remains. A proposal for a mild reform of the system unexpectedly came up to discussion at the 4th session of Vatican Council II. The work of the conservative curial body, the Sacred Apostolic Penitentiary, was meant to forestall any attempt toward a more thoroughgoing reform. The proposal met with such strong criticism, however— particularly from Julius Cardinal Dotefner of Munich, who urged drastic revision of the document by a reconstituted commission—that debate on the subject was halted as abruptly as it had begun."

But, as the *Christian Century* points out, progressive Catholics have already updated their thinking concerning indulgences. Here is an encouraging sign.

Consider this editorial by Dale Francis, editor of the Catholic weekly *The Sunday Visitor and Operation Understanding*, when he wrote:

> I was invited to speak on Reformation Sunday at a Methodist church. What the pastor wanted me to speak about was the modern Catholic view of the Reformation. . . . That is what I did, although I suspect I did not give the kind of talk he had in mind. I suspect he thought I would approach the new historical insights, the new attitudes toward the Reformation—but I didn't. I reflected instead on what I believe is the authentic modern attitude toward the Reformation; that is, that it simply isn't relevant. As a matter of fact, it has not been relevant for a long time

now. What in the name of common sense is the use of going back 400 years every year and reexamining old wounds? The wounds left scars, but reexamining them every year did nothing except reopen them.

Pope John said that we should forget historical encounters and deal with the situation as it exists now. Discussion of the Reformation has lost its relevancy primarily because the Catholic church of the day of the Reformation and the Protestant churches today aren't the churches of the Reformation.

One of the big fusses at the time of the Reformation was over something called *indulgences*. Indulgences simply have no relevancy now. Maybe the basic theological concept—the idea that we should do good works and that God rewards good works—still exists; but I doubt if there are many Catholics today who think about indulgences at all. They know they should do good works; they believe God wants them to do good works; they believe God somehow rewards good works; but there must be few Catholics who would do good works today for the sake of the reward. And just so there will be no mistake, there are no Catholics—or there should be no Catholics—who believe that it is good works that merit heaven. They know it was our Lord's redemptive death upon the cross that opened the way to heaven, and that all the good works in all the world couldn't gain heaven for one soul without Christ's redemption of man.

The point is—the world has made quite a few turns since the Reformation and, while the world has been turning, the people—Catholics and Protestants—have been changing attitudes too.

This is a startling statement, yet others as startling are being made by prominent Catholic theologians today. The same American theologian who said, concerning indulgences, that

Luther was right also said: "His teaching on justification is more palatable to me than that of Thomas Aquinas."

We shall review these statements with sympathy and an attempt to reach a better understanding.

In the present dialogue, it is a Christian obligation for both Catholics and Protestants to learn what each is saying about the essentials of our Christian faith in the hope that we might arrive at a larger measure of doctrinal unity than has been known in the past 450 years.

Justification by Faith Alone
Part Two

The Two-foldness of Divine Truth

There is no question but that there are apparent contradictions in the Holy Scriptures. Ofttimes they become vexing issues of bitter controversy even among those who profess faith in the Word of God. One such issue is that of justification. From the days of the Reformation it has been a divisive doctrine. The conflict arises because the Scriptures seem to teach two sides of justification: justification by faith and justification by works.

In our consideration of the biblical teaching on justification, we start with the premise that genuine Christians most certainly believe *both* sides of what the Scriptures teach about this important truth. This is not easy, however, because there does seem to be an inconsistency here which is not easily overcome, if finally overcome at all. Furthermore, such inconsistency affects our minds adversely in their innate quest for unity and harmony in truth. We are disturbed.

But need we be? Perhaps our disturbance arises from the fact that we have not assumed the right intellectual posture. Perhaps, after all, we have assumed a philosophical posture rather than a biblical one. What is the philosophical posture? Let's put it this way: it is the glory of the philosopher to develop a system of thought that is *whole* and *unified*. His ambition is to trace all possible knowledge about "all things" to one universal principle. He must show how, through varied appearances, one universal law prevails. There can be no ambiguity in his system. Einstein attempted such a task in the physical realm.

What the physicist attempts in the physical realm, the philosopher attempts in the metaphysical realm. If in checking his theory of unity he comes upon something that seems to violate it, he recognizes it as a check in his thinking and starts over again. There is ever the danger that a philosopher will begin with a basically wrong assumption. It is just at this point that he is most vulnerable, for, generally, the philosopher assumes that his intellect, although finite, can encompass the infinite. He really assumes that he can "know it all." He does not seem willing to admit with the apostle Paul that "we know in part." He tries to pour the eternal into the temporal and, in so doing, attempts what someone has called "the finalization of the temporal." He forgets that only in the realm of the eternal are "all things" finalized, and generally his failure to recognize his limitations leads him into the trap of deceitful pride.

Christians must ever be on their guard against accepting the false assumption of the philosopher. Like the philosopher, the Christian diligently seeks for as much unity and harmony as possible in his system of thought, but he starts with the premise that ultimate unity is found *in God alone.* This does not preclude his diligent pursuit after truth. He recognizes the responsibility of thinking God's thoughts after Him, for he knows that God puts no premium upon ignorance or intellectual slothfulness. He believes that God's children should be more interested in His world, His works, and His Word than non-Christians. He believes that Christians should be the best scientists, the best philosophers, and the best historians, as well as the best theologians, that it is possible for them to be.

But the Christian should never forget that his little mind is finite. He should always be ready to say with the Apostle: "Now we see through a glass darkly." Humility should ever be the mark of Christian scholars.

The history of theology is replete with records of tragic and futile battles that have been fought by theologians in their attempt to resolve these apparent theological contradictions. For instance, what unwholesome debates have been engaged in over the two conceptions of divine predestination and human free will—the teaching of St. Augustine on the one hand and Pelagius on the other, or of Calvin and Arminius. From the report of the Theological Committee of the Faith and Order Movement, I extract this comment:

> Many theological attempts have been made on philosophical lines to reconcile the apparent antithesis of God's sovereignty and man's responsibility, emphasizing too exclusively one side or the other; thus causing much strife among Christians. But these speculations are not a necessary part of the Christian faith. . . . The mistake that has been made has been that theologians have named a philosophical consistence. . . . Whereas our religious convictions demand a dependence upon God, our ethical convictions demand human freedom. Both concepts must be held because they represent the only basis on which the spiritual life can be built up.

But what is true of these two conceptions, namely divine sovereignty and man's responsibility, is true also of the doctrine of justification, as we shall observe in later chapters. At this juncture, I shall propose a principle of biblical interpretation which I shall apply to our treatment of each part of our general theme of justification by grace through faith. This principle of interpretation is "The Two-foldness of Divine Truth."

This principle may be illustrated in several ways. Let me draw first upon some facts from nature. In nature, God continually acts according to two seemingly opposed principles. For instance, what keeps the planets moving in beauteous order around the sun? Not one force, but two—two forces pulling each particle of matter in opposite directions at the same instant. Consider again how physical life is preserved. It is supported by two gases of opposite qualities. If we breathe one of them alone, we would die quickly from the intense expenditure and exhaustion of our vital forces. But place us in an unmingled atmosphere of the other, and life would be extinguished in a few seconds. Again, what is the salt we put upon our foods? Sodium chloride, a compound of two substances either of which, alone, would kill us. And, still again, our physical bodies are subject to the opposite action of two forces: by one, flesh, blood, and even bones are broken down; by the other, new particles are being constantly built up.

Now let's draw some illustrations from Christian doctrine. To the question, "Is God one?" the church responds biblically, "Yes." Is this one God revealed in three persons, and is each of these three persons Deity? And again the church responds biblically, "Yes." Without hedging a bit, Christians must face the fact that there is a metaphysical contradiction here that no finite mind can solve; yet all who subscribe to the authority of God's Word believe that the Scriptures teach both the unity and the plurality of the Godhead. If we are asked: "Come, now, in which do you really believe, God's oneness or God's plurality?" we give what we consider a true biblical answer: "Both." We cannot fully explain it, but we discover that when we let this truth dwell in our thinking and control our living, it becomes reasonable enough to our faith.

Again, consider the person of our Lord Jesus Christ. To the question, "Is He God?" the church has always responded biblically, "Yes." "Is He man?" and again the church has responded biblically, "Yes." But how can this be? No matter how many theological books one may read in which the authors seriously attempt to explain how Jesus Christ can be both God and man at one and the same time, one lifts his weary head from the perusal of these works still baffled by the mystery of it all. Yet, strange as it seems, when this truth is *accepted by faith* and allowed to govern the mind and the heart of the Christian, he finds a sweet reasonableness in this amazing and magnificent truth that Jesus Christ is both "very God of very God, and very man of very man," and that He was manifested for our salvation.

Let me come back to the issue which we mentioned earlier concerning the conceptions of the sovereignty of God and the responsibility of man, for it is vitally related to the general theme of these lectures, namely justification by grace through faith.

Consider the teachings of the Scriptures concerning the change of man from enmity against God to love of Him. Here are some Scriptures which really indicate that this change is brought about by the power of God:

Acts 16:14: "Lydia . . . whose heart *the Lord opened,* attended unto the things which were spoken of Paul."

Acts 13:48: "As many as were *ordained* to eternal life believed."

Ephesians 1:4: "He hath *chosen us in Him before the foundation of the world,* that we should be holy and without blame before Him in love."

Now consider the Scriptures which indicate that this change is brought about by the action of the man himself:

Acts 17:11–12: "The Bereans were more noble than those in Thessalonica, in that *they received the word with all readiness of mind,* and searched the Scriptures daily whether those things were so. *Therefore* many of them believed."

John 5:40: "Ye will *not come* to Me, that ye might have life."

Here we have two sets of scriptures which seem to suggest two opposing sources of man's salvation—a divine choice and a human choice. Now which should Christians believe? The answer is, both!

But it is just at this point that we get into trouble. In our quest for unity of truth, we attempt to effect reconciliation between these apparent contradictions. We choose one set of texts and, in doing so, we reject, or at least minimize, the other. As someone has said, "We torture the passages and bring them into as near an accordance with our own views as we can." Most of the time those who over-emphasize man's part in salvation have ofttimes fallen into vain self-reliance and idolatry of the "means." They have regarded man's will as solitarily free. Man's powers and activities in the doing of good works have come prominently into view. God's infinite foreknowledge, His predestinating grace, and His boundless power have been injured. The result has been the exaltation of man and robbing God of the praise and glory due unto His holy Name as the sole Author of our salvation.

On the other hand, those who have over-emphasized God's sovereignty in salvation have fostered an equal mischief. Accustomed to regard God only as the sovereign Benefactor, and man as passive and utterly helpless, they have, to a marked degree, fallen into spiritual indifference and idleness. Indeed, at times they have looked with suspicion and frowned upon those who use "means" to advance the salvation of man. Furthermore, by their unbalanced teachings they have laid God open to the charge that He is the sole author of sin and that the damned in hell are there because God ordained their damnation.

In our dilemma we fitfully ask, "But which of these two views is right?" Now it is just at this point where we are at fault. We take it for granted that we have the right to make a choice between two positions, to hold fast to the one and reject the other. In my opinion this is disastrously wrong, for we set ourselves up as judge of the Holy Scriptures rather than as "believers" in them. We forget that God who spoke the one spoke the other. To the question, "Which am I to believe?" the biblical answer is "both," in spite of all of the philosophers' protests.

At this point I would interpose a practical word. It is quite understandable that in our state of perplexity we should want some "practical solution" to our problem of interpreting the Scriptures in a way most pleasing to God. And I think we find that practical solution in the adoption of a basic presupposition, namely that God comes *before* man and therefore should have the priority. After all, the Scriptures commence with the affirmation: "In the beginning God" and not "in the beginning man." This would mean that while we recognize that we can never fully comprehend God's mysteries, we will be enabled to steer a safe course between Scylla and Charybdis, and thus avoid making a "shipwreck of our faith." In my opinion, by applying the principle of the "two-foldness of divine truth," we shall have found at least a "working solution" in our efforts to understand as much as our finite minds are able to understand of the "whole counsel of God." It is this principle that we shall apply in our pursuit of the study of the teaching of the Holy Scriptures regarding justification by grace through faith.

The chief issue responsible for the theological conflict between the Reformers and the Catholic church in the 16th century was the doctrine of justification. Other bases of theological differences existed then, and still exist, but in Luther's day no question was more divisive than "how a man can be just with God?" It seems strange, therefore, that in all of the dialogue that is presently going on between Protestants and Catholics there has been little consideration given to the discussion of this doctrine by the ecumenical leadership. Protestant theologians, with few exceptions, have bypassed dialogue on this issue. Here and there one finds a magazine article in which justification is the primary theme. On the Catholic side, however, we get the impression that this issue is once again gaining the attention of some of her leading theologians. The most unexpected and scholarly work yet produced from the Catholic standpoint is by the brilliant young theologian Hans Kung. Robert McCarthy Brown, Professor of Religion at Stanford University, and an invited observer to the Second Vatican Council, has said of Kung's work, simply titled *Justification,* that sympathetic attention should be given to this book not only by Protestant theologians, but by clergy and laity as well. Consider this startling statement made by Professor Kung on page 284: "Today there is a fundamental agreement between Catholic and Protestant theology precisely in the theology of justification, the point at which Reformation theology took its departure."

Naturally we Protestants are led to ask, "Can this be true?" and we also ask a second question, "Is this pronouncement attested to by the official statements on justification by the Catholic church?"

To obtain answers to these questions, I turned to several recent and authorized Catholic sources, and here are my findings. First, in the index of the latest *Handbook of Catholic Faith*, I found no listing at all of the word "justification." Second, in the 1966 *National Catholic Almanac* there is but one reference to this doctrine—a reference of only thirty words! And, finally, in the documents of Vatican II, there is no reference whatsoever to the word "justification" in the index. In the face of these facts, one feels led to ask: "Is this issue of justification no longer crucial in the eyes of the Catholic church? Is the all-important question of how a man may be just with God no longer of such great importance as it was in the days of the Reformers? Or are we to conclude that the pronouncements of justification as set forth in the Council of Trent in 1545 are still binding upon the church today?"

In all fairness to Catholic theologians, it should be pointed out that in Catholic theology justification is considered but one phase of the larger work of what is called redemption. Nor is this theological structure peculiar to the Catholic position. Karl Barth subsumes justification under the title of "reconciliation." One must conclude, therefore, that to understand the teaching of either Hans Kung, the Catholic theologian, or Karl Barth, the Protestant theologian, on the subject, one must study the larger truth of "redemption" or "reconciliation." I have no quarrel with this theological procedure of justification, but I am not prepared to admit that the teaching of the Scriptures on justification is of so little importance that, first, it can be submerged under a larger revelation of truth to the point where it is itself obscured; or, second, that it is a truth, though intimately related to other redemptive truths, that cannot stand on its own feet.

I will now present the contrast between the Catholic view of justification and that of the Reformers. Perhaps the quickest way to get at our problem is to recall that in our previous lecture we stated that the Reformers taught that justification meant to "*declare* one righteous," whereas Catholic teaching is that it means to "*make* one righteous." The Reformers insisted that justification came about when God *imputed* righteousness to the sinner, whereas Catholics hold that righteousness is *imparted,* or, as they say, "infused into" the sinner when he enters upon the "state of grace" which will ultimately lead to his final justification.

Let me dwell first upon the Reformers' position. They held that justification denotes an act of God whereby, on the basis of the redemptive work of Christ—that is, His death for our sins, His burial and His resurrection "for our justification"—God declares the sinner righteous and *accepts* him immediately as righteous in His sight. It is an *act* which is completed at once, and not a work that is gradually accomplished by successive acts, and *certainly* not by anything the believer does. This act of God takes instant effect and produces an immediate and complete change in the sinner's whole relationship to Him. It bestows the full and free pardon of sin and translates the sinner at once from a state of condemnation into a state of favor and peace. Paul writes in Romans 5:1: "Being justified by faith, we have peace with God through our Lord Jesus Christ."

The justification of the sinner includes forgiveness and acceptance, that is, full pardon of sin, admission into God's favor, and a title to eternal life. The fact that the Gospel proposes to every sinner free pardon of sin and the privilege of immediate acceptance with God, including the gift of eternal life, is so evident from innumerable testimonies of Scripture that it is seldom if ever denied in express terms by anyone: "For God so loved the world, that He gave His only begotten Son, that whosoever believeth in Him should not perish, but have everlasting life" (John 3:16); and "In whom we have redemption through His blood, the forgiveness of sins" (Ephesians 1:7). But the believer is not merely forgiven, he is also "accepted in the Beloved" and "made the righteousness of God in Him."

Justification does not have to do primarily with deliverance from the defilement and dominion of sin. We have used the word "primarily" because we do not want to imply at this point that there is no relationship whatsoever between justification and sanctification. Of this we will speak later. But deliverance from the defilement and dominion of sin is the result of our sanctification and not primarily of our justification. Justification has to do strictly with the guilt and demerit of sin, and the making it possible for God to accept the unrighteous as "righteous in His sight." Sometimes, in our over-enthusiasm, we speak of sin as being blotted out, as if, in some way, sins, as actual and historic facts, cease to be. This is not so. The fact of sin remains a fact forever. It can never become an "unfact," if you please. For instance, suppose I lied about a friend, and that lie was carried by the four winds of gossip to all parts of the world. One thing is sure. That lie can never be recalled; but thanks be to God, the guilt that I contracted because I told that lie, and the demerit of it which deserved punishment, can both be put away. Forgiveness presupposes both the reality and the demerits of sin, and frees us from the charge of guilt and a sentence of condemnation without impairing our sense of either. It is only by forgiveness that sin can be cancelled. It cannot be cancelled by repentance, or even by regeneration. The divine sentence of condemnation of sin can only be reversed by the divine action in the remission of sins. In this way, and in this way only, sins are "blotted out."

And while the pardon of sin is an indispensable and important part of the sinner's justification, it is not an adequate or a complete description of justification. Justification also includes "the acceptance of the sinner as righteous in the sight of God." He is admitted to divine favor and becomes the possessor of the gift of eternal life. As the Westminster Confession of Faith puts it:

> Justification is an act of God's free grace wherein He pardoneth all our sins, and accepteth us as righteous in His sight, only for the righteousness of Christ, imputed to us, and received by faith alone.

So much for a brief statement of the Reformers' position. Let us now consider the Catholic view. First of all, let me give the thirty-word definition of justification which appears in the 1966 *National Catholic Almanac*:

> Justification—the remission of sin *and* the infusion of sanctifying grace at baptism; or, the recovery of sanctify-

ing grace by an act of perfect contrition or in a sacrament
of penance.

As we have noted previously in Catholic theology,
"sanctifying grace" is that which produces justification. In the
Catholic Glossary we find this definition of "sanctifying grace":

> Sanctifying grace is a supernatural gift *infused* into the
> soul at baptism. It remains as a permanent quality of the
> soul making it pleasing to God and capable of supernatu-
> ral merit. Sanctifying grace is lost by mortal sin, recov-
> ered by repentance and the sacrament of penance, in-
> creased by reception of the sacrament and the perfor-
> mance of good works (p. 334).

But what is the grace to which reference is made? The
Catholic catechism replies: "Grace is a supernatural gift of God,
freely bestowed on us for our sanctification and salvation."
Observe here that there is no reference whatsoever to justification. While it is true, as we have pointed out, that in the structure of Catholic theology the teaching of justification is included
in the teaching of redemption or reconciliation, it should be
pointed out that in the definitions and descriptions of salvation
in Catholic theology there is little or no reference to two words
which appear again and again in Paul's letters, especially his
Epistle to the Romans. These two words are "righteousness"
and "justification." What is the significance of these omissions?
In my opinion, the failure to recognize the significance of these
two words in biblical teaching constitutes a further example of
how Catholic theology confuses justification and sanctification;
or, to put it in another way, which we have done earlier, Rome
insists that a man may be made righteous through the new
birth and the infusion of God's grace into his soul before he can
have a title deed to eternal life and the assurance that he will get

to heaven. This infused grace, so it is taught, operates within the soul from the time of baptism throughout one's lifetime (and, I suppose, even in purgatory) in order to effect one's final justification which will make it possible for him to enter heaven. To support this statement, let me quote again from the *Catholic Glossary*:

> The life of grace itself is a continuous movement towards a definite goal. . . . Growth and effort are its characteristics. Any coming to rest entails inevitable loss, a shrivelling up of vitality and a diminution of our life force. . . . This condition cries out for increasing help from God. . . . The church calls this supernatural influence actual grace. This *actual* grace issues in good works which lead to our justification.

The *Glossary* continues:

> All good works which lead to our justification . . . receive their first impulse and initiative from the grace of God. . . . Everyone receives sufficient grace in order to reach heaven. . . . But the state of grace is not a condition of rest in God. . . . He must produce good works. It is upon his good works, upon his own efforts, that a man is judged. Good works, therefore, are the reason why God gives the reward of eternal life. . . . The state of grace is not only a sanctifying state, but it also demands that we should earn the wages of supernatural life by our own labors. . . . Salvation hangs upon our manner of life.

In subsequent chapters we shall see that Catholic theology substitutes the *works* of the believer for the *work* of Christ. Rome does not deny that we are redeemed through the merits of Christ's death, burial, and resurrection; but it is denied that we are redeemed *only* through the merits of Christ's death, burial, and resurrection. To be finally justified, and to have a

sure entrance into heaven, one must add his own merits to the
merits of Christ in order that he might be acceptable to God.
Thus we see that justification is only possible *after* this life is
lived in "obedience to the church," *after* "satisfaction by temporal punishment is made for sins already forgiven," *after*
"cleansing for unrepentant 'venial sins' have been effected," and
after "the soul has been *perfectly* prepared to enter into
heaven." What does this mean? It means clearly that only the
"godly" are finally justified, whereas the Scriptures affirm with
great force that "To him that worketh not, but believeth on
Him that justifieth the *ungodly*, his faith is reckoned for
righteousness" (Romans 4:5).

But it is still true that there is a two-foldness of divine
teaching on this momentous truth of justification and, in coming chapters, we shall explore both sides.

Justification by Faith Alone
Part Three

The Two-foldness of Justification

According to the received tradition, it was on October 31, 1517, that Martin Luther fixed his Ninety-Five Theses to the church door at Wittenburg. Ever since, most Protestants have commemorated this event in an anniversary celebration on the last Sunday in October. It was one of the great events in the church calendar. Mass choirs sang in convention halls; powerful sermons were preached on salvation themes; the courageous Reformers of the 16th century were eulogized for their devotion to Christ and His Word; and everyone joined in the heroic strains of "A Mighty Fortress is our God." Many people went away from these great services uplifted, with new commitment to the "faith of our fathers," and to the principles for which they lived and died.

Now it is quite different. In some Protestant circles—even among a few Lutherans—it has not been fashionable to celebrate the birth of the Protestant Reformation. To do so, we are told, would be to put roadblocks in the progress of the ecumenical dialogue that is now taking place between Protestants and Catholics. A protest is being made by both Catholics and Protestants against opening old wounds and inflicting new ones. The general feeling is that enough blood has been spilt over religion. In truth, a modern day "Reformation" service is quite apt to turn into an ecumenical festival in which the events of the 16th century are comfortably glossed over. Common celebrations of the 450th anniversary of the Reformation between Lutherans and Catholics have been held. I am among those who are highly in favor of a moratorium on religious quarrels and the thawing of the icy attitudes among those who call themselves the people of God. The world has been waiting a long time for Christians to treat one another with love. Perhaps that is what the world has been waiting for most from the church. Perhaps this is our mightiest weapon in evangelization. Ruth Bell Graham said: "A saint is one who makes it easy to believe in Jesus."

Does this mean that we Protestants must scuttle the Reformation of 1517? By no means. To do so would be a spiritual disaster unparalleled in the history of the church. But why? Certainly not because of the dishonor that could be done to the great Reformers—Luther, Zwingli, Calvin, Melanchthon, Bucer, Latimer, Knox and many others; not because of our repudiation of the invaluable "Protestant principle" that frees the conscience to seek after truth without the pressure of prohibition. As great as were the Reformers themselves, and as great as were the principles of Protestantism that led to the liberating of the conscience from unholy tyranny, the greatness of the Reformation must be found in its recovery of the profound theological and indispensable truth of justification by grace through faith. Yet we have read recently of some Protestant religious leaders who said they did not know what to make of the Reformation teaching of justification by faith. After Paul Tillich wrote "Protestantism was born out of the struggle for the doctrine of justification by faith," he added these significant words:

> This idea is strange to the man of today, and even to Protestant people in the churches. Indeed, as I have had over and over again opportunity to learn, it is so strange to modern man that there is scarcely any way of making it intelligible to him.

In the introduction to this series, I announced that in these chapters we would attempt to make this timeless truth intelligible to serious-minded Christians. In order to do so, I will have to review the theological situation in the 16th century. In later chapters I will show the relevance of this truth in our individual lives, and in the church of Christ today.

In the 16th century, the Roman Catholic church became frighteningly aware of the fact that when the Reformers plunged the knife of criticism into the body of the church, they were not only tearing her flesh, but striking at her very heart. If Luther's teaching on justification was right, her whole system of salvation had to be recast, if not totally abandoned. She became alarmed that the Reformation was not only sweeping throughout Germany, but reaching into other lands as well. Consequently she launched her own "counter reformation." This was formally done in the 19th Ecumenical Council held at Trent over a period of 18 years, from 1545 (a year before Luther's death) to 1563. The Council's actual sessions occupied only four years, but what is most significant is that seven full months were devoted solely to the question of justification. The result was 16 chapters setting forth the doctrine of justification, and 33 canons denouncing the errors which were judged to be opposed to it. That we might sense something of the spirit of these pronouncements, let me quote three of the 33 canons concerning justification.

> CANON IX: If anyone says that a sinner is justified by faith alone, meaning that nothing else is required to cooperate in order to obtain the grace of justification, and that it is not in any way necessary that he be prepared and disposed for the action of his own will, let him be "Anathema."
>
> CANON XI: If anyone says that men are justified either by

the sole imputation of the justice of Christ, or by the sole remission of sins to the exclusion of the grace and *charity which is poured forth in their hearts by the Holy Ghost*, and remains in them, or that the grace by which we are justified is only the good will of God, let him be "Anathema" (italics added).

CANON XII: If anyone says that justifying faith is nothing else than confidence in Divine blessing which remits sins for Christ's sake, or that it is this confidence alone that justifies us, let him be "Anathema."

So we see that the battle line of the Reformation was the issue of justification by grace through faith.

We have already observed that to Luther the issuance of indulgences was more than practical abuse. It was the visual embodiment of a whole system of teaching that subverted the scriptural grounds of faith and hope towards God. Luther came to this knowledge through years of soul agony. None of us will ever know the spiritual struggle that he had to obtain the forgiveness of God. He could not believe that man could provide forgiveness of his sins in any way. This was *God's* sovereign right and prerogative. He was thus led to compare the Bull of Indulgences which Pope Leo had issued with the Gospel of God, of which he had an ever-increasing apprehension as being the good news of the unmerited favor of God. He saw that the Bull and the Gospel set forth two doctrines of justification which were not only different, but diametrically opposed. The Gospel presented a doctrine of pure grace, the Bull a mixed doctrine of divine grace and human merit. One was founded on the finished work of Christ, and the other depended on the imperfect works of sinning man to supplement the work of Christ. In my analysis of these differences, let me point out four basic points where Rome and the Reformers differed on what the

Scriptures teach concerning justification:

The *nature* of justification, or what that is which is denoted by the term in Scripture;

The *ground* of justification, or what that is to which God has regard as the grounds upon which He "justifies the ungodly";

The *means* of justification, or what that is through which God bestows and man receives forgiveness of sin, a standing in righteousness, and a title to eternal life; and

The *effect* of justification, or what consequences must follow from this change in a man's relation to God.

In regard to the *nature* of justification, or what that is which is denoted by the term in Scripture, the Reformers held that a fundamental error of the church of Rome consisted in confounding justification with sanctification. Rome taught that one was not truly justified until he had first experienced sanctification, and that to the full. That is why, according to Roman dogma, justification is often spoken of in terms of "sanctifying grace."

G. H. Joyce, in his book *The Catholic Doctrine of Grace*, writes that:

> Man is justified by the infusion of sanctifying grace into his soul, and his justification is nothing else than the change effected in him by this gift, and through it, his sins were forgiven and he is transformed into a new creature, and made a child of God (p. 44).

The author continues:

> The Council of Trent, in its decree regarding the revealed doctrines of justification, defines it to be "not merely the remission of sin," but the sanctification and the renovation of the inner man by the free acceptance of grace and the accompanying gifts; whereby man from unjust is

> made just, and from an enemy is made a friend of God
> that he may be an heir according to the hope of life ever-
> lasting (p. 44).

In opposition to these and similar errors on this point, the Reformers held and taught that justification is "an act of God's free grace whereby He pardoneth all our sins and accepteth us as righteous in His sight." It is an act of God *external* to the sinner of which he is the *object*—not an *inward* work of which he is the *subject*. Justification is not a change in the sinner's moral and spiritual character.

The instant a sinner (not a "perfected saint") believes, however weak his faith and however imperfect his holiness, he may say with Paul in Romans 5:1: "Being justified by faith, I have peace with God."

We shall consider these points more fully in subsequent chapters, but this suggests how widely the two parties differed with respect to the *nature* of justification.

In regard to the *ground* of justification, or what that is to which God has regard as the foundation for His "justifying the ungodly," the Reformers believed that a fundamental error of the church of Rome consisted in substituting the inherent righteousness of the regenerate for the imputed righteousness of the Redeemer.

Now let it never be said that the Roman church has denied that the sufferings and death of Christ—and therefore His atoning merits—have nothing to do with our justification. But what they did deny was that God's righteousness which He wrought out in Christ's death, burial and resurrection is *imputed* to us so that it becomes the immediate and *sole* reason on account of which God forgives our sins and accepts us as righteous in His sight. The merits of Christ were rather, according to Rome's doctrine, the procuring cause of that regenerating grace by which we are *made* righteous, and the inherent personal righteousness which is thus produced is the real approximate grounds of our justification. Or, to put it in another way, while they did count upon Christ's righteousness which He wrought out in His death, burial and resurrection, they refused to allow that God's righteousness in Christ is the sole and all-sufficient ground of our justification through faith, which *neither requires, nor admits of any addition being made to it in the form either of suffering or obedience on the part of the believer.* It is this fundamental error, in regard to the ground of the sinner's justification, that explains and accounts for many collateral and subordinate teachings of the Roman church to which the Reformers took exception.

The Reformers believed that the Scriptures taught that we were justified only on the grounds of the righteousness of God imputed to us. In the penetrative language of James Buchanan in his work *The Doctrine of Justification,* the Reformers based their doctrine on such considerations as these:

> A righteousness of some kind is indispensable if God is to accept us as righteous;
> It must be such a righteousness as is adequate to meet and to satisfy all of the requirements of that perfect law which is God's rule in judgment;
> Its requirements were fulfilled by the obedience—passive and active—of the Lord Jesus Christ;
> He thus became "the end of the law for righteousness to everyone that believeth in His name";
> Our inherent personal righteousness as believers—even were it perfect—could not cancel the guilt of our past sins, or offer any satisfaction to divine justice on account of them;
> So far from being perfect, even in the regenerate, it is defiled by indwelling sin, and impaired by actual transgression;
> The work of the Spirit in us, indispensable and pre-

> cious as it is for other ends, was not designed to secure our justification in any other way than by applying to us the righteousness of God and enabling us to receive and rest upon it by faith.

Again, we shall have occasion to develop these points more fully in subsequent chapters.

In regard to the *means* of justification, or what that is through which God bestows and man receives forgiveness of sin, and his standing in righteousness and eternal life, the Reformers believed that a fundamental error of the church of Rome consisted in denying that we are justified by that faith which "receives and rests upon Christ alone for salvation which He has freely offered to us in the Gospel."

Her theologians affirmed that we are justified not simply by faith in Christ, but by faith that, coupled with love, provided "the germ of new obedience." Furthermore, they affirmed that this faith was first infused by baptism so as to "delete" all past sins—original sin in the case of infants and both original sin and acts of sin in the case of adults—of those who were duly prepared to receive baptism. They taught also that in the event of post-baptismal sin, confession and absolution effectually delivered the sinner from all punishment, except such as is endured in penance or in purgatory.

What does all this mean? It means that, after all, it is how one lives that determines whether he is justified or not, contradicting the truth of Scripture which says that justification is "not of works, lest any man should boast!" Rome thus taught that justification can only really come *at the end of one's life,* or, more specifically, only when one is loosed from purgatory rather than at the beginning of his "life of faith." Only *after* he believes, loves, obeys, produces good works according to the requirements of the Catholic church, and gives satisfaction to

God by way of purgatorial sufferings, can he ever hope to be justified so as to be able to stand in God's presence and be acceptable to Him.

In opposition to this form of teaching, the Reformers held and taught that we are justified by faith alone, simply because faith receives and rests upon Christ *alone* for salvation, and apprehends and appropriates God's righteousness in Him as the ground of acceptance. It involves the whole mind and soul of the sinner who receives Christ, and looks to Him only for forgiveness. It might be a very weak faith, but if it was a heart response that was truly penitential and which, having abandoned all hope of self-salvation, turned only to Christ, then that faith was immediately and invariably effectual for salvation insomuch that he in whom it exists may be fully assured that he has "passed from death unto life," and that he will never "come into condemnation" (John 5:24).

The Reformers did not deny—indeed, on the contrary they affirmed—that this faith "worketh by love" and through love, as the mainspring of a new obedience, and produced all "the peaceable fruits of righteousness." This was a "justification unto life" (Romans 5:18), they strongly emphasized, but it was not the new life that brought justification. It was the death of the Son of God who, having put away sin, offered a righteousness by which alone man can appear in the presence of God and be "accepted" of Him.

Finally, as to the *effect* of justification, they held that a fundamental error of the church of Rome consisted in believing that it was neither so complete in its own nature, nor so infallibly secure as to exempt a believer from the necessity of making some further satisfaction for sin, or to warrant the certain hope of eternal life. In short, the Christian had to become perfect through "satisfaction" of his own as well as the satisfaction of Christ, before he would ever be received into heaven. If he could reach perfection in this world, happy was he; if not, he would have to come to it through the distresses of purgatory. In any case, he would have to become perfect before he could be declared righteous by God and be received by Him. This of course meant that there was no point at which a sinner, or a believer, could believe that he was actually justified. He could never be sure that he had attained to a state of Christian perfection. Justification, then, cannot be a present privilege. The believer cannot rejoice in it as of now. He has no assurance that he will finally persevere and merit justification. He is certainly bowed down with the burdensome thought that he must endure temporal punishment in purgatory as a "satisfaction" due for post-baptismal sins. In other words, he lives his whole life in doubt, in fear, and, certainly, in some measure of bondage.

In opposition to this soul-distressing teaching, the Reformers taught that as justification properly consists in the forgiveness of sins and a sure title to eternal life, so it is the present privilege of every believer *from the instant when he receives and rests on Christ alone for salvation, and forever afterwards*. He continually "joys in God through our Lord Jesus Christ, by whom we have received the reconciliation" (Romans 5:11).

The act of God in justification is a complete, final, and irreversible act of divine grace by which the sinner is transferred once and forever from a state of wrath and condemnation into a state of favor and acceptance. But this act does not stand alone. God performs other acts based thereupon. Justification, fully appropriated by the sinner, gives him such an assurance of God's love, such peace of conscience, such joy in the Holy Spirit that, in recognition of and response to God's act in justification, he seeks to glorify God in his life, longs for "growth in grace" and strives manfully to persevere in faith even unto the end. He believes that the eternal purpose of God in his complete re-

demption will not fail, for he believes that "whom God did predestinate, them He also called; and whom He called, them He
also justified; and whom He justified, them He also glorified"
(Romans 8:30).

I am painfully aware that, in presenting so brief an outline
of the teachings of both the Roman Catholic church and the
Reformers of the 16th century, I have not done justice to either
side. I am also regretfully aware that there have been no really
serious efforts on the part of either Protestant or Catholic theologians to attempt some reconciliation, if possible, between
the two positions of justification, during the past 400 years.

But what is the situation today? Amazingly different! Let
me refer to the comments of several outstanding theologians
which indicate a changed attitude on the part of some Catholic
scholars. The Reverend Harry J. McSorley of Washington, D.C.,
an authority on Luther, and a Paulist scholar of note, said recently:

> Ten or fifteen years ago Catholics did not like to speak of
> Luther and when they did, his activity was referred to as a
> rebellion or revolution. Now as a result of the Second
> Vatican Council, it is recognized that the Roman Catholic
> church must always undergo reformation of which she
> always stands in need.

Research has demonstrated, according to this Paulist
scholar, that "the Catholicism which Luther rejected was not
truly Catholic. . . . There was real error in time and in place.
The church in Germany was guilty of serious doctrinal errors.
The chief error was a view that maintained a sinner, by doing
everything he was capable of doing by his own natural powers,
could win the grace of forgiveness of sins from God. I maintain
that Luther rightly criticized and rejected this error. In doing so,
he was a Catholic reformer."

There, you have it. Luther is now being claimed by the Catholic church. In fact, Bishop Hans Martensen of Copenhagen, a Jesuit authority on Luther, said, "Many documents of the Second Vatican Council contain ideas that would not have been formulated except for the influence of Martin Luther."

An American theologian teaching in Rome has openly said that "Luther was right on indulgences and on most theological points," and that his teachings on justification "are more palatable to me than Thomas Aquinas."

The late Catholic theologian, Jesuit John Courtney Murray, one of America's most influential theologians, calls Luther a "religious genius—compassionate, rhetorical and full of insights."

But the most complete and scholarly work on justification in recent times, from the Catholic viewpoint, is by the brilliant young theologian Hans Kung. In his volume, *Justification*, his procedure is unique. He first presents what he considers to be a legitimate and probably widely accepted Protestant view by presenting in the first one-third of his volume an outline of what is taught on justification by the Protestant theologian who is more respected by Roman Catholic theologians than any other, Karl Barth. Kung evidently thought that if he allowed Karl Barth to be the spokesman for Protestantism, he would then be able to make a response to the Protestant teaching on justification that would be considered seriously by Protestants. In the latter two-thirds of his book, under the heading "An Attempt and a Catholic Response" he gives his reply. I shall quote quite copiously from Kung's work, but let me now give you his conclusion:

> There is a fundamental agreement between Karl Barth's position and that of the Catholic church in regard to the theology of justification seen in its totality (p. 277).

Then on page 284 he writes:

> It is without doubt . . . there is a fundamental agreement
> between Catholic and Protestant theology precisely in the
> theology of justification—the point at which Reformation
> theology took its departure. Despite all the difficulties, can
> we not—after these 400 years—come closer to a meeting of
> the minds, and this in a way which is theologically deci-
> sive?

Let me conclude this chapter on justification by quoting
some paragraphs from Kung's article on justification in
"Christianity Divided," which rejoices the hearts of the sons of
the Reformation:

> We are justified through God's grace, and thereby *every*
> human achievement is excluded when justification is in
> question. "If it is by grace, then it is no longer on the basis
> of works: otherwise grace would no longer be grace"
> (Romans 11:6). If by grace, then it will be impossible to
> speak of a justification because of *any* obligation (p. 322).

> Justification through "faith alone" bespeaks the complete
> incapacity and incompetence of man for any sort of self-
> justification. . . . Thus no work, not even the work of love,
> justifies man, but only faith, justified through God
> Himself (p. 323).

> Sacred Scripture never speaks about justification by love.
> It always speaks emphatically about justification by faith.
> This is understandable if we think with the legal charac-
> ter of justification in mind. Justification is the declaration
> of justice by God in the court of judgment, and the appro-
> priate human attitude is obedient submission to this
> judgment. Justification is the declaration of justice by the
> merciful Judge, and the human attitude appropriate to this
> is one supported by fear and, above all, by trust—the

abandonment which affirms one's own unworthiness before God's grace under the divine judgment of grace. In
short: *Faith!* (p. 324).

The sinner is pronounced just, and he ought to submit
himself in faith to this judgment. It is not up to him to
pass a sentence in his own case to his own advantage. As
a sinner in need of justification, he is completely and
wholly unqualified to do that. But this is true even *after*
God's justifying judgments. Without any merit of man,
indeed, contrary to his whole sinful being, this judgment
becomes an acquittal which brings salvation. Justification
purely from the grace of God! How then could he who has
been graciously judged and justified by God subsequently
dare to set himself up as a self-justifying judge as if grace
does not *remain* just that—grace! (p. 327).

One concludes his reading of such views from one of today's leading theologians with amazement, and with no small
degree of cautious hopefulness. That Karl Barth felt this way is
evident from his letter to Hans Kung after reading his
Justification, a letter printed on the first pages of that book. He
wrote:

If what you have presented in Part Two of this book is actually the teaching of the Roman Catholic church, then I
must certainly admit that my view of justification agrees
with the Roman Catholic view, if only for the reason that
the Roman Catholic teaching would then be most strik-
ingly in accord with mine! Of course the problem is
whether what you have presented here really represents the
teaching of your church. This you will have to take up
and fight out with biblical, historical and dogmatic ex-
perts among your co-religionists. I don't have to assure
you that I am keenly interested in discovering what recep-
tion your book will find among them. For my part, I can
only acknowledge and reflect upon the fact that you have

presented considerable evidence in support of this sort of understanding and interpretation of the teaching of your church. . . . Involved as you are with a subject so crucial as justification, you have taken a rather sizable step; how feasible a step remains to be seen. . . . Significant and sufficiently rewarding for the day is this, that the view in both directions (in this division within the self-same faith between people who believe otherwise but in no other!) will open up and brighten up again. For this, we on both sides can give thanks.

And I, too, would give thanks and hope for greater light to come to the people of God through further study on the part of both parties of the grand theme of justification by grace through faith.

Justification by Faith Alone
Part Four

The Two-foldness of Grace

It may come as a surprise to some Protestants to learn that the Roman Catholic church teaches that salvation is wholly of grace. Her theologians refuse to relinquish to the Reformers, and to Protestants, the expression "sola gratia"—only of grace. Louis Bouyer, an outstanding Catholic theologian, in his work *The Spirit and Forms of Protestantism* (p. 43), makes this strong assertion:

> Luther's basic intuition—sola gratia—on which Protestantism continually draws for its abiding vitality, so far from being hard to reconcile with Catholic tradition, or inconsistent with the teaching of the apostles, was a return to the clearest elements of their teaching and is in the most direct line of that tradition. . . . If both Protestants and Catholics could be persuaded of it, the object of the basic antagonism of Protestants to the church would cease to exist.

Bouyer is particularly qualified to speak concerning the doctrine of justification by grace because he was formerly a Lutheran minister. But when he makes the statement that the teachings of grace of the Roman Catholic Church and those of Protestantism are substantially the same, a Protestant naturally questions whether he truly understands what Protestants actually believe about justifying grace. We are not left in doubt, however, as to what he does believe. Here is another important extract from his book: "Salvation is a grace, a gift of God, not the work of man. Therefore man can be saved by faith in God the Saviour, and by this means *alone*." How is this to be understood? Bouyer answers, "First, salvation depends not on one's own strength, but on God's. In this realization where radical distrust of self is but the obverse of absolute confidence in God, consists faith; nothing else can possibly replace it."

Second, "faith *alone* saves us." But what does this mean? He replies:

> It means, if it means anything, that we, on our part, have nothing to add to it, nothing outside or independent of it. Any such addition would result of necessity in a denial of the essential. For if, believing in principle in the saving action of God, we were obliged to add something of our own initiative, what would be the result? We would fall back at once into the impossible situation from which grace had rescued us; we would have to accomplish our salvation in part, in the hope that God would do the rest. . . . In other words, either we are not saved by divine grace, acknowledged and accepted by faith, or this grace, which is in God, is the sole cause of our salvation and faith which is in us, the sole means of access to it. For if there is something needed for salvation which has a source other than grace received by faith, we are confronted again with the impossible task of the salvation of man by man. The Gospel, however, is the good news that Someone else—God in Christ—has done for us what we could not do (p. 12).

Then Bouyer makes this strong statement:

> *All* is grace, and consequently *all* in our salvation comes to us by faith. If this *all* is compromised, the very heart of Protestant spirituality is wounded mortally. . . . We can see that Luther's view of salvation so understood is in perfect harmony with Catholic tradition, the great Conciliar definitions on grace and salvation (p. 13).

Now I submit to you that a casual reading of these statements seems to indicate that the Catholic position on justifying
grace is identical with the Reformers' position. But we cannot
let the matter rest here. We must raise a basic question about
Bouyer's use of the word "grace." Does he use the word in the
same way in which the Reformers used it when they proclaimed that man was justified "by grace through faith; and that
not of yourselves: it is the gift of God—not of works, lest any
man should boast" (Ephesians 2:8–9)?

In order to answer this question we must inquire how the
word "grace" is used in Scripture and throughout the history of
Christian theology. Probably all Christian scholars will agree
with Staudenmaier who wrote:

> Grace is distinguished in many different ways; not as
> though there are various kinds of grace; but rather the va-
> riety is determined by the various human situations and
> relationships that rest on the nature of the human recep-
> tion of the one and only divine grace.

There is a sense in which grace might be considered to be
universal in that *everything that God has done* to manifest His
glory and give evidence of His goodness is a revelation of His
grace. This view of grace is strongly held in the Greek
Orthodox church. Dr. Nicholas N. Gloubokowsky, a well-
known orthodox theologian, has written: "All of God's acts are
grace in creation, providence and redemption; each person of
the Trinity having His part in every act" (*The Doctrine of
Grace*, p. 61.

Read with delight the eloquent words of the early Church
Father, Chrysostom:

> What belongs to the law of Moses was itself the work of
> grace as well as our very creation out of non-existent

> things. . . . And not only our creation out of non-existent things, but also the fact that after creation we were immediately taught what to do, that we have this law in our creative nature, and that our Maker deposited in us an unbribable judgment of the conscience—all this was the work of the greatest grace and unspeakable love towards man.

Another early Church Father, Gregory of Nyssa, wrote: "Grace embraces everything good and fair, descending from the Father, through the Son, in the Holy Spirit."

The Fathers referred to this grace as "original grace." They consistently taught that *this* grace would not enable a man to enter the kingdom of God. For that, "specific grace" was needed, "a grace that was manifested only in Jesus Christ." The revelation of God's grace in redemption is without question the highest and the fullest manifestation of His love towards His creatures. But the New Testament teaches that there are two phases of "specific grace" which we describe as "declarative grace" and "operative grace."

How are we to understand the two-fold character of "specific grace"? As taught by the Reformers, "declarative grace" is that grace which God exercises when He *declares* a sinner "righteous" the moment he truly believes that "Christ was delivered for our offenses, and was raised again for our justification" (Romans 4:25). It is all the same as God's imputation of righteousness to the unrighteous when the sinner believes in Jesus. It is an act of God accomplished once and for all which puts the sinner in the state of acceptance with God because God, "for Christ's sake," forgave him his sins.

On the other hand, "operative grace," as the term implies, is that grace which operates within the believer, beginning with his "new birth" and continuing throughout his entire lifetime, and (the Catholic would add) even in purgatory. It produces holiness in his life and obedience in his service. By this operative grace, he performs "good works." I summarize:

"Declarative" grace accomplishes the justification of the sinner. "Operative" grace brings sanctification to the believer.

The confusion of these two phases of grace has been the cause of the continuing controversy over the issue of justification for the past 450 years. Catholic theology has so joined them and, in so doing, has confused justification with sanctification. But happily, in our time, there are an increasing number of Catholic theologians who now distinguish between these two forms of grace in such a way as to bring them closer to the Reformers' view. On the other hand, many Protestant theologians are recognizing that these two skeins of truth—justification and sanctification—are not to be so disassociated the one from the other that they do not sustain a vital relationship to each other.

Let us now return to the question: What did Bouyer mean when he attributed all of the work of redemption to the grace of God, and thereby excluded any addition on the part of man as the means to effect man's salvation? For he does put this with emphasis when he says that God achieves *all* through His grace, and that there isn't a single thing that man can do by way of good works that is not attributable to the grace of God. In support of this affirmation and, as the teaching of the church, he quotes Canon 5 of the Second Council of Orange in 529 A. D.:

> If anyone says that the increase, or even the beginning of faith, or the inclination to believe which leads to faith in Him who justifies the ungodly, and to regeneration by baptism, are innate in us, and are not the effective grace, that is, of the Holy Ghost who, by His inspiration, turns our wills from unbelief to faith, from ungodliness to piety, such an one must be held to oppose the doctrines of the apostles.

He also quotes Canon 18: "Whatsoever good works we do are deserving a reward not through any merit anterior to grace; their performance, rather, is due to a prior gift of grace to which we have no claim" (*Spirit and Forms of Protestantism*, Bouyer, pp. 48–49).

These strong affirmations help us Protestants understand why Catholic theologians today will not relinquish the phrase "sola gratia" to the Protestants. They believe they magnify the grace of God in salvation as much as we Protestants do—indeed, more!

Bouyer seems anxious to prove that what he calls the "positive principles of Protestantism" are "not only valid and acceptable, but must be held to be true and necessary *in virtue of Catholic tradition itself,* and in virtues of what makes up the authority of the church both of today and of all time." He writes:

> Salvation as the pure gift of God in Christ, communicated by faith alone, in the sense that no other way can be thought of apart from faith, or even along with faith; justification by faith in its subjective aspect, which means that there is no real religion where it is not living and personal; the absolute sovereignty of God, more particularly of His Word as contained in the inspired writings—all these principles are the heart of Protestantism as a reforming movement. Yet, if we go to the root of them all, to what the Reformers considered most essential, to what is retained by living Protestantism, today and always, we are bound to say that they are all corroborated by Catholic tradition and maintained absolutely by what is authoritative, in the present, for all Catholics (p. 137).

Thus Bouyer pays tribute to what he calls the "positive elements of Protestantism." Observe his reference to "justification by faith in its subjective aspect." He does not deny the objective aspect of salvation, for he has previously written of two aspects of the principle of salvation in this manner: "The objective aspect being the gift of God; the subjective, the appropriation of the gift of man."

While he treats of both of these aspects, we believe he does not do justice to the scriptural teaching on the "objective aspect" by speaking of it disparagingly as a negative element in Reformation theology. He refers to Luther as "identifying his affirmation about 'sola gratia' with a particular theory known as extrinsic justification"—a justification that is *external*. To enforce his teaching, he argues that the Reformers taught first, that "grace alone saves us," and, second, "it changes nothing in us in so doing." This is a contradiction, he argues, for "the second negates the first." Then he uses Luther's simile to underscore what he thinks is his error, for Luther wrote: "The grace of God envelops us as in a cloak, but this leaves us exactly as we were. The sinner after receiving the grace and so saved is no less a sinner than before."

In short, Bouyer does not see that the moment a sinner believes in Christ, he is given a righteous standing in God's eyes *not because of some change that has taken place in him, but because of changed relationship to God Himself.* The moment before he believed he was "ungodly," that is, "unrighteous," but now, having believed, he stands before God in "the righteousness of Christ." The glorious truth broke upon Luther that it was this "faith" that was "reckoned to him for righteousness" (Romans 4:3).

The issue was quite clear. Rome refused to recognize that God exercises His grace "declaratively" as well as "operationally." She did not admit that God *declares* a sinner righteous before *making* him righteous.

The Reformers believed in *both* declarative and operative grace. Those who charged them with believing that when a man was justified "it changed nothing in him in so doing" falsified their teaching. Thirty years after Luther's death, the Lutherans drew up the *Formula of Concord* in 1577 and, in Article IV, they clearly stated the Reformers' position:

> Good works certainly, and without doubt, follow true faith
> if it be not a dead but a living faith, as the fruit of a good
> tree. . . . We believe, teach and confess also that all men,
> and those especially who are born again and renewed by
> the Holy Spirit, are bound to do good works.

The *Formula* goes on to affirm that "good works may become injurious when we rely upon these good works to merit justification before God." They did not believe for one moment that a sinner who truly believes is not regenerated, but they did not equate regeneration with justification. They did not for one moment believe that the Christian should not be sanctified, but they did not equate sanctification with justification. They did not for one moment believe that the Christian should not do good works, and that these good works were the result of the operative grace of God working in him, but they did not, and dared not, identify justification with these "good works of faith." They truly taught that justification did indeed anticipate regeneration, sanctification, and the accomplishment of good works, but they did not identify it with any one of these acts of God's operative grace. They magnified the "declarative grace of God" as did Paul in Romans 4:5 where he plainly teaches that "Unto him that worketh not, but believeth on Him that justifieth the ungodly, his faith is reckoned for righteousness."

At this point, it would be well if we should inquire as to whether there are some encouraging signs that indicate a better understanding upon the part of Catholic and Protestant theologians concerning this great Reformation issue. Personally I believe there are such signs. For at least a decade, not a few reputable Catholic theologians (especially some of the younger ones) have been making a reappraisal of the teachings of the church on justification. One of them, Hans Kung, has authored a volume, *Justification,* that should be read by every Protestant. All of the following quotations are from this work, and are selected because they touch particularly upon the two aspects of God's grace to which we have been giving our attention. He assents to the fact that according to the original biblical use of the term "justification" it must be defined as a *declaring just by court order.* In the Old Testament, it meant "a divine act of judgment." In the Septuagint it generally means "forensic justification" (p. 209). Then he quotes Cardinal Newman on "the primary sense" of the term "justification": "Justification is, in the proper meaning of the word, a *declaration* of righteousness" (Newman, *Lectures of Justification,* p. 66).

He also quotes Newman as setting forth three principles concerning justification founded on sacred Scripture: "Justification is, in the proper meaning of the word, a *declaration* of righteousness; it is *distinct* from renewal; it is the *antecedent or efficient cause of renewal.*"

On page 212 we choose some selected statements by Kung which support Newman:

> The term "justification" mean a *declaring just.* It really implies a declaring just in the sense of leaving out of account, a not imputing. . . . God does not *reckon.* . . . God does not impute sin and its guilt. . . . Despite the sin, God declares the sinner just. Then he quotes Psalm 32:1–2: "Blessed is he whose transgression is forgiven, whose sin is covered. Blessed is the man unto whom the Lord imputeth not iniquity, and in whose spirit there is no guile."
>
> The term "justification" as such expresses an actual declaration of justness, and *not an inner renewal.*

> The divine declaration of justice has this quality in con-
> trast to any human judgment—that it does not justify the
> *just* man, but the *sinner*. Romans 4:5 says that we must
> "believe in Him who justifies the *ungodly*."

And then Kung makes several affirmations that make us
hopeful as we consider future dialogue:

> Put without polemics, the justification of the sinner
> means a declaration of justice by God Who, at the cross,
> and in the resurrection of Jesus Christ, declares all sinners
> free and just. Thus the accent is not on the "subjective,"
> but on the "objective" aspect of justification. . . . It is true
> that only he who believes is "actually (subjectively)
> justified," yet *the decisive element in the sinner's justification
> is found not in the individual, but in the death and
> resurrection of Christ.* It was there that our situation was
> actually changed; there the essential thing happened.
> What happened afterwards in the individual man would
> be impossible to conceive of in isolation. It is not man in
> his faith who originally changes the situation, who does
> the essential thing. It is not a matter of completion of the
> central salvation event in Jesus Christ, but rather an
> active acknowledgment, and this solely by the power
> stemming from the central event. In the death and
> resurrection of Christ, justification is established with
> final validity. It happened once for all, and irrevocably
> (pp. 230–31).

This really is an amazing statement for a Catholic theologian
to make. It is to be questioned, of course, whether this is a
definitive statement of the Catholic church. We must wait to
see whether or not, in the theological dialogue of the coming
days, the teaching of an *extrinsic or objective justification* as
taught by the Reformers becomes a part of the official teaching
of the church of Rome.

In conclusion, we Protestants must admit that, in the tremendous upheaval of the church which took place in the 16th century, Luther and some of the other Reformers placed so great an emphasis upon "declarative grace" that, in some cases, they minimized "operative grace." On the other hand, not a few Catholic theologians are admitting today that, in a violent reaction to this over-emphasis of the Reformers, the Council of Trent countered by over-emphasizing "operative grace" altogether. But if present trends continue, we may yet see, in our time, closer theological agreements between Protestants and Catholics with respect to the two aspects of divine grace— "declarative grace" and "operative grace." God grant it! For if such agreement were reached, it would, in my judgment, do more to unite the people of God, renew the church of Christ and bring "sola Deo gloria"—"glory to God only"—than any and all other agreements that might be achieved in the pursuit of a larger measure of "unity in doctrine."

Justification by Faith Alone
Part Five

The Two-foldness of Faith

In the two previous chapters we considered the teachings of justification and grace from the standpoint of the interpretive principle of "The Two-foldness of Divine Truth." In our treatment of justification in the third chapter in this seven-part series, we observed that Rome says the word means principally "to *make* a sinner righteous"; the Reformers said it meant "to *declare* the sinner righteous." In our consideration of the two-foldness of divine grace in the last chapter, we observed that there are two kinds of redemptive grace: "declarative grace", by which God *reckons* a man righteous in His sight, and "operative grace," by which God *makes* a man righteous.

We then observed how, in our time, both Protestant and Catholic theologians, in friendly and helpful dialogue, are making a serious attempt to bring about as much harmony between the two viewpoints as possible.

In each of these lectures we have emphasized the fact that the justification of the sinner is the work of God, *and of God only,* supporting our contention by the scriptural truth in Romans 8:33: "It is God that justifieth."

But we are led to ask: is there not a human side to justification? The answer is "yes." Man must have *faith.* It might well be said that the critical issue of the 16th-century Reformation revolved around the Latin words *sola fide,* which mean "faith alone." We can hardly realize today how radical and bitter was the controversy that raged around this word "alone." If we

were to pinpoint a historical event when the theological controversy began in earnest, we would place it in 1521 when Luther
translated the New Testament into German and rendered
Romans 3:28: "Therefore we conclude that a man is justified by
faith *alone* without the deeds of the law."

Great abuse has been heaped upon him because he was
charged with falsifying the Scriptures when he inserted the
word "alone" in his translation. There is no such word in the
original Greek text. But happily in our day, fair-minded Catholic
theologians are conceding, as does Hans Kung in his work on
Justification (p. 249), that "the translation of this text with the
inclusion of the word 'alone' was not Luther's invention."

He then refers to several translations in which the word
"alone" occurs as the Nurnberg German Bible's reading of
Galatians 2:16: "Gerechtfertigt . . . *Nur* durch Den Glauben"
(produced in 1483, the year of Luther's birth). The same reading occurs in three Italian translations, according to Oltramare:
"ma *solo* per la fede" or "per la *sola* fede" (Genoa 1476, Venice
1538 and 1546).

Furthermore, Dr. Kung says that the Catholic Council of
Trent, which condemned many teachings of the Reformers,
"did not intend to say anything against the formula (*sola fide*)
in itself." And what is even more significant, he adds: "The
formula definitely belongs in Catholic tradition." He refers to
Cardinal Bellarmine (who probably wrote the ablest refutation
of the Reformers' teachings) as citing the following Church
Fathers as having used the expression "faith only" in their
writings: Origen, Hilary, Basil, Chrysostom, Augustine, Cyril
of Alexandria, and especially Ambrosiaster and Bernard.

It is becoming increasingly apparent that one of the wholesome results of the present theological dialogue is that there is a
clarification upon the part of both Protestants and Catholics

concerning what is *the faith that justifies*. The contemporary Catholic theologian Louis Bouyer, in his work *The Spirit and Forms of Protestantism* (p. 13), writes:

> What it (the formula *sola fide*) aims at rejecting is, *alone*, the idea that we have to add our personal quota, that is *external to these two things*: grace which gives; faith which receives. Understood in this way, such an addition amounts to saying that we are saved neither by grace nor faith. . . . The insight of Luther is that *all* is grace, consequently *all* in our salvation comes to us by faith. If this "all" is compromised, the very heart of Protestant spirituality is wounded mortally.

This, then, is the true biblical position, namely that man is justified through God's grace alone, and through faith alone in God's grace. Man achieves nothing. There is no human meritorious activity in the act of justification. "It is God that justifies" (Romans 8:33).

Bouyer then goes on to assert that there is nothing in this position that is not supported by the decrees of the Council of Trent. He quotes one of them:

> We may be said to be justified freely in the sense that nothing that precedes justification, neither faith nor works, merits the grace of justification.

At this point the question might well be raised: If this, then, is the official teaching of the Catholic church concerning justification by faith, why should there be any further controversy over this issue? Are not Protestant and Catholic theologians saying the same thing?

Unfortunately, our reply must be "no," and, in support of this negative position, we must take a brief excursion into church history.

In order to get our chronological bearings, let me remind you that it was in 1517 that Luther nailed the 95 Theses to the door of the Castle Church in Wittenburg. In 1521 he made his famous declaration, "Here I stand," at the Diet of Worms. The die was cast and the garment was rent. Following the Diet, the conflict took on political overtones as the German princes sided with Luther against the Pope. For the next decade there were debates, disputes, and intrigue growing out of a series of councils or diets called by either the Pope or the Emperor, Charles. The Emperor had to keep the German princes in line because of his war with the Turks. Therefore, he was somewhat conciliatory toward the "evangelicals," as the Lutherans were called in that day. So, at the Diet of Augsburg in 1530, he allowed the evangelicals to present their "confession of faith."

The Augsburg Confession was carefully composed by the learned, prudent, and conciliatory Melanchthon. It was revised and cordially approved by Luther and his prince, the Elector of Saxony, Frederick the Wise.

What we are particularly interested in is Melanchthon's statement of the method of justification by the free grace of God, through faith alone, and based solely on the merits of Christ. He did this in moderate terms, and in the most inoffensive terms, yet the two Catholic divines—Faber and Eckius—rejected his statement on justification and advised strongly against the acceptance of the "confession." The chief ground of their opposition was its alleged *novelty* as "a method of teaching which is now introduced for the first time, and which was at direct variance with that which had prevailed in the Roman church."

The Reformers were made to feel that unless they would consent to abandon, or at least modify, their teaching on this point, they would expose themselves and their cause to "imminent danger" (the sword)! But the Reformers stood fast.

The great breach had come! Bainton comments in *Here I Stand* (p. 375):

> One might take the date June 25, 1530, the day when the Augsburg Confession was publicly read, as the death day of the Holy Roman Empire. From this day forward the two confessions stood over against each other, poised for conflict.

The two camps threatened the unity of both the church and the Empire. One might almost think that from that time on there would be no more efforts toward conciliation and reunion. But a decade later, in 1541, the Diet of Ratisbon was held in which a marked and striking change in the policy of the Catholic party took place. Instead of denouncing the Protestant doctrine of justification as a dangerous novelty directly opposed to the teaching of the Roman church, the Catholic delegates were now prepared ostensibly to adopt it as their own—to claim it even as a portion of that truth which they had always held in part. James Buchanan, in his *The Doctrine of Justification* (p. 144), writes:

> That the original charge against the Protestant doctrine as a *novelty* and their (the Catholics') subsequent claim to it as the old doctrine of the church could not both be true is evident because they are manifestly contradictory, and it might seem incredible that they could have been adopted by the same parties in good faith.

The Emperor Charles, who had called the Diet of Ratisbon, presented a new statement to the assembly, and then named three divines on each side—Eckius, Gropper and Pflug for the Romanists, and Melanchthon, Bucer, and Pistorius for the Protestants—to examine it and report. What a momentous hour! The tide of the church's destiny might have turned here so that there never would have been a division in the church, nor a movement known as Protestantism. Strange as it seems, these six divines agreed upon the article on justification. Indeed, this agreement seemed so promising that one of the Catholic representatives, Contarini, sent the joyful message to Rome: "God be thanked. Both sides have united on the dogma of justification." Tragically, both Rome and Wittenburg later repudiated this agreement. A few years afterwards, at the Council of Trent in 1543, the curtain was drawn on this dialogue when the Fathers pronounced their anathema upon the Protestant teaching of "justification by faith alone."

At this point, we are led to ask—and not without a bit of irritation—why was it, if they were so close together, they could not fully agree? What terrible things the church would have been spared if the dialogue at the Diet of Ratisbon had been successful! The answer to the above question lies in the fact that, while concessions and compromises in times of controversy are often wise and profitable, to make a concession of *the essential point* in question is not only dangerous, but calamitous. The Roman theologians did make concessions, but in all of these concessions one point was carefully reserved (or expressed in ambiguous terms) which was of such vital and fundamental importance that, according to the sense in which it was understood, it would definitely be in favor of the old Catholic position. To discover this point, we will have to consider the following statement made by the Catholic representatives:

> Sinners are justified by a living and effectual faith which is a motion of the Holy Spirit whereby, repenting of their lives past, they are raised to God and are made real partakers of the mercy which Jesus Christ has promised. . . . Which no man attains but, at the same time, love is shed abroad in his heart and he begins to fulfill the law, and

> that this is not to hinder us from exhorting the people to increase their faith and this love by outward and inward works; so that though the people be taught that faith alone justifies, yet repentance, the fear of God and of His judgments and the practice of good works ought to be preached unto them.

Why didn't the Reformers fully accept this statement? Because it set forth, in their understanding, *a wrong view of justifying faith*. It is true that the article speaks much of faith, but it is not of *the faith that justifies the sinner, but rather of the faith that sanctifies the believer*. It diverts the mind from the external object of justifying faith which is the death, burial, and resurrection of Christ, on the grounds of which *alone* God's perfect righteousness is imputed to the sinner the moment he believes. It directs the mind toward the inward effect of faith by which the character and conduct of the believer is changed, and an inherent righteousness is produced in him. The Reformers readily admitted that this second element of teaching is sound and wholesome in its own place and in its proper connection, but it becomes unsound and dangerous when it is mixed with the truth which related to the ground and reason of the sinner's acceptance with God. Buchanan comments:

> By introducing the sanctifying effects of faith into the definition of it as if it were the *means* of justification, the Roman divines made provision for falling back on their favorite doctrine of an inherent, as opposed to an imputed righteousness; and for ultimately setting aside all the concessions which they had apparently made (p. 148).

No wonder, then, that the article was not satisfactory to either Rome or Wittenburg. It had too much of the Gospel in it to be palatable to the consistent adherents of Rome, and too much of disguised legalism to be acceptable to the Reformers at

Wittenburg.

But what of today? Has the cycle come round again? Will there be another Council of Ratisbon? Are we witnessing in the efforts of Hans Kung, Bouyer, Rahner, and other Catholic theologians another attempt to arrive at some agreement on this whole important issue which caused the great rift 450 years ago? We hope so! At least we see some trends in that direction.

Thus far we have considered the issue of justifying faith. Let us now consider the teaching of Scripture with respect to *sanctifying* faith. The Reformers strongly affirmed, with their Catholic counterparts, that there is a "sanctifying faith" as well as a "justifying faith." The whole of Christian salvation, as far as the human side is concerned, is conditioned by faith; for not only do the just stand before God in a faith begun, but they continue to live their entire lives in a "faith continued," for "without faith it is impossible to please God" (Hebrews 11:6). The Reformers admitted that justification is not only a judicial act by which the sinner is declared righteous, but it is the beginning of subsequent acts of God. The justified one becomes the regenerate one, but only because he *is* the justified one! He receives a new life from God, a life that needs not only to begin, but to be continued.

The just *always* live by faith, but faith looks in two ways. The faith of the sinner looks to Christ on the cross who, by His death, burial, and resurrection, made it possible for God to forgive his sins and accept him as righteous in His sight; but it also looks to the indwelling of Christ who, by the operative grace of the Holy Spirit, produces in him a life of sanctification. The Reformers affirmed that the work *for* us on the cross and Christ's work *in* us by the Holy Spirit cannot be disassociated; but they would not consent for one moment that these two operations of God are one and the same thing.

In speaking of justifying faith, John Calvin (and more recently Karl Barth) speaks of the "emptiness of justifying faith." By this he meant that this faith is *empty of any work that could be considered meritorious*. Obviously it is a human act, but it lives from, and is directed by, the grace of God, and can therefore *never stand in competing relationship to grace*. On the other hand, sanctifying grace looks to the Holy Spirit through whose operative grace the believer is enabled to maintain good works. His faith cooperates with God to fulfill God's will. It is a "living faith," such as Abraham had when he offered up Isaac. It is an "obedient faith" that glorifies God in the eyes of men. The world sees their good works, and glorifies their Father which is in heaven (Matthew 5:16).

The charge brought against Luther again and again was that he was an advocate of a "dead faith." Surely no one who has read the preface to his commentary on the Epistle to the Romans could so accuse him!

> Faith is a divine work in us which transforms and begets us anew. It makes us in heart, temper, disposition, and all our powers, entirely different men than we were before and brings with it the Holy Spirit. It is a *living, busy, mighty, active thing*. It is impossible that it should not be ceaselessly doing that which is good. It is impossible to separate good works from faith.

When we acknowledge Christ by faith, we must also acknowledge that, to be a living faith, it must have in it the *full purpose of obedience*. We must insist that obedience is not and cannot be the ground of our acceptance with God in righteousness, but obedience is the unfailing fruit and an inseparable accompaniment of that faith through which we obtain acceptance. Faith which comes to Christ for forgiveness and does not come, at the same time, with the sincere purpose of wanting to be obedient, and coveting that grace which will make obedience possible, is not the faith which obtains justification. Faith—a living, dynamic faith—is the only faith by which we are justified, and is the only faith by which we are sanctified. To live continually by faith is possible only when that faith is inspired by the matchless love of God in Christ. When faith in Christ is so excited by the Holy Spirit in the heart of a sinner, it becomes an operative, energetic, and productive faith.

Abraham became the "father of all them that believe" (Romans 4:11), because his faith was a "living, busy, mighty, active thing." That is why he has this testimony: "He was strong in faith, giving glory to God" (Romans 4:20). We who are Abraham's children by faith (Galatians 3:7) should know, as he did, a "faith that justifies" and a "faith that sanctifies," and then we, too, will be "strong in faith, giving glory to God."

Justification by Faith Alone
Part Six

The Two-foldness of Merit

It seems fitting, as we come to the sixth part of this series, that we review the teaching of justification by grace through faith as held by the Reformers and the Roman Catholic church in the 16th century. And we should keep in mind that these two positions are still held by the orthodox in both groups today. The two systems may be briefly characterized as follows:

As to the Doctrine of Rome:
Rome claimed to attribute *all* of salvation to the grace of God. In so doing, however, she made the exercise of grace dependent upon man's free will, teaching that the sinner had some predisposing qualifications which fitted him to receive the grace of God.

She also taught that a believer so cooperated with God's grace as enabled him, through such cooperation, to merit eternal life.

She did recognize the merits of Christ, but they were reckoned not as the immediate and all-sufficient ground of a sinner's justification, but only as the remote "procuring" cause of that infused personal righteousness which, when *perfected* in this life, and in purgatory, was the real reason for the sinner being accepted as righteous in the sight of God.

We must conclude, therefore, that Rome fluctuated between the free grace of God and the free will of man, between the merits of Christ and the merits of His people. In attempting to combine these two elements in one system, she taught that justification depended partly on grace and partly on works, even though she claimed that these were the "works of grace."

There are other features (which, unfortunately, we have not had time to consider) which were related to justification, such as the mediation of saints, additional satisfaction for sin in the austerities of penance and the pains of purgatory, and the imposition of penance upon the penitent. Ofttimes these teachings led man to look to something which he could do himself by which he could provide some merit for salvation instead of relying solely on Christ and His finished work.

The Doctrine of the Reformers:

The doctrine of the Reformers offered a striking contrast. It proclaimed the glorious truth that every sinner to whom the Gospel comes has, the moment he believes in Christ's expiatory work:

Direct and free access to God through the sole mediation of Christ;

The full pardon of all sin;

The full acceptance with God as a son; and

A sure title to eternal life.

All these wonderful gifts are his, and may be immediately appropriated and enjoyed by faith. Furthermore, being united to Christ by faith, he will be made partaker, in due time, of all the blessings of a complete and everlasting salvation.

Perhaps the contrast can be pointed up succinctly if we say that the Reformers taught that the sinner was justified wholly on the basis of Christ's merits due to the mercy of God, whereas Rome taught that the sinner was justified on the grounds of both the merits of Christ and his own merits, which merits were based upon his good works done as a believer, thus mixing the mercy of God with the merits of man.

Rome, then, insisted on "good works," and such good works were merits. But did not the Reformers also? Indeed they did! But they believed that there are two kinds of merit, and that these should always be distinguished: there are the merits of Christ and there are the merits of the believer.

These are not one and the same, although, like justification and sanctification, they should never be disassociated. Christ's merits are the merits which God attributed to His voluntary death for sin, His burial, and His resurrection—all of which He accomplished in behalf of sinners. These merits are His and His alone. They cannot be ours by any meritorious act upon our part; but they can be ours by faith. However, such faith is not meritorious; it is a "gift of God." As we cannot obtain forgiveness by any merit of our own, so we cannot obtain justification before God for anything we have done, or ever will do. Only on the merits of Christ, and for Christ's sake, are we justified in God's holy eyes. Justification of the sinner is the result of the merits of Christ, whereas the merits of the believer are the results of his sanctification. The merits of Christ are infinite, eternal, and undiminishable, while the believer's merits are not.

How wonderful is the truth that freely, by His grace, through the redemption that is in Christ Jesus, God has declared us righteous in His sight. Hear again this wonderful text in Romans 4:5: "Unto him that worketh not, but believeth in Him that justifieth the ungodly, his faith is counted for righteousness."

As we think on the subject of "merits," we are keenly aware that the scriptural teaching on the subject of divine rewards is too little understood by God's people. Perhaps one reason is that he who is set for the defense of the doctrine of divine grace is fearful lest that truth be impugned by the teaching of merit. The Reformers were particularly sensitive at this point; but if the Romanists have exalted merit to the minimizing of grace, evangelicals must be aware of the danger of exalting grace to the exclusion of merit.

The late Dr. A. J. Gordon once wrote:

> Just as the legalist resents the doctrine that good works can have no part in effecting our forgiveness, so evangelicals recoil from the idea that they constitute any ground for a recompense. On the contrary, we have the feeling that such requital of faithful service and obedience is absolutely necessary to satisfy our instinctive sense of justice. We cannot think of a final divine reckoning which shall assign the same rank in glory and the same degree of joy to a lazy, indolent and unfruitful Christian which is accorded to the ardent, devoted and self-denying Christian.

When our Lord would point up the solemnity of what would take place at His second coming, He quite frequently referred to the work of His disciples. In Matthew 16:27 we read: "For the Son of Man shall come in the glory of His Father with His angels; and then He shall reward every man according to his works." In the closing verses of Revelation (22:12), we read: "Behold, I come quickly; and My reward is with Me, to give every man according as his work shall be."

Evangelicals must never neglect to set before the people of God a positive injunction to self-denial, for it is by a life of self-effacement that the faithful receive the "recompense of reward." That we have given the impression to some Romanists that we do not teach self-abnegation is brought to light in a letter sent out by the Society of Evangelical Missions of Paris, the Director of which is M. Wilfred Monod. In an appeal to Protestant Christians for self-denial, he inserted the following in his letter:

> How is it that Protestants have reduced upon a man like Pere Gratry the impression which he formulates as follows: Protestantism is, in essence, the abolition of sacri-

fice? To abolish mortification, abstinence and fasting; to abolish the necessity of good works, effort, struggle, virtue; to shut up sacrifice in Jesus alone and not let it pass to us; no more to say, as St. Paul did, "I fill up that which is wanting in the sufferings of Christ," but rather to say to Jesus on His cross: "Suffer alone, O Lord"—there is Protestantism.

We know that this is not true of all evangelicals; yet no one can live in the heart of evangelicalism without a profound discomfort over the truth which it discloses.

Scriptural testimony to the fact that God rewards His faithful children is particularly evident when we learn what it is that God rewards:

In Matthew 6:6, we read that God rewards secret prayer;

In Luke 6:35, loving our enemies and lending to the poor;

In Matthew 5:12, suffering persecution as the prophets suffered in their day;

In Hebrews 10:35, steadfastness in Christ;

In Matthew 6:3–4, unselfishness;

In 1 Corinthians 9:17, a willing spirit in service.

A passage that has provided Rome with what they would call a proof text of their dogma of purgatory is found in 1 Corinthians 3:8–17. Pope Innocent IV, in his letter to the Bishop of Pusculum in 1254, spoke of those who have gone to purgatory because their "lesser sins which still weigh upon them, although forgiven in this life, have not been purged."

Paul, in 1 Corinthians 3:13 and 15, writes: "The fire shall try every man's work . . . of what sort it is"; and "If any man's work shall be burned, he shall suffer loss, but he himself shall be saved, yet so as by fire."

This is indeed a solemn Scripture, but it should be interpreted in the light of the context and not wrenched from its moorings. A careful examination of this passage leads one to consider it a part of a larger passage commencing at 1:10 and concluding at 4:6. Provocation for the Apostle's words of rebuke and correction was their sectarian devotion to the "ministers of Christ"—that is, Paul, Apollos, Peter and others (see 1:12). The Corinthians were pitting one over against another and playing favorites. This was "carnal" (1 Corinthians 3:1), and revealed their sad immaturity. In 3:5–9, Paul says that he, Apollos, and Peter are fellow-workers together and should not be made to be "opponents" to each other. He then recognizes the solemnity of being a minister at all when at firsthand he says, "I laid the foundation in Corinth when I preached Christ, and Christ alone; but since I laid the foundation, others have built thereupon."

By that he means, particularly, other teachers and preachers. Therefore, in this particular text, he has an exclusive group in mind, namely those who are charged with the building of the "church of God," as if it were a building. That is why he says that if any, by the introduction of hay, wood and stubble—in the form of false teaching or corrupt admonitions—destroy or do harm to the church of God, God will see to it that they lose their rewards for such evil deeds. He is not talking about a servant's "work." In fact, he says that after all of the combustible materials such as wood, hay, and stubble will be consumed in the day of Christ, even the unfaithful minister shall "himself be saved, yet as by fire" (1 Corinthians 3:15). It is not the minister's soul that is at stake, but his works. What an awful revelation it will be when some servants of Christ find that much, if not all, of their ministry, is consumed by fire because they built but hay, wood and stubble upon the foundation of Christ.

It is true that, since there is a principle of judgment announced in this text (even though it has to do primarily with ministers), it is quite evident that God will judge the works of all His children in the same way. But it is their "works" that shall be judged; and, even if all of them are consumed in fire, yet they "shall be saved." And why? Because by faith they built upon Christ, and Christ alone, as the only foundation for their salvation.

The brighter side of the picture, of course, is that God rewards His faithful servants for their services that will survive the ravages of that terrible conflagration because they are like unto "gold, silver, and precious stones."

So we see that the Scriptures plainly teach two justifications, one by faith and one by works, and, while they are not unrelated, they should never be disassociated; they are to be distinguished. One rests solidly and only upon the merits of Christ and His redemptive work—on His merits alone; the other upon our works of obedience and love that grow out of our living faith in the risen Son of God. These "works" are recognized by our Heavenly Father as worthy of being rewarded, though they are not reckoned by Him as worthy of being compared with the "merits" of His Son. The great error of the Roman theology is that they mix Christ's merits and the merits of the believer.

Perhaps an illustration will help us understand the motive and purpose that prompts God to reward His faithful servants. Let us begin by a general statement. Just as a human father rewards a faithful son, so does our Heavenly Father reward His faithful servants. But why should an earthly father reward his son, we might ask? For after all, when the son does "good works," isn't it the father (and I might include the mother in this illustration) who really does those "good works" in him? Isn't the very life of the son the gift of the father? Aren't the inherent capabilities of the son—his physical strength, his mental acumen and his latent capabilities—really attributable to the father? To such questions we would probably answer in the affirmative; but, at this point, we can look at another side of this illustration. If the son has reached maturity, and has accomplished some outstanding work which has been assigned to him by his father, could he not legitimately look for some kind of recognition, and even reward, for his services? We might well expect, then, that he would come to his father and ask if he was not to be paid for this work.

Now suppose for a moment the father took the position that he was himself the sole author of what the son had done; he might well put some such questions to the son such as these: "Why should I reward you for your services? Do you not recognize that all of the physical strength, mental acumen, and innate capabilities by which you were able to accomplish these tasks would not have been yours if I had not given you my life? It is really I who am working in you. Shouldn't I get all the glory?"

But the boy might reply: "Well, father, I recognize that I owe my very life to you and, if it were not for you, I would not even exist. Furthermore, I am grateful for the strong body, healthy mind, and innate capabilities that you have bequeathed to me. But on the other hand, father, was it not I who did the works? Did I not choose to do them of my own free will? You did not force me to do them. In fact, you didn't even ask me to do them as a duty. Therefore I took pleasure in doing them because the only thing I really wanted to do was to please you. In fact, if you are pleased, that is all the reward I ask."

Whereupon the father (if he is a noble father, as our God is a noble God) might say, "Well spoken, son. I deeply appreciate your gratitude for the gift of life which you received from me, but, because you chose to use my gifts—my gift of life, wisdom, innate skills—to do these good works, and all because you knew I would be pleased with what you did, I am going to find the greatest joy showing you my appreciation for your loving service by rewarding you handsomely for them."

And so it is with our Heavenly Father and His willing servant.

Once again we see that there are two related, yet opposite, ideas that should ever be kept before us. Only the Father could give life; only our Heavenly Father can give us the title to eternal life. This He does of His own sovereign will, and through the merits of Christ's work alone; but the believer who had received life as a "gift of God" now chooses to express that life in good works which the Heavenly Father recognizes within the framework of the family economy and lovingly rewards. There is no thought, however, that these "works" have anything to do with the "inheritance of life."

The charge was brought against the Reformers, in their day and ever since, that they despised "good works." David Shaff, in his work, *Our Fathers' Faith and Ours*, writes:

> The charge that Luther and the Protestant system have reduced the obligation and value of godly living, and taught that salvation is offered through faith, independent of good practices, was made from the first, as by Cardinal Sadoleto, and has been repeated even to our own day.

One of the chief opponents of the Reformers was Sir Thomas More, Chancellor under Henry VIII of England. How far he was from understanding the teaching of the Reformers is seen by the words he used in *The Supplication Souls* (p. 309). Speaking of a false Gospel, he writes:

> Which Gospell is Luther's Gospell, and Tindale's Gospell, telling you that there needeth no good workes, but that it wer sacrilege and abomonation to go about to please God with any good workes and that there is no Purgatory.

Another leading Catholic theologian of the time, Bellarmine,

was so unfair as to represent Luther's position in this fashion:
"If you come with a bag full of good works and lay it down, you
will not be able to enter the kingdom of heaven." We might
point out that this statement would have expressed Luther's
position, and the position of Protestants, if Bellarmine had but
added the words: "And have not faith."

The Reformers did magnify faith, but not as an intellectual
element only. Faith did not merely mean "belief," but trust. All
saving faith is trusting faith. Faith, to be a saving faith, must
have in it a living quality.

When James, in his epistle, speaks of "faith," he is contrasting two kinds of faith: dead faith and a living faith. His illustrations, both negatively and positively, clearly indicate this.
Negatively, he says that a man may *say* that he has faith, but if,
when a brother who lacks daily food asks him for some, he
says: " 'Good luck to you, keep yourselves warm, and have
plenty to eat' (James 2:16, NEB), without giving him the things
needed for his body, what does it profit?" That kind of faith,
because it does not issue in works, is dead.

But when James presents the positive proof of Abraham's
faith, he recounts the total obedience of the patriarch when he
offered up Isaac upon the altar. By no suggestion whatsoever
did James mean to imply that Abraham did not have faith before he committed this act of dedication. In fact, he knew the Old
Testament Scriptures well enough to know that his "faith was
reckoned to him for righteousness" (Genesis 15:6) before Isaac
was even born. His faith stood naked before God whose
"promise" he had believed that "out of his own loins" God
would give his "seed" in which "all the nations of the earth
would be blessed." But Abraham's faith, James insisted, was a
living faith, and the proof of it is that when it was challenged to
demonstrate positively, actually it was such a faith that he
showed openly by the offering up of his son.

So James says, "you see that a man is justified by works and not by faith alone." Here he was not contrasting works with faith, but works with dead faith; and dead faith never justifies anyone. But a "living" faith does justify because it not only trusts in Christ and His merits, but proves its trusting quality by allowing the Holy Spirit to produce good works in the believer and thus demonstrates that the faith which is in him is a "living" faith.

To settle once for all, we could hope, the question of whether Luther believed that a Christian should be "zealous of good works," as Paul admonishes in Titus 2:14, let me quote a brilliant historian in the 19th century, Charles Beard, who has given us an excellent volume on the Reformation. The reason I quote him is that he was a Unitarian, and therefore cannot be charged with being biased toward the Reformers. He writes:

> On no account could Luther be charged with being *indifferent to the sanctity of moral law* or that the good works on which he poured contempt and scorn, were those without which the manly or the Christian character cannot be conceived. Only those critics who have utterly failed to understand both the great Reformer and his characteristic position can accuse him of a personal tendency to Antinomian heresy. . . . He delighted in preaching a moral sermon; he expounded the Decalogue more than once.
>
> Faith was to Luther no mere intellectual acceptance of Christ in His atoning death, even if that acceptance were of a strictly personal kind: it was a spiritual incorporation of the soul with its Saviour as involved a changed individuality, a renewed and strengthened nature out of which all the fruits of righteousness naturally grew. For the Christian so transmuted, it was no longer a question of doing good works in obedience to an external law, so to speak, to order; they were the natural expressions of a new man as inevitable as breathing and speaking. The doc-

> trine so stated has the advantage of being true to two well-known and indisputable facts of human nature: First, that the motive power of character lies in the affection, and that to produce a cleansed, strengthened, renewed man, there is no other way than to inspire into the heart a passionate love and trust of some worthy object; and, second, that actions do not so much determine character as are determined by it, and that, to go back to the familiar phrase of the New Testament, "If you would have good fruit, you must make the tree good."

And then Beard pays a high tribute to the purity of Luther's teaching on redemptive grace when he writes:

> It was admirably adapted to work the great change of which I have spoken, for it led the soul straight to its divine object. It made religion a matter only for the believer in Christ.

And what Luther taught, Calvin taught. In answering Cardinal Sadoleto, the Genevan Reformer said that:

> This calumny our opponents have ever in their mouths, namely, that we take away the purpose of well doing from the Christian life by recommending gratuitous righteousness. It is true that we deny that good works have any share in justification, but we claim that full responsibility rests upon the righteous to do good works.

The Reformers taught, then, the reality and the necessity of good works in the case of every true believer. They saw that in Scripture they are not only required of all believers, but recognized as being truly acceptable to God, and even rewarded by Him. They are acceptable to God for three distinct reasons:

Because they are acts of beautiful obedience upon the part of His children who have been "accepted in the Beloved";

Because they are agreeable to His revealed will; and

Because they are the "fruits of the Spirit" and, as such, are very precious in themselves and very pleasing to Him.

Paul writes of the giving of the Philippians that their contributions were "an odor of a sweet smell, a sacrifice acceptable, well-pleasing to God" (Philippians 4:18); and Peter also writes that all believers are "a spiritual house, a holy priesthood, to offer up spiritual sacrifices acceptable to God by Jesus Christ" (1 Peter 2:5).

From these testimonies, and many more that could be advanced, it clearly appears that for believers to exhibit both the graces of the Spirit and the works of faith holds an important place in the scheme of grace and redemption—that they are, in their own nature, intrinsically good, as contra-distinguished from those which are morally evil; that they are acceptable to God both as being in accordance with His revealed will, and also as being the fruits of His Spirit. And let it be plainly said that such good works are rewarded.

The Reformers feared that to extol good works, and attribute any merit to them, would encourage those who performed them to think that by the doing of them they contributed some merit toward their justification and eternal salvation. This fear is justified because this is what is taught by the Roman Catholic system. It teaches that the believer's life, in proportion as it is good, merits reward in God's sight which reward is final justification and the beatific vision. Merit is acquired by obedience to the rules laid down by ecclesiastical authorities as well as by obedience to the plain precepts of the Scriptures; or, as the Council of Trent put it, "by the observance of the commandments of God and the church."

Trent also claimed that "through the most holy Sacrament, all true justice and righteousness either begins or is being begun, is increased, or being lost, is repaired." It pronounced its

anathema upon those who claim that by good works performed through the grace of God and the merit of Jesus Christ,
the justified man does not truly merit increase of grace, eternal
life and also increase in glory. The following is taken from the
Canons and Decrees of the Council of Trent, Chapter 16, under
"Justification":

> Hence, to those who work well *unto the end*, and trust in
> God, eternal life is to be offered both as a grace, mercifully
> promised to the sons of God through Christ Jesus, and, as
> a reward, promised by God Himself to be faithfully given
> for their good works and merits. . . . For since Jesus Christ
> Himself is the head of the members, and the vine in the
> branches continually infuses strength into those justified,
> which strength always precedes, accompanies and follows
> their good works, and without which they could not in
> any manner be pleasing and meritorious before God, we
> must believe that nothing further is wanting to those jus-
> tified to prevent them from being considered to have, by
> those very works which have been done in God, fully sat-
> isfied that divine law according to the state of this life, and
> to have truly merited eternal life.

Now what is this but adding human merits to Christ's
merits in order to inherit eternal life? How can this be reconciled with the teaching of Paul: "By grace are ye saved through
faith, and that not of yourselves; it is the gift of God, not of
works, lest any man should boast"?

And then we see that again there has been confusion with
respect to the teaching of justification and sanctification. These
two doctrines can be reconciled, provided it is admitted, without any equivocation, that Paul's conclusion in Romans 3:28
was right, when he said: "Therefore we conclude that a man is
justified by faith without the deeds of the law."

We have contended from the outset that the chief error of

Roman Catholic theology is its failure to distinguish between justification and sanctification. Moeller, a Catholic theologian, in his work *Theology of Grace* (p. 41), writes:

> Of central importance is the distinction introduced by Calvin between justification and sanctification. This distinction was not taken into consideration in the definitions at Trent. The Council is said to affirm, in regard to *justification*, a series of things which the Reformation refused to admit, preferring to attribute them instead to sanctification. This point must be carefully considered.

It seems fitting then that we should conclude this chapter on merit by pointing up similarities and dissimilarities between justification and sanctification. As you read, keep in mind that we associate justification with *imputed* righteousness, and sanctification with *imparted* or *infused* righteousness.

As to similarities:
Both are sovereign favors, bestowed on us by the God of divine grace. Both come to us through the redemption that is in Christ Jesus.
In both, the operation of the Holy Spirit applies the work of Christ. They are both essential to our salvation from the state in which we find ourselves as sinners, and from the dangers to which we are exposed as believers. Both of them, therefore, are enjoyed by all genuine believers, and by believers only.

As to dissimilarities:
Justification rests back upon God's just dealing with our sin in Christ on the cross. *Sanctification* relates to God's work in the heart of the believer by the Holy Spirit.

Justification is an instantaneous act of God.
Sanctification is a process of which the Holy Spirit is the agent.

Justification changes our standing before God.
Sanctification is a change of our nature or character.

In *justification* we are pronounced righteous.
In *sanctification* we are empowered to become increasingly holy.

Justification is the acceptance of our person into God's favor.
Sanctification is the renewal of our heart into God's image.

Justification gives a title to heaven.
Sanctification helps to fit us for it.

Justification is complete as soon as we believe.
Sanctification then commences and is carried on amidst great imperfections.

In *justification* there is no difference between believers.
In *sanctification* there are great differences between believers.

Justification means that God's perfect righteousness is credited to our account the moment we believe.
Sanctification means that God works in us to will and to do of His good pleasure, thus producing a righteous life through the agency and operation of the Holy Spirit.

The believer has a perfect standing in a perfect righteousness because he trusts in a perfect Redeemer who accomplished a perfect act in His death, burial, and resurrection upon the grounds of which God could sovereignly declare us perfectly justified in His sight!

No wonder the child of God may joyfully sing:

Jesus, Thy blood and righteousness
My beauty art, my glorious dress;
'Midst flaming worlds, in these arrayed,
With joy shall I lift up my head.

Justification by Faith Alone
Part Seven

The Two-foldness of Righteousness

Both the Old and the New Testaments speak of righteousness in a two-fold manner: first, they teach an *imputed* righteousness; and, second, they teach an *imparted* righteousness.

As we consider the teaching of imputed righteousness, we observe that one Scripture links both Old and New Testaments together with respect to the truth of imputed righteousness. Romans 4:6–8:

> As David also describeth the blessedness of the man unto whom God imputeth righteousness without works, saying, "Blessed are they whose iniquities are forgiven, and whose sins are covered. Blessed is the man to whom the Lord will not impute sin."

Our first task is to inquire as to the meaning of the word "impute." Webster defines it: "To charge, to attribute, or to ascribe." It is also defined theologically as "to ascribe vicariously" or "to experience or suffer something that benefits others."

But now a serious question arises of an ethical character. How could God, morally or ethically, fail to impute sin to the one who had actually committed it? And here we come to the heart of the Gospel, for the answer to this profound ethical problem is in the mystery and wonder of the truth set forth in 2 Corinthians 5:21: "For God made Him to be sin for us who knew no sin, that we might be made the righteousness of God in Him."

Observe that we have another evidence of the two-foldness of divine truth, for we have presented here the two-foldness of the doctrine of imputation:

God imputes our sins to Christ; and

God imputes His righteousness in Christ to us sinners.

Here we see the basic character of the scriptural teaching of imputation, and it may well be said that he who does not understand this doctrine does not understand Christian faith. But he who understands it glories in this truth, as did Chrysostom, one of the early Church Fathers, who wrote in these heartwarming words of this blessed truth:

> God made a righteous person to be a sinner that He might make sinners righteous. . . . For what he says is not "God made Him to be a sinner," but "God made Him to be sin." Not merely Him who will never sin, but who did not even know sin, and all this that we might be made righteous— but more—righteousness—yea, the righteousness of God. For truly this is the righteousness of God when we are justified not of works . . . but of grace, for all sin is wholly taken away.

Let us consider the first of these two acts of imputation, namely that God imputes sin to Christ.

Our first observation is that obviously God can charge sin to a righteous man only by an act of *imputation*. Christ was a righteous man. He had no sin, nor had done any sin, nor would ever do any sin. Therefore, for Him at a given moment in history to be "made sin" was possible only by imputation. He was made what He was not—*sin!*

Consider, further, what was involved in this act of God's imputation of sin to Christ. Did Christ actually commit the sin of lying when He was there on the cross, or the sin of stealing, or the sin of blasphemy, or any other sort of sin? No, a thousand times, no! He committed none of these sins, for He was the "Holy One of God." But, the fact is, He was made sin, and this by the act of imputation. So we see that the whole scheme of eternal redemption rests solidly on an act of imputation.

Our second observation is that, similarly, when God credits righteousness to the sinner, this too must be in the very nature of the case an act of imputation. If a man has never been, nor ever could be, righteous in and of himself, then for God to declare him righteous in His sight would not be possible except by an act of imputation. In this act, God does reckon the sinner to be what he was not—righteous.

But now we ask: What is the righteousness that God imputes to the sinner? First, let it be grasped that the expression "the righteousness of God" is one of the most important to be found in the Holy Scriptures. It frequently occurs in the Old Testament; it occurs 92 times in the New Testament; it occurs 36 times in the Epistle to the Romans.

Let us now consider a most familiar text—Romans 1:16: "For I am not ashamed of the Gospel, for it is the power of God unto salvation to every one that believeth; to the Jew first, and also to the Greek."

Paul here declares that the Gospel is "the power of God unto salvation." But why? Few have given a clear and unfaltering answer to this question. Few have ever observed what Paul's basic reason was as to why the Gospel was the power of God unto salvation. He affirms it clearly in verse 17: "For therein is the righteousness of God revealed."

Therefore, if the gospel is the power of God unto salvation only because in it the righteousness of God is revealed, then it behooves us to ask most seriously the question: Of what "righteousness of God" did Paul here speak?

The answers to this question have been manifold. There are those who have said that the phrase simply indicates a moral manifestation of the righteous nature of God. They say: "In the Gospel there is a pure scheme of morality revealed."

We reply, were this explanation the true one, so far from being the reason why the Gospel should be the "Good News" to sinners, it would rather be the cause of universal and hopeless condemnation. This concept of the righteousness of God was what drove Luther to despair.

Some have said it was God's "method" of justification.

We reply, the righteousness of God cannot mean God's method of justification, nor can it be the justification which God bestows. Righteousness and justification are two quite different things.

Robert Haldane, in his *Epistle to the Romans*, writes: "The righteousness of God, then, is not a method of justification, but *the thing itself* which God has provided, and which He confers through faith" (p. 127).

To teach that the Gospel is the power of God unto salvation because in it is revealed a divine method of justification, or the justification which God bestows, leaves the question unanswered as to what the Gospel reveals. The implication is that the Gospel is only a divine scheme of justification, but the language of Romans 1:17 shows that the Gospel is the power of God unto salvation because it reveals God's righteousness. We repeat Haldane's words: "It is not a method of justification, but the thing itself."

Others claim that the "righteousness of God" is an attribute of God. But this can hardly be so, for no one can possess an attribute of God in the same sense and measure as God Himself does. Therefore, man will never have, naturally, that same kind of righteousness that God possesses because he is not an eternally righteous being. Therefore, this righteousness must be different; and it is. The righteousness of God of which Paul speaks here is something which becomes *the property of the believer*. Furthermore, it comes through Christ's death, burial, and resurrection, and finally comes on the grounds of faith, and faith alone. If it were an attribute of God, then in what possible way does it have any relationship to the death, burial, and resurrection of Christ? And if it has no identical relation with those events, how can it possibly become the righteousness of His people, who can only obtain it through faith in the death, burial, and resurrection of His Son?

Let me quote these discriminating words of Haldane, whom I consider to have the fullest light on this subject:

> The righteousness of God, which is achieved by faith, denotes something that becomes the property of the believer. It cannot then be here the divine attribute of justice, but the *divine work* which God has wrought through His Son. This, therefore, determines that phrase in this place as referring immediately not to the divine attribute, but to the divine work. The former, that is, the righteousness of God as an attribute, cannot be ours. To be ours, we would have had to possess it as God does from the very beginning, and throughout our entire existence. God cannot sin, because He is inherently righteous. Man could, and did sin, and therefore is not inherently righteous as God is righteous; and of course, since man has sinned, it clearly argues that he could not have had the kind of righteousness that God has as an attribute.

There is another interpretation of the "righteousness of God." It takes different forms, but the essence of it is that God has, through the Gospel and through the death, burial, and resurrection of Christ, made another way by which man can perfectly fulfill His law and thus merit salvation.

In essence, this is the Catholic view, and we will have more to say about it later. But now we ask the question: Does this mean that the Gospel reveals a way by which man may himself fulfill the law so as to be perfectly righteous? This seems to be the obvious sense of this teaching. Man must become "perfect" before he can be justified! If this is judged to be the righteousness of God, "Who then can be saved?"

But now it is time for us to attempt an answer to the question: What is the "righteousness of God" which is revealed in the Gospel, and to which Paul devotes the first five chapters of his grand Epistle to the Romans?

Let it be established at once that, according to Romans 3:21, it is the righteousness that is revealed in—and only in—Jesus Christ. But if it is through Jesus Christ, then it is through Christ *as a man*. When He was born He, the divine Son of God, was given human life. Therefore it is only in the human/divine One that this righteousness has been made manifest. There is only one Mediator—"The Man, Christ Jesus" (1 Timothy 2:5).

Therefore Christ is our righteousness. But how did He become so? In two ways:

By doing what we did not do, namely, He kept the righteous law of God; and

By doing what we could not do, namely, He put away sin by paying its penalty.

Concerning point one, let us consider a seeming contradiction. According to Romans 3:21, the righteousness of God was "manifested *apart* from the law," yet it was "witnessed *to* by the law and the prophets." But why? Because in providing this righteousness for the sinner, God had to do it righteously or consistently with His former revelations in the law and the prophets. This meant that Christ had to keep the precepts of the law. That is why we read in Galatians 4:4 that He was "born under the law." But, unlike sinful man, He could and did keep the law in every one of its precepts. He never broke it.

We see now why it was that Christ had not only to keep the law, and thus prove Himself the righteous One (as a man), in order that He might qualify as man's Redeemer, but at the same time He had to come under the broken law and suffer the penalty that that broken law imposed upon man because man had sinned. Therefore, in that moment when, on the cross, He was made sin, He came under the curse of the law and was judged by God in the sinner's place.

So, I repeat, on the one hand Christ fulfilled the law in that, as far as He Himself was concerned, He kept all of the law, not breaking one single precept. On the other hand, because He was to rescue man from sin and death, He suffered the curse of the broken law, namely death, when He was made sin on the cross.

But, then, something happened which, if it had not taken place, would have meant that there would be no Gospel to offer to sinful and condemned man. What was it? Christ's justification from sin! What do we mean by this expression? The answer lies in Romans 6:7: "For he that is dead is justified (marginal reading) from sin." It has been rendered in other ways: "He that has died is free from sin" (RSV) and "A dead man is no longer answerable for his sins" (New English Bible).

What does this mean but that the "sin" which had so shortly before been imputed to Christ was no longer His? He was now clear of it, freed of it, justified of it. For one terrible moment He was what He had never been in Himself, nor ever will be again, namely, *sin*. But, having died *for* sin, He died *to* it, and God attested to that glorious fact by raising Him from the dead. That is why Paul writes in Romans 4:25: "He was delivered for our offenses and raised again for our justification."

We turn now to Romans 3:21–28, in which we have the fullest revelation of what is the character of the "righteousness of God." Every word in these wonderful verses points to the righteousness that is imputed and not a righteousness that is infused.

Note, in the first place, the persons who are justified are sinners (v. 23); a justification is bestowed freely by God's grace (v. 24); and the procuring cause of justification is the "redemption that is in Christ Jesus" (v. 24). But in this case the "redemption that is in Christ Jesus" (which, we admit, may include every phase of God's redemptive purpose and plan for man) is particularly limited, as far as the doctrine of justification goes, to the grand fact set forth in the 25th verse, namely that "God set forth Christ to be the propitiation through faith in His blood" in order that He might declare Himself just in dealing with man's sin, and the justifier of him who believes in Jesus.

So we conclude our teaching on "imputed righteousness" by saying that man is justified when God acts in accordance with His own holy nature, manifested not in demanding righteousness of the sinner, but in setting the believing sinner in His own presence in the very standing in which Christ is with him. This God does because of the righteous judgment of man's sins visited by Him upon man's substitute, Christ, at the cross. So we see that God's imputed righteousness is wholly apart from the law, wholly apart from works, wholly apart from any merit of man, and only upon the merits of Christ's death, burial, and resurrection. Therefore the believing sinner sings joyfully:

> Not the labors of my hands
> Can fulfill Thy law's demands;
> Could my zeal no respite know,
> Could my tears forever flow,
> Thou must save, and Thou alone.

We turn now to consider the teaching of Scripture on *imparted* or *infused* righteousness.

When God adopts a sinner into His family and gives him an inheritance among His children, having bestowed upon him the gift of eternal life, He does not leave him to continue such as he was before, but bestows upon him an abundance of grace. Indeed, divine grace is infused into his soul in order that he, who now has a righteous standing before God by faith in Christ's death, burial, and resurrection, is now enabled to arise in "newness of life" and accomplish good works before men, and thus "glorify his Father who is in heaven." And how is this brought about? It is when God effects the union of the believer with the resurrection; it is the basis upon which God effects a vital union between the believer and the risen Son of God. The believer then becomes a living member of Christ's mystical body, and thus a partaker of the Spirit of God. The believer is not merely accounted righteous, but has a principle of righteousness implanted in his heart which operates to bring forth the fruit of actual righteousness in his life and conversation.

The charge was brought against the Reformers that they said the sinner was declared righteous without being made righteous; but it is not so. The Reformers warned again and again that if anyone would say that he was "righteous" and failed to produce works of righteousness, then he deceived himself. Ofttimes they quoted: "My little children, let no man deceive you; he that doeth righteousness is righteous even as He is righteous" (1 John 3:7).

They taught that it is not sufficient to merely say, "I believe in Jesus Christ and His death for me on the cross." For if one believes in Christ, the living Son of God comes to live in him and, by a work of grace which the Bible calls "regeneration," produces in him the fruits of righteousness. As one already justified, he is called to sanctification.

If I were concerned principally with the grand theme of sanctification, I would develop this point of imparted righteousness with greater fullness. Since our major concern in

these lectures has been to teach on justification, we must return again to the all-important question: Is man justified, as
Catholic theology teaches, by having righteousness infused in
him, which righteousness works in him to produce sanctification, without which he cannot truly be justified?

To point it up once more, let me quote G. H. Joyce, who
represents the Catholic view clearly when he writes:

> A man is justified by the infusion of sanctifying grace
> into his soul; and his justification is nothing else than the
> change effected in him by this gift and, through it, his
> sins are forgiven and he is transformed into a new crea-
> ture and made a child of God.

In this statement, we see once again the way in which
Catholic theology confuses sanctification with justification. But
to do this is fatal. We can lose the joy of our justification if we do
not recognize how easily possible it is to confuse this issue of
justification and sanctification, of imputed and imparted righteousness.

James Buchanan writes:

> There is perhaps no more subtle or plausible error on the
> subject of justification than that which makes it to rest
> on the indwelling presence and the gracious work of the
> Holy Spirit in the heart. It is a singularly refined form of
> opposition to the doctrine of justification by the imputed
> righteousness of Christ, for it merely substitutes the work
> of one divine Person for that of another. . . . Nothing can
> be more unscriptural in itself, or more pernicious to the
> souls of men than the substitution of the gracious work of
> the Spirit in us for the vicarious work of God. . . . If we are
> justified on the ground of the work of the Holy Spirit in us,
> we are called to rest on a work which, so far from being
> finished and accepted, is not even begun, in the case of
> any unrenewed sinners; and which, when it is begun, in

> the case of a believer, is incipient only—often interrupted in its progress by declension and backsliding—marred and defiled by remaining sin . . . and never perfected in this life, even according to the low standard of the relaxed law, if that law is supposed to require any definite amount of personal holiness in heart and life.

One of the most common deficiencies in Christian thinking is to confuse the work of Christ and the Holy Spirit, which confusing carries over especially into the realm of justification. In order to help our thinking here, let me make this observation: The Holy Spirit did no part of the work by which our justification was secured; it was Christ's work alone which provided the grounds of justification. The Scriptures are replete with attributing to Christ certain works which are never said of the Spirit and His work.

Let me put it negatively. The Spirit did not take upon Himself "flesh and blood." The Spirit did not satisfy the demands of the law. The Spirit did not become subject to the limitations of humanity. The Spirit did not "suffer the contradiction of sinners." The Spirit did not bear our sins in His own body on the tree, for He had no body. The Spirit was not "made sin for us"; nor did the Spirit cry: "My God, My God, why hast Thou forsaken Me?" The Spirit did not expiate human guilt by making propitiatory sacrifice for our sins. No blood of the Spirit was shed; no life was poured out in death. No Spirit was buried with criminals in His death, and no Spirit was raised from the dead. But Christ knew all of these experiences. That is why the Gospel is, as Paul writes in Romans 1:3–4:

> Concerning His Son, Jesus Christ our Lord, who was made of the seed of David according to the flesh, and declared to be the Son of God with power according to the Spirit of holiness by the resurrection from the dead.

But what is the work of the Spirit? The work of the Spirit consists in bearing witness to Christ, and applying to men the redemption which the Savior obtained for them, so as to make it effectual for their complete and everlasting salvation. Our Lord Himself said, "Ye shall testify of Me," and this is what the Spirit continually does. It is the Spirit who convinces men of sin, of righteousness, and of judgment. It is the Spirit who awakens the conscience. It is the Spirit who burdens the soul with its guilt. It is the Spirit who quickens faith in the heart of the sinner when he hears the good news of Christ's death, burial and resurrection. It is the Spirit who regenerates him and makes him alive toward God. But so far from leading a sinner to rest on his own works in Him as the ground of his acceptance with God, the Spirit constantly points away from Himself to Christ as the only One who made possible the forgiveness of his sins, acceptance with the Father and the inheritance of eternal life.

The weakness in Rome's teaching that justification results from the operation of infused righteousness in the believer is revealed when we ask the question: "When is a sinner justified?" Bennett discovered the Achilles' heel in the theology of Rome when he wrote:

> The error of Rome is betrayed by a total silence concerning any definite period in which a person is completely, or indeed really justified, either in their own sense or in ours. The indefiniteness of their doctrine places it in striking contrast with that of the Apostles, who speak of a blessing received at a definite period, when we believe; obtained by a definite means, faith; producing a definite effect, peace with God; and followed by a definite consequence, title to eternal life.

It was this unbearable uncertainty and lack of assurance

that drove Luther to despair until he rightly understood the teachings of the Scriptures on the "righteousness of God."

The *Chronicles of the Schonberg-Gotta Family, a Contemporary Record*, states:

> His great terror was the thought of "the righteousness of God" by which he had been taught to understand His inflexible severity in that "the righteousness of God" is not *against* the sinner who believes in the Lord Jesus Christ, but *for* him—not against us to *condemn*, but for us to *justify*.

"I felt very angry," Luther said, at the term 'righteousness of God,' for, after the manner of all the teachers, I was taught to understand it in a philosophic sense—of that righteousness by which God is just and punishes the guilty. . . . At last I came to apprehend it thus—through the Gospel is revealed *the righteousness which availeth with God*—a righteousness by which God in His mercy and compassion justifieth us, as it is written: 'The just shall live by faith.'

"Straightway I felt as if I were born anew; it was as if I had found the door of Paradise thrown wide open. The expression 'the righteousness of God' which I so much hated before, became now dear and precious—my darling and most comforting words. I see the Father—inflexible in justice, yet delighting in mercy—He justified me, a sinner!"

I conclude this series with a tribute to the "righteousness of God" which should rejoice the heart of every child of God who knows that the "grace that is greater than all our sins" is a "*grace that reigns through righteousness to eternal life* through Jesus Christ our Lord" (Romans 5:21), and upon which he can confidently rest for time and eternity.

I close with Haldane's tribute:

No explanation of the expression "the righteousness of God" will at once suit the phrase and the situation in which it is found in the passage before us [Romans 1:17 and Romans 3], but that which makes it that righteousness, or obedience to the law, both in its penalty and requirements, which has been yielded to Him by our Lord Jesus Christ. This is indeed the righteousness of God for it has been provided from God and from first to last, has been effected by His Son Jesus Christ. Everything that draws it off from this signification tends to darken the Scriptures, cloud the apprehension of the truth in the children of God, and to corrupt the simplicity that is in Christ. To *that* righteousness is the eye of the believer ever to be directed; on *that* righteousness must he rest; on *that* righteousness must he live; on *that* righteousness must he die; in *that* righteousness must he appear before the judgment seat; in *that* righteousness must he stand forever in the presence of the righteous God.

"I will greatly rejoice in the Lord; my soul shall be joyful in my God: for He hath clothed me with the garments of salvation. He has covered me with the robe of righteousness" (Isaiah 61:10).

Singing the Words God Has Put in Our Mouths

A Personalized Account of the 1551 Genevan Psalter

I believe that the story of the Genevan Psalter can be told in terms of four men. John Calvin championed the principle of the congregational use of the Psalms, which he called "singing the words God has put in our mouths."[1] Clement Marot and Theodore Beza provided the poetical versification. Louis Bourgeois supplied the tuneful melodies for the words which God has put in our mouths.

1. *Calvin lays the foundation for the Genevan Psalter*
If Gothic architecture can be called theology in stone, it is even more true that the Genevan Psalter is theology in music. To say that John Calvin was the father of this Psalter is to say the same thing. And he was the father of Reformed music, although, unlike the other two great Reformers, Martin Luther and Ulrich Zwingli, he was not himself a musician. Luther was even called the Palestrina of the Reformation—but a similar claim could not be made for the great Genevan, although, let it be quickly observed, he was by no means devoid of musical appreciation. No less competent a music critic than Sir Richard Terry takes sides with Calvin against the French composer, Goudimel, in favoring the dropping of a fourth rather than a

---

[1] Preface to *Opera* of 1545.

second in a certain composition.[2] Calvin also made the statement, not unlike Luther who rated music next to theology itself, that "among the other things which are suitable as a means of recreation, and of giving pleasure, music has a primary place. . . . And in truth we know by experience that music has a secret, and almost incredible power to move hearts."[3] Nevertheless, Calvin's musical significance lies not in his own skill in that field but in his laying the theological foundation on which competent musicians could build.

These theological foundations which account for the development of Reformed music in general, and the Genevan Psalter in particular, are at least four in number. First, the principle of the authority of the Word of God. Calvin was a great defender of the idea that nothing should be used in the public worship of God which was not prescribed by God Himself in the Scriptures. Hence, his advocacy of the use of the Psalms in worship as indicated by his words, which we have chosen as the theme of this paper, "Singing the words God has put in our mouths." That is, let us sing to God's praise only that which God has provided for the purpose through the inspired words of the sweet singers of ancient Israel. In enunciating this principle, Calvin was reverting to the earliest practice of the Christian Church as indicated, for example, in the fifty-ninth canon of the Synod of Laodicea about 360. We forbid *"the singing of uninspired hymns in the church,* and the reading of uncanonical books of Scripture." It is worthy to note the difference between Calvin and Luther at this point. Luther used the Psalms, but favored the Latin hymns of the Christian Church, and composed many based on the New Testament. In other words,

---

[2] Davies, *John Calvin*, p. 43.
[3] *Opera* VI, 170 and VIII, 469; cited by Davies, *op. cit.*

Luther inclined to purely human compositions based on the gospels especially while Calvin insisted on the inspired poetry of the Old Testament Psalter. Where he deviated from this principle he still confined himself to inspired literature elsewhere—such as the *Magnificat* of the Virgin and the *Nunc Dimittis* of Simeon. The first principle, then, nothing but divinely inspired literature for use in the worship of God, virtually created the Genevan Psalter.

A second Calvinistic principle of basic importance for the emergence of the Genevan Psalter is the Reformation doctrine of the priesthood of all believers. According to this, there is no difference of kind between laity and clergy—all have immediate access to God through their common and final priest, Jesus Christ, who opened up a new and living way to the Father in His own blood and made it accessible to all who believe. This trust spelled the emancipation of church music from the clergy and a return of it to the congregation. Congregational participation in the liturgy in general, and singing in particular, had been reduced, through the development of the Romish hierarchical system, to a negligible minimum. Calvin gave back to the people of Geneva their right of congregational singing—singing of the Psalms, of course. So during his first stay in Geneva he and Farel came to Council with the request to grant this right to all believers. It is also significant that he encouraged the use of popular tunes so that the people would be able to exercise their restored privilege. While he retained the choir, he employed it not to entertain or perform, but to lead the people so that they would learn once again how to sing the songs of Zion in concert.

The third theological foundation of the Genevan Psalter was the doctrine of common grace. By this it was recognized that there are two types of divine gifts—supernatural and natural. The former are the virtues wrought in the soul by a special work of grace; the latter are those which pertain to secular matters and are distributed to all, not to saints only; as a matter of fact, often to sinners. But, wherever they were, Calvin recognized these and used them for his purposes. Skill in music is a natural rather than supernatural skill, but Calvin was ever on the alert to capture this for the worship of God. Thus, at his Academy in Geneva, he made music required four hours each week. The choir thereby trained in this skill was to lead the people so they could, under its leadership, cultivate the same skill. Acting on this same principle, Calvin was quick to appreciate the able—though not excessively orthodox—Marot, and to stand by the gifted composer, Bourgeois, who was thrown into prison for breaking some of the rigid disciplines of Geneva of which Calvin was himself the main author. Abraham Kuyper, in his admirable *Lectures on Calvinism,* so aptly remarks, "Music . . . would flourish, henceforth, not within the narrow limitation of particular grace, but in the wide and fertile fields of common grace."[4]

The fourth and last theological foundation we will consider is Calvin's magnificent theo-centricity. Possibly no man in history was more determinedly devoted to the glory of God. All he thought, all he did, had to be directed to the exaltation of the sovereign majesty of almighty God. I think it is this principle which explains some surprising and unfortunate musical idiosyncrasies of our Reformer. Why, for example, did he oppose the accompaniment of the organ in congregational singing? Why was he, unlike Luther, opposed to four-part singing? Why was the choir allowed to sing the parts, but the people, quite against the wishes of the composer, Bourgeois, restricted to unison singing of the melody? This is a surprising position

---

[4] *Lectures on Calvinism,* p.228.

for a man of culture to take who exhibited and championed as much natural talent as Calvin did. It has been suggested that the reason for Calvin's unexpected opposition to harmony was the fact that the people were not yet trained for it. But this does not seem true, nor would it explain his opposition to the use of the organ. The explanation is to be found, I believe, in his constant concern for the glory of God, and his fear that too elaborate a musical service would draw the minds of simple worshipers from the glorifying of God to the admiring of human skills. Many a church father had expressed this fear before Calvin.

2. Marot and Beza build the framework of the Genevan Psalter
The metrical versions of the Psalms were put to general popular use by the court and people of France in the 1540s. Instead of the secular and frequently vile *chansons* so commonly sung hitherto, a musical revival exhibiting itself in widespread Psalm-sing-spirations had broken out. Each courtier and lady had claimed one particular Psalm tune as his own special song, taking their cue from the future King and Queen, Henry II and Catherine d'Medici, themselves.

Unlikely as such a widespread popular use of the Psalms may be today, this had happened before—in the early days when the Psalter was the hymnal of the Church. John Chrysostom, in the fourth century, writes, for example, "David is always in their mouth, not only in the cities and churches, but in courts, in monasteries, in deserts, and in the wilderness. He turned earth into heaven and men into angels, being adapted to all orders and to all capacities."[5]

But the question is, what caused this general outburst of

---

[5] *The Psalms in Worship*, edited by J. McNaughter, p. 170.

popular—if not pious—Psalm-singing in sixteenth-century France? The answer is Clement Marot. Marot was born in 1496, and the muse must have been transmitted from his poet father's bloodstream, for the youth quickly exhibited great skill. In 1519 he entered court life and, at the establishment of Margaret of Angouleme, he also learned evangelical principles, which he confessed in 1527. It was these which were to cause him some trouble, and he had to flee to Cahors. He returned to favor again. "In 1530," as one writer has it, "he married. Next year he was again in trouble."[6]

In 1535 came his worst trouble, however, for he was involved with the Placardists, who posted signs which vilified the mass in the main streets of Paris. This time Marot fled to the Duchess Renee in Ferrara, Italy, at whose court at this same time was another French Evangelical refugee by the name of John Calvin. When Marot finally was free to return to France in 1539 he was received cordially by King Francis I and actually given a house and lovely grounds at Lyons. Here it was (was it as a result of Calvin's influence, perhaps even suggestion?) that Marot began to versify the Psalms which so quickly became the rage we have previously described.

But this popular triumph became Marot's undoing. In 1539 the first Calvinistic Psalm book was published at Strasbourg consisting of eighteen versified Psalms, twelve of which were by Marot. In 1542, thirty Psalms by Marot were published and dedicated to the King. All was going well for the French poet— but unfortunately it went too well. His Psalms appealed not only to the good Catholics, but, alas, to the heretical Protestants as well—as a matter of fact, especially well. Soon the Huguenots were outsinging the Catholics, who suddenly found that their

---

[6] *Encyclopedia Britannica*, 14th ed., vol. XIV, p. 936.

fashionable court theme-songs had become the hallmark of the dangerous heresy. As the Huguenots sang more lustily, the orthodox Sorbonne condemned the Psalms, the Catholics swallowed their mirth, and the hitherto popular Marot was suddenly in an embarrassing situation. Expeditiously, in 1543 he fled to Geneva where another French Evangelical refugee was now the dominant figure, one John Calvin by name.

The relationship of the two refugee Frenchmen in Switzerland is an interesting story. Calvin, the stern moralist, bending all his genius to glorify his God, and Marot, at best a casual Evangelical without deep attachment to the Reform, and merely a light-hearted poet of genius, or, at worst, an opportunistic free-thinker, were not, shall we say, a natural choice for roommates.[7] But this team lasted a year because Marot liked his job of versifying more Psalms and Calvin recognized a genius, even if he weren't a Puritan, when he saw one. So Marot, encouraged by Calvin, completed twenty more Psalms before he found the restrictions of Geneva more than his courtly past and poetic sensibilities could endure.

When Marot left Geneva, he also left many Psalms unfinished and no one to succeed him. But in the providence of God, which in the creation of the Genevan Psalter showed a distinct predilection for refugee Frenchmen, came Theodore Beza to Geneva. A comparison of Beza, who was to complete Marot's work, with his predecessor reminds one of George Bernard Shaw's little play, *The Doctor's Dilemma*. In this story the doctor has only one vacant bed and two desperately ill applicants. One of these is an artistic genius of no moral account and the other is a very good man who, at the same time, is the essence

---

[7] It is interesting to note that Douen, Marot's main biographer, has a distinct preference for his hero, and no little aversion to Calvin's type of person.

of mediocrity. The doctor's dilemma, of course, is which of these men should be saved. They could be Marot and Beza, except that Marot was not altogether worthless morally, and Beza was not without some poetical merit. There was, however, no comparison between the deep evangelical character of Beza and the cavalier nature of Marot; nor, on the other hand, between the poetic genius of Marot and the relatively modest gifts of Beza. When, however, Calvin once accidentally (how Calvin must roll in his grave at the use of the word "accidental") stumbled on a versification of a Psalm by Beza he realized he had the man to continue the work of Marot and soon persuaded Beza and the Council of that fact.

So it was that in 1551 thirty-four of Beza's versions together with those of Marot were published and the Genevan Psalter, whose four-hundredth anniversary we celebrated in 1951, was born. It was to be completed eleven years later.

3. Bourgeois finishes the structure

So Calvin had laid the foundation; Marot and Beza had built upon it. The Genevan Psalter was largely done except for one all-important element—the music. Words without music were like a skeleton without life, as far as congregational singing was concerned. To be sure there were tunes employed for Marot's very first verses. But many more tunes needed to be provided, and for this vital contribution to the making of the Psalter God brought another Frenchman to Geneva—Louis Bourgeois. We do not know whether Calvin had anything to do with this musician's coming to the Swiss town, but he had everything to do with his recognition. Bourgeois appreciated music and Calvin appreciated Bourgeois.

Indeed, Calvin appears to have been about the only one who *did* appreciate Bourgeois. When he came to Geneva it was to fill the musical post left by Franc. Bourgeois was not thought to be able to do the job alone, but another man, Fabri, was also appointed. The hundred-florin salary which Franc had received was divided, with Fabri receiving forty and Bourgeois sixty florins. Later, the *Geneva Register* informs us, Bourgeois's pay was reduced to fifty florins. When he pled for more, two measures of corn were granted in view of an expected increase in his family; but not even the intercession of Calvin could get the tight Council to give Bourgeois a raise. Calvin was successful, however, in rescuing him from jail where he had been preemptively thrown when he dared to introduce some musical innovations without the permission of the town Council.

Under these trying circumstances, with Calvin supporting him, Bourgeois developed the melodies of the Psalter. Where he got these melodies is a matter of speculation. Grove's *Dictionary* states: "How far the other tunes adapted by Bourgeois are original it is impossible to determine. A few can be traced to a German original, some are constructed out of fragments of earlier melodies, while others are adapted from secular songs popular at the time. It is not improbable that every tune in the Genevan Psalter belongs to one or other of the above categories."[8] Of "Old Hundredth," for example, Millar Patrick approves the statement that "its component parts are found over and over again in various combinations, and, while one of the most effective, it is also perhaps one of the least original tunes in the Genevan Psalter."[9]

Be all this as it may, it is clear that the attractive melodies of this Psalter are mainly traceable to the work of Louis Bourgeois who, serving as editor from 1542–1557, added some seventy

---

[8] *Dictionary of Music and Musicians*, Vol. I., p. 375.
[9] *Op. cit.*, p. 23.

tunes to the Psalter. All this is well known and commonly recognized, but Kuyper calls our attention to achievements of this Calvinistic composer which are not so well known. It was Bourgeois who exchanged the eight Gregorian modes for the two from popular music, the major and minor. He also wedded melody to verse in what is called expression, developed solfeggio or singing by notes, reduced the number of chords, distinguished the various gamuts more clearly and generally simplified the knowledge of music, all, apparently, under the aegis of Calvin.[10]

There was, however, one point of basic and irreconcilable difference between the theologian and the musician. The musician was right, but unfortunately the theologian won the argument. This concerned part-singing. Bourgeois, who strongly favored it, would have had no trouble with Luther or Knox, but Calvin was resolutely opposed. His opposition not only ultimately dismayed Bourgeois so much that he left Geneva in 1557, but the use of unaccompanied melodies characterized the Reformed singing of Psalms, in most places, for centuries.

Nevertheless, before Bourgeois left Geneva he had bequeathed to the Psalter the lovely melodies which helped to make Psalm-singing a thing of beauty. Bridges remarks, "Historians who wish to gain a true philosophical account of Calvin's influence at Geneva ought probably to refer a great part of it to the enthusiasm attendant on the singing of Bourgeois' melodies."[11] True enough—Calvin owed much to Bourgeois; but how far would Bourgeois have gotten without Calvin? He did not, to be sure, get harmony because of Calvin, but without him he likely would not have been able to develop even

---

[10] Kuyper, *op. cit.*, pp. 228f.
[11] Patrick, *Four Centuries of Scottish Psalmody*, p. 26.

melodies in Geneva. As Kuyper also aptly observes: "If Bourgeois was the great master whose works still assure him a front rank among the most noble composers of Protestant Europe, it is also worthy of note that this Bourgeois lived and labored in Geneva, under the very eyes of Calvin and even partly under his direction."[12]

There, then, in brief, is the story of the Genevan Psalter of 1551. The idea itself came from John Calvin, the poetry and verse from Clement Marot and Theodore Beza, and many of the melodies from Louis Bourgeois. But all of it, as each of these men knew, came from God in order that His people could sing the words which He has put in their mouths to the praise of His glory who put them there.

---

[12] *Op. cit.*, p. 228.

Total Depravity

W. G. T. Shedd, the eminent professor at Union Theological Seminary, New York, in the last century, while it was still an institution of the Presbyterian Church, once wrote: "The most important conviction which a person can have is the conviction of sin." David had it. He was convicted of sins, of gross sins. "I acknowledge my transgression . . . I have sinned and done this evil." But, more important than that, he had a conviction of sin: "Behold, I was shapen in iniquity and in sin did my mother conceive me." He knew that God desired truth in the inward parts of David, and that that was precisely where God would not find it. David needed nothing less than a new nature; the old one was beyond repair. "Create in me a clean heart, O God, and renew a right spirit within me." To desire radical grace, you must be convicted of radical guilt.

"Conviction," with Shedd and other Puritans before him, was an existential word long before "existential" was a word. It meant the total experience of the total person—in this case, the conviction of sin. It meant that the total person was aware that the total person was a sinner. No, the total person was aware that the total person was depraved. It will not do to say "sinner"; the word "sinner" has been sanctified. We feel rather holy today when we confess that we are sinners. After all, the best people confess that they are sinners. When I confess myself to be a sinner, I am associating with the best people. It is rather fashionable to become a self-confessed sinner. This makes it almost impossible to feel sinful while confessing that one is sinful. The word is too well perfumed. We need a nasty word like "depraved." Try that for size. Call yourself depraved and see how you like it. If you like it, it is no good; but in all probability you will not like it because the best people do not call themselves depraved. After all, "depraved" is reserved for the worst people. You know—sadists, masochists, homosexuals, perverts. "I may be a sinner, but, thank God, I am not one of those!" But that is precisely the point—you *are* one of those. I am one of those. I will not say that we are all sadists, etc., because then you will feel relieved and say, "You see, he is just generalizing."

I am universalizing, but I am not generalizing! You are a sadist, a masochist, a homosexual, a pervert. Every one of you—the refined girl and the well-brought-up young man—without exception, you are a dirty, filthy, lousy, stinking lot.

Yes, I am too, but I see no reason why my filthiness should make you feel less ashamed of your filthiness. You are sadists, masochists, homosexuals, perverts, and incestors. I am too. Here, before all of you, I confess that I am a pervert. That shocks you, doesn't it? Yes, I mean it. I am a pervert. You really are shocked now, aren't you? I can hear you thinking, "Does he mean it? Is he really a pervert? Of course, he doesn't really mean it. Even if he were, he would never tell the world about it."

I mean it, all right. The trouble is, you do not believe in sin. You cannot really stomach a full confession of total depravity. When I stand up here and say that I am a pervert, I mean that and *more* than that. I am anything you can mention. I am worse than anything you can mention. I am worse than anything you can conceive. And you are filthier than anything that I can imagine.

Now, let me say this: I have never committed an act of perversity in my life. You are relieved, are you not? You didn't think that I really meant it, though I did have you scared for a moment. There you are. You see, you do not really believe in sin. I *did* mean it. No, I never committed an act of perversion in my life, but I am a pervert. I have the nature of a pervert. The nature of the man who commits acts of perversity is my nature. The depravity of his nature may have been developed by different circumstances, outer and inner, than mine, but it was the same depravity. Putting me in comparable inner and outer conditions, I would have committed comparable acts. There, but for the grace of God, go I. I am personalizing all this not because I am unique, but because I am not. What I have said about myself I could say (and, what is more important, you could say) with equal truth about yourself. Moreover, if you cannot say this there is only one reason, and that is because you do not really have a conviction of sin. You may have a conviction of the pervert's sin, but you do not have a conviction of your sin until you see that the pervert's nature and yours are one and the same. Wherein it differs, it differs because, and only because, of the grace of God.

If you can listen to someone speaking of some particular criminal as not fit to live among decent people, and see nothing wrong with that sentiment, you do not know what sin is. Criminals must be punished, imprisoned, or segregated from the rest of society. There can be no sober denying of that grim fact. But the criminal must be cut off not from decent people, but from other *depraved* people. The more depraved must be isolated from the less depraved because there is the greater danger that the more depraved will make the less depraved more depraved than that the less depraved will make the more depraved less depraved.

"I came not to call the righteous to repentance." Sinners do not bear the call of Christ because they do not think they are sinners. So men are unsaved not because of their sins, but because of their "righteousness." No sinner is ever lost; only the righteous perish. "Sinners" go to heaven while the "righteous" go to hell. All is well if only we can realize that all is not well.

We will live if only we can see that we are dead. But, alas, as long as a man remains a sinner, he will never have a conviction of being a sinner. One must begin to be righteous before he ever suspects that he is not righteous. Oh, come to Jesus! Call His name "Jesus," for "He shall save His people from their sins." If you realize your radical guilt, He will give you His radical grace.

What Every Adult Church Member Should Know

Introduction

In my introduction I wish to say not so much what every church member should know, but *that* every church member should know. There are two outstanding and painfully obvious reasons why a return to a more faithful *teaching* ministry is imperative for the church. First, religious illiteracy among our professing Christians is staggering. Second, the inevitable result of religious illiteracy, namely religious indifference, is manifest in the same proportions.

Some Evidences of Religious Illiteracy*

Religious illiteracy is a fact—a sad fact, a dangerous fact, but a fact. Dr. Wilbur Smith in his recent book, *Therefore Stand,* relates these two typical instances: "Some years ago the distinguished professor Kittredge of Harvard was hearing a class in Macbeth and during the class a student reading aloud came upon the word Golgotha. The professor asked his students what Golgotha meant, to which he replied, 'I don't know, in fact I never heard the word before.' 'Do you know what Calvary means?' 'I have never heard the word.' As may easily be believed by those who knew Kittredge, the learned and frequently sarcastic professor simply bowed his head and said, 'The class is dismissed.' "

---

* The first part of this article is also included in the chapter entitled "Religious Illiteracy." —Editor

"A certain individual went to a post office in the city where I am writing, to mail a small package to a soldier, and the one weighing the package asked what was in the package. She replied, 'A New Testament.' 'What is that?' he asked. 'It is a part of the Bible.' To this the clerk replied, 'Do they call it the New Testament because someone just wrote it?'"

This writer himself, as an erstwhile grader of Bible examinations in a Christian college, has been informed that Nathaniel was thrown into the lions' den, that Matthew was a Republican and that Dan and Beersheba were man and wife like Sodom and Gomorrah. This gross ignorance is so widespread in its extent, so ghastly in its nature and so perilous in its portent that the church must begin again to teach her people—and thoroughly.

Religious Illiteracy Produces Religious Indifference
Furthermore, this is a day of relative religious indifference although a higher percentage of the population than ever before are members of the Christian Church. In 1890 there was but 22.5 % of the population on the rolls; in 1942 there was 52.5%. We have had a growth but it has been a fig-tree growth—leaves without a corresponding amount of fruit. This is true of our own denomination. It can be shown—and I heard it demonstrated by one of our leaders—that over the past 25 years our church has declined considerably in numbers of missionary aspirants, amount of giving and such significant indices of spiritual tone. The usual explanation is that we are not still getting "old-line UPs." But "old-line UPs" are not born, they are made—they are taught. We have as good material today as we had in 1900, but what are we making of the souls God has entrusted to our spiritual care and perfecting?

Now if we are to remedy the present situation, it seems we must act in a *fundamental* manner. The ax must be put to the root of the tree. The logic of the *dilemma* is clear: religious indifference results from religious illiteracy which in turn results from lack of instruction. The logic of the *solution* seems equally clear: religious instruction will result in religious literacy (generally) which in turn will result in religious interest and activity (inevitably).

Religious Knowledge Intensifies Christianity

That a man's Christian life will be proportionate to his grasp of Christian truth may require proof. Many will say: "The most pious person I have ever met was a poor old lady scarcely able to read." Such cases, however, do not disprove but rather demonstrate our point. We must not forget that knowledge has not one but two dimensions—both breadth and depth. Of the woman in question, her knowledge was undoubtedly scanty in its extensiveness, but profound in its intensiveness. She may only have grasped a few articles of faith, but these she understood deeply and experientially. So she really *knew* more than some student who had a broad general acquaintance with the whole field of systematic theology, but had assimilated very little of his knowledge. A container that is only two feet wide but ten feet deep will hold more water than one that is ten feet wide and only one foot deep. Our contention is that the *more real* knowledge, the *more real* Christianity. Show me a religious person and I will show you a person who has some knowledge of God in Christ and one who could be made more saintly still by even more knowledge.

Fundamentals included in a Teaching Ministry

There are various things which our church can do toward "*teaching* all nations in the name of the Father, the Son and the Holy Ghost." First of all, it would be well for the minister in his preaching to adopt the advice of a popularizer of science who once said: "Never overestimate the knowledge of your audience; but never underestimate their capacity for knowledge." Second, officers of the church who are obliged to give assent to the Reformed creed of the church could reasonably be expected to know, before they assent, what the creed is. Third, should any Sabbath school teacher, the shortage of such not forgotten, be asked to teach who has not first been trained in *what* to teach? Fourth, is it right to admit a child to the communion table without first having established his faith and the practice of church attendance with reasonable thoroughness? And can such be done in six half-hour periods?

Examinations Required before Church Sessions

Fifth, new adult members are, according to our Book of Government, to be examined by the session, and "in this examination special attention should be given to the doctrine of the Trinity—Father, Son, and Holy Spirit; the inspiration of the Scriptures of the Old and New Testaments; the atonement; the necessity of repentance and faith in Christ; the duty of separation from the world, of household religion, including family worship, of Christian giving and the evangelization of the world, of diligent attendance on the ordinances of divine worship, public, private, and family, and of conformity to the laws and usages of the church." Can this be done with any adequacy unless these persons have been reasonably well instructed beforehand? We fear not.

I. A Survey of the Bible

The Bible is that indispensable book in which God has deposited the record of the revelation of His redemptive words and acts which He communicated to the world by divinely inspired writers. If we will notice the ingredients of this definition we shall have a fairly general understanding of the Bible.

The Bible Is the Indispensable Book

In the first place it is the indispensable book. It is not the exclusive source of information about God, for nature and providence bespeak the divine existence. It is, however, the exclusive source of a "saving" knowledge of God. In the words of our Confession: "Although the light of nature, and the works of creation and providence, do so far manifest the goodness, wisdom and power of God, as to leave men inexcusable; yet they are not sufficient to give that knowledge of God, and of His will, which is necessary unto salvation; therefore it pleased the Lord, at sundry times, and in divers manners, to reveal Himself (in the Bible), and to declare His will unto His Church."

The revelation of God in nature is very much like a department-store bill. A study of the bill will reveal that it has an author and that the author is fair, honest, efficient, wise and powerful enough to bring effective prosecution if we do not pay the bill. In fact, there is only one thing the bill does not tell and that is where we are going to get the money to pay it! So nature leaves us with the knowledge of a fair, honest, efficient, wise and powerful enough Person to bring effective prosecution against us for our failure to pay all our debts of righteousness. It also tells us everything, but how that debt, which troubles our conscience, can ever be paid. Only in the Bible are we given the "saving" knowledge that "God so loved the world that He gave His only begotten Son, that whosoever believeth in Him should not perish, but have everlasting life."

The Bible Is a Single Book

In the second place, the Bible is a single book. It is one book although more than 40 different persons wrote it over more than a thousand years. Through the plurality and diversity of human authorship there are a unity and consistency in its teachings that have persuaded multitudes of the most learned that behind the different men there was always the same God.

But while the invisible reason for the unity of the Bible is the one ultimate Author, the visible reason is the one Story it tells. The Bible, we repeat, is the record of God's "redemptive acts and words."

Redemption, in the deed or its explanation, is the one and only theme of the Book. Hence Luther referred to it as *Heilgeschichte*, the history of salvation. Likewise, we sing of the cross that "all the light of sacred story gathers 'round its head sublime."

The Bible Is the Story of Salvation

How true this is is better seen from the contents of the Bible itself than from what believers have said about it. In its opening chapters it tells of the creation. Why? To set the stage for the appearance of man. Why? To show that man was created good, sought out evil and fell from Paradise. Why does it tell all this which the sinning, suffering, aspiring man of blood, sweat and tears could know without being told? In order to show what God intended to do about perishing sinners who would repent. When the Bible in the opening chapters of Genesis has described the creation of man and his fall it has merely set the state for his salvation, with which it is then concerned to the last chapter of the Revelation. Notice how God intimates, in His preference for Abel's blood sacrifice, that salvation will be by the death of God's sacrifice, Christ. Notice how a little later He calls Abraham apart to become the father of a people to whom He is going to teach the way of salvation so that when they have learned they may teach the world. All the rest of the Old Testament is concerned with nothing but teaching Israel by a sacrificial system, by providential dealings, by miraculous intervention, and by prophetic revelations, the ABC's of the salvation story.

"One Book, One Story, One Savior"

Came the day of examination in the appearance of Christ. And, as in all examinations, some students failed and some passed. In this case most of the class failed. Israel, as a nation, rejected the Savior they had been taught to welcome and crucified the Lamb of God whose redemption they had been prepared to herald to the world. But some Jews, the apostles and others, passed the test, believed on Christ and spread the story of redemption by His blood, until the world in general had heard. That church, Jews and Gentiles, which had been called out of the world was further trained in advanced matters concerning salvation. The lessons which the apostles, or apostolically sanctioned writers, gave them are the gospels and epistles of the New Testament. There is your Bible—as simple as that—one book, one story, one Savior.

The Bible Is a Divinely Inspired Book

Not only does the Bible contain an inspiring story—it is itself an inspired account of that story. "Holy men of God spake as they were moved by the Holy Spirit."

When God inspired a man to write, that man did not cease to be himself. There are those who construe inspiration in such a way that if God inspires, man expires—loses all his individualities and becomes a mere empty instrument. Such could not be the case for the Scripture writers have grammatical constructions, etc., which are all distinctive and individualistic. Inspiration did not protect a man from himself, but from his sins. He was kept from error and from idiosyncrasies.

The Bible is a Foundation Book

So, then, the Bible is that indispensable book in which God has deposited the record of the revelation of His redemptive words and acts which He communicated to the world by divinely inspired writers. And what more convincing proof is there than the effect of the Bible on society. And what more true, succinct, and dramatic statement of that influence do we have than from the pen of James Russell Lowell who once wrote: "Show me a place on this planet ten miles square where a man may live in decency, comfort, and security, supporting and educating his children, a place where age is reverenced, infancy respected, womanhood honored, and human life held in due regard, and I will show you a place where the gospel has gone before and laid the foundation."

II. A Survey of the History of the Church

The Bible tells but one story—the story of redemption. Now we will observe the response of people to that story. It is as you might expect: some respond favorably and some unfavorably. Some welcome their Savior while others resent the implication that they need a Savior. The former class, the believers, constitute what we call the church.

It is the story of this church we wish briefly to sketch. As soon as there was one sinner who responded to the gracious overtures of God there was the church. Adam, Abel, Seth, Noah and the other early Genesis heroes evidenced their faith in God by the sacrifices they offered. The church existed there. But the church was not organized until Abraham was called out of Ur of the Chaldees to become the father of the faithful who were now to be set apart from the rest of the world by a sign, circumcision, and a place, the land of Palestine.

The Church Existed before Christ

Then we had the church; yet an institution different from the church as we know it today. It differed in various respects. First, church and state were one rather than separate. Second, the church was restricted almost completely to one national group rather than being universal. Third, the church was preparing for and anticipating the first coming of Christ rather than rejoicing in it as an accomplished fact and now looking forward to His return "to judge the quick and the dead." Fourth, the church was in a state of childhood and discipline rather than maturity and freedom. Fifth, the emphasis, consequently, was on the external form which symbolized Christ rather than upon Christ, Himself, manifest. Sixth, knowledge of God was through a special group, the prophets; and access to God in worship through another special group, the priests. Today, the Word of God is completely revealed and access is free to all by the last properly ordained priest which is Christ Himself, "who ever liveth to make intercession for us."

But in both dispensations it was one church, i.e., a body of believers, though administered under the very different circumstances and modes which we have described. The Christian church, therefore, is the continuation of the Jewish church, just as the oak is the fruition of the acorn or as the butterfly emerges from the chrysalis.

Christianity Is the Continuation of Judaism

If, however, the Christian church is the Jewish church reorganized along its modern lines, what is present-day Judaism? For that matter, what was the status of the majority of the Jews of Jesus' time who did not receive Him? Do they not claim to be the continuation of the Old Testament church? They do; especially the Orthodox Jews do. What then? The answer is, they are and they are not. They are the lineal descendants of the

Old Testament priests and prophets; they maintain Old Testament sacrifices; they observe the Old Testament law. And yet they are not the Old Testament church. The Christian church is that, although it is not generally of the same nationality, does not maintain the Old Testament sacrifices, and has done away with the most of the Old Testament ritual laws. How then can we substantiate our claim to be of Abraham's seed and the continuation of the Old Testament church? The answer is, we are the same in spirit. The Old Testament looked forward to Christ, and we believe in Him; the Jewish church was saved not by works but by grace and so are we; the Jewish church saw in the sacrifices and rituals so many pointers to Christ and so do we; and while the Old Testament continued them because Christ had not yet come, we have discontinued them because He has come.

To Deny Christ Is to Deny Judaism

For a Jewish friend, therefore, to deny Christ is to deny not only Christianity, but also Old Testament Judaism. It is to reveal that he who is a lineal descendant of Abraham is not of his spiritual seed. Here is an interesting illustration of the principle of Christ: "To him that hath it shall be given, and to him that hath not shall be taken away even that which he hath." To the Jew who has not Christ even the Old Testament itself is his no more; the Christian who has Christ, has the Old Testament also.

This needs special emphasis because we are often beguiled into judging by appearances. It would *appear* that the Jew is the heir of the Jewish church. Especially, it would appear so when it is remembered that the vast *majority of Jews in Christ's day and still today do not believe in Christianity* and did not and will not join the Christian church. Majorities, however, do not determine truth. It was that handful of original apostles and disciples, all of them Jews, that constituted the Jewish church and not the majority who did not believe.

The Reformation, Last Great Epoch of the Christian Church

The last great epoch of the Christian church was the Reformation. At that time something occurred rather similar, in one respect, to the great reorganization at the time of Christ. The Jewish church just before Christ and the Christian church before Luther had one thing in common—they both degenerated. True, they had done great things for God, had produced great prophets and saints, had kept the testimony of the Word alive. Yet they had declined through the gradual infection of false doctrine, the toleration of immorality, the development of a hierarchy of religious leaders who were not orthodox in teaching and were less so in example. Christ appeared and the true remnant followed Him; Luther appeared and the true remnant followed him. And as the church of which the apostles were the head was the true *Jewish* church now made universal, so the church of which the Reformers were the head was the true *Christian* church made pure. And just as the Jewish majority that did not accept Christianity ceased to be the true Jewish church, so the majority that did not accept the Reformation of Christianity ceased to be the true Christian church. But in each case the true church was made out of the remnant of the previous one.

The Real History of the Church

When people ask me, "When did Protestantism originate?" my answer is "with Adam." It was the Roman church which originated in the 16th century A.D. But we do not read it so in history books. According to most of them, Catholicism began with the first pope and Protestantism with Luther. Books say such things, however, because they almost necessarily judge by majorities and externals, and not by underlying principles and attitudes.

There, then, is the vital history of the church. Founded in Adam, organized with Abraham, reorganized, spiritualized and universalized by our Lord, and purified by the Reformation. What will be the next epoch?

III. A Survey of Presbyterian Doctrine

You remember that the little girl came home from Sunday School and said: "Mother, the teacher said Jesus was a Jew."

"That is right, my dear," answered mother.

"But," the perplexed daughter replied, "isn't Jesus the Son of God?"

"Why, of course," the mother said.

"Well, then, how could Jesus be a Jew when God is a Presbyterian?"

Now we Presbyterians do not believe God is a Presbyterian, nor do we believe that an individual must be a Presbyterian in order to be acceptable to God. One does not even need to be a Presbyterian to be in a Presbyterian church. That is, a prospective member of our church is required only to believe the great catholic doctrines of the church to be admitted. However, it is understood that the new member is disposed toward the Presbyterian doctrine to which he will be exposed as a member of our communion. Furthermore, in order to become an officer of the church he must know and believe in Presbyterianism.

Four Distinct Levels of Doctrine

There are four distinct levels of doctrine in our church's creed. Let us present these diagrammatically:

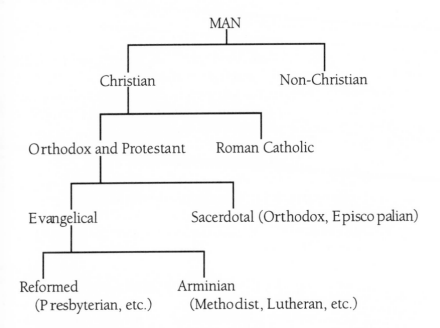

First, there are the universally held Christian doctrines in distinction from the non-Christian. Second, there are the general Protestant and Orthodox doctrines in distinction from the Roman Catholic. Third, there are the Evangelical doctrines in distinction from the Sacerdotal. Fourth, there are the Reformed doctrines in distinction from the Arminian. All of these terms will now be explained.

Doctrines Distinguishing Christians and Non-Christians
In the light of the diagram let us examine the four levels of doctrine. First, the Presbyterian Church champions the universally held Christian doctrines. That is what we mean when we say as Presbyterians, "I believe in the holy catholic (univer-

sal) church." The Apostles' Creed from which this is quoted is itself universally confessed—the common denominator of Christianity. These "essentials" of Christianity, which all historic Christian churches teach, include:

1. The existence of a personal, intelligent and moral God.

2. The supernatural revelation of God in the Bible.

3. The subsistence of three persons, Father, Son, and Holy Spirit, in the one divine substance.

4. The manifestation of the Son of God in human flesh in which He died to atone for the sins of the penitent.

5. Christ's resurrection, ascension and return in glory to judge the quick and the dead.

6. The privilege and obligation of every person to repent, believe and live a Christian life.

Doctrines Distinctive of Orthodox and Protestant Churches

The second set of doctrines which distinguish Orthodox (generally) and Protestant from Romanists are fundamentally two: the authority of the Bible and justification by faith.

1. The authority of the Bible. The Bible, being the Word of God, is the final authority in the faith and practice of the Protestant, especially. The Bible is not, however, authoritative for the Catholic. Only the church's interpretation and application of the Bible have validity for him. The Bible itself is a closed book, and that is no figure of speech, for the loyal Catholic who awaits the word of God from the lips of man. The Protestant churchman, however, has a "paper pope"; the Bible is the Word of God for him. It is his duty and privilege to study it, and when, like the Bereans of Bible times, he searches the Scriptures he is called "noble," not "heretic,"

2. Justification by faith. The Protestant churches teach that a man who exercises faith in Christ as his Intercessor and Sin-Bearer is justified before God. The Roman churches teach that a

man is not justified by faith in Christ but that his own works added to Christ's work of grace are the basis of justification. Both churches, of course, insist that the Christian must do good works; but the Catholic church teaches that these works produce our justification, while the Protestant church teaches that our justification by the grace of Christ produces our good works. We might state the matter graphically:

Roman doctrine: faith + works ➜ justification

Protestant doctrine: faith ➜ justification + works

Works are part of the root of justification in Romanism, and are the fruit of justification in Protestantism.

The far-reaching effects of this difference are obvious. How can a Catholic ever know that he is justified before God? When is he sure that he has added enough good works? Answer: Never. Result: No peace or security. It was this inevitable fear and perturbation that drove Luther back to biblical doctrine so that he could say with Paul: "Being justified by faith, we have peace with God through our Lord Jesus Christ, through whom we have access into this grace in which we now stand, and we rejoice in the hope of the glory of God" (Romans 5:1–2).

Doctrines Distinguishing Evangelical Sacerdotal Churches

The third level of doctrines includes those which distinguish the sacerdotal or sacramental Protestant churches from the evangelical. The sacerdotal churches—mainly the Orthodox and Episcopalian—maintain an apostolic succession of clergy. They believe that the first bishops of the church ordained their successors by the laying on of hands and that these have in turn, and by the same manner, ordained others down to the present time. Only, therefore, by the bishops is ordination valid or regular. This is the crux of the difficulty of union between Episcopal and Presbyterian churches today. How can the Episcopal church recognize Presbyterian clergy unordained by a bishop? How can Presbyterians regard ordination by a bishop as necessary? The evangelical churches, such as the Presbyterian, believe in an apostolic succession, but transmitted via the congregation, presbytery or other church unit; not a succession of priests ordained by bishops.

The other characteristic of the sacerdotal churches is the tendency to believe that the sacraments are indispensable to salvation and that they are effective by an inherent power—*ex opere operato*. The evangelical churches differ with their brethren here in believing that the sacraments depend for their efficacy on the faith of the participant and that they are not indispensable to salvation but are the proper signs of it to be administered when and if possible.

Doctrines Distinguishing Reformed and Arminian Churches

Finally, the fourth level of doctrine, which distinguishes the Reformed churches from all other evangelical churches, is Calvinism. These doctrines have been reduced to a system and a convenient acrostic invented for them. The acrostic is the word "TULIP":

T = *total depravity*. This means that man's sin affects every phase of his being: thought, feeling and will. It does not teach that man is utterly sinful and therefore a devil, although his depravity penetrates each area of his personality.

U = *unconditional election*. This means that God chose to save some of mankind even though they themselves, because of sin, were not able, on their own initiative, to supply the conditions of acceptance.

L = *limited atonement*. This teaches that Christ came into the world with the specific or limited purpose of saving these elect persons by Himself bearing their sins in His body on the tree.

I = *irresistible grace*. Sinful men being averse to God would naturally not accept the overtures of Christ or His gospel. Hence, God changes the heart and makes them a new creation so that their eyes are opened to the glory of Christ, and, seeing Him as He is, they are, of course, irresistibly drawn to Him.

P = *perseverance*. This teaches that the Christian will persevere in good works because God having begun a good work (irresistible grace) will continue it to the last day.

The Arminian churches differ on these five points. But among the other Reformed, or Calvinistic, churches which teach these truths, such as the Baptists and Congregationalists, generally, the only characteristics which distinguish them from the Presbyterian family are their form of church government with which we will deal in the next section.

A Survey of Presbyterian Church Government

It has been said that the man who knows but one religion knows none. In a sense that principle is true and applies to Christian denominations also. He who knows but one of them knows none. At any rate this much is unqualifiedly true: The better we know other denominations the better we shall understand our own; and, conversely, the better we know our own the more we shall understand others.

Let us therefore approach a brief survey of Presbyterian church government by first examining hastily the general types of church government. The following diagram will illustrate graphically these various types:

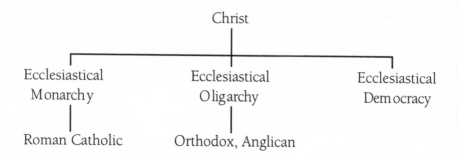

PATTERNS OF CHURCH GOVERNMENT

Christt

Ecclesiastical	Ecclesiastical	Ecclesiastical
Monarchy	Oligarchy	Democracy
Roman Catholic	Orthodox, Anglican	

All Churches Recognize Headship of Christ

It will be noted, in the first place, that all Christian churches officially regard Jesus Christ as their supreme Head. Whatever other differences there may be, agreement on this point is general. One church or another may maintain that one form of government or another detracts from the actual Headship of Christ. But this much is certain, each church *professes* to reverence Christ as its own ultimate King.

Second, there is, therefore, authority in all churches. They may not all exercise it, but all regard Christ as *ruling* through a particular form of government. There is no logical reason why a monarchical church should be thought of as possessing more authority than a democratic one, for each professes to derive authority from Jesus Christ.

Third, it is clear that the difference among churches is not on the *fact* of authority but on the *instrument* of authority. All agree that Christ rules; but "By what means?" is the question. Some maintain He rules by means of an earthly monarchy; others by an oligarchy; and others by a democracy. Let us examine each briefly.

Churches Conceding to Central Authority

The Roman Catholic church is unique in holding to an absolute monarch as the head of the Church. He is called the Pope and when he speaks *ex cathedra,* or officially from the pontifical throne, the Holy Father's words are infallible and not to be questioned. He rules the church by divine right and the ecclesiastical royalty (the various orders of priests) administers the affairs of the church under him.

Oligarchy is government by a group of church nobles who constitute a ruling class. The ecclesiastical oligarchy prevails in a pure form in the Orthodox and Anglican churches and in a mixed form in the Episcopal and Methodist churches. In the pure form of ecclesiastical oligarchy this spiritual royalty belongs to a class apart—set apart by an apostolic succession and not by choice of the membership. In the mixed form of ecclesiastical oligarchy, the selection of the ecclesiastical royal family is, in part, by the membership of the church or representatives of it. Oligarchy, in general, differs from monarchy in not having one head, but is like it in possessing a religious nobility selected more or less independently of the will of the people ruled.

Churches Practicing Democratic Form of Government

Democracy is a rule of the people, by the people and for the people. A pure political democracy, which does not actually exist, would require all the people directly to make and enforce all the laws. Such a procedure being impractical, all democracy is limited, or republican, in form. In this the people elect representatives to whom they delegate authority to act in their stead.

Church government knows both forms of democracy: absolute (or approximately so) and limited. The Congregational, Baptist and Independent churches usually conceive the individual congregation as retaining all governmental rights and being the functioning governmental unit. Of course, this procedure is not and cannot be adhered to completely, but the attempt is made to approximate it. In the Presbyterian and Reformed churches, especially, there is the limited democracy or republican form of church government. In the Presbyterian system the congregations elect ruling elders who together with the teaching elders (ministers) constitute the session. The eldership once selected is for life and exercises authority over the church by means of various courts.

Presbyterian Church Government Is Described

Let us observe a few things. First, Christ is Head of the Church. He it is who calls the sinner out of the world and into His Church. From these called-out ones He selects His elders who form the session, which is the governing unit of the congregation. Each session in a given area sends two delegates, one of whom is always the minister, to form the presbytery which meets quarter-annually. The presbytery in a given area annually sends delegates to form the synod (of which, for example, there are 11 in the United Presbyterian Church in this country). Also annually commissioners from all the presbyteries are sent to form the highest court of the denomination—the General Assembly.

It should be remembered that the diagram represents the order of origin and not of authority. In point of origin, first the congregation; second, the session; third, the presbytery; fourth, the synod; fifth, the General Assembly. In point of authority, first, the General Assembly; second, the synod; third, the presbytery; fourth, the session; fifth, the congregation. In each case, however, Christ is supreme, both from the point of originating the government of His church and also from the point of governing His church. No authority whatever may supersede that of Jesus Christ and the Presbyterian is never expected to acquiesce in any ecclesiastical decree, however imposing, unless it be in accord with the will of Christ as given in the Scriptures. He must choose excommunication rather than acquiescence in such a decree.

Scriptural Authority for Presbyterian Government

Why does the Presbyterian prefer this system of government? Not because it is most sensibly democratic or efficient, although it may lay claim to both. He prefers it because he believes it is the system of government set forth in the Scriptures. First, he maintains that it was the system that prevailed among the Jews among whom the church originated (Exodus 3:16, 4:29, 18:24–26; 1 Samuel 8:4; 2 Samuel 5:3; Ezra 8:14; Acts 4:5). Second, he believes that there is no New Testament warrant for a monarchical or episcopal form of authority. The word "bishop," or *episkopos,* he concedes, is used in the New Testament, but obviously as a synonym for "elder," or *presbuteros* (compare Acts 20:17 and 20:28). Third, he finds more than mere congregational authority in the New Testament (Acts 15:23–29; 20:28; Matthew 16:19, 18:18).

The question will be asked, are there not more officers than elders in a Presbyterian church? Yes, there are, and these officers, which almost always include trustees and frequently deacons also, are very important. The trustees who deal with matters "purely financial," and the deacons who are "messengers of the gospel in the homes of the people," are not listed in this pattern of government, not because they are unimportant, but merely because they are part of the local rather than the denominational fabric of government.

IV. A Brief Survey of the
United Presbyterian Church

The United Presbyterian Church is one of the "Big Three" Presbyterian bodies. The Northern Presbyterian Church is the largest with some two million members; the Southern Presbyterian Church has about one-half million on its rolls; and we are about a quarter of a million strong.

It has not always been so, however. Our origin is humble and our formal organization recent (1858). The story has been told briefly and well by Dr. William J. Reid, late pastor of the First United Presbyterian Church of Pittsburgh, in his book, *United Presbyterianism.*

In 1733 certain ministers seceded from the Established Church of Scotland, on the ground that there were corruptions in the doctrines of the church, and tyranny in the administra- tion of its government. Soon after, they organized themselves as a presbytery, which was called the Associate or Secession presbytery. For a time they performed no judicial acts; but after waiting for three years, and seeing no prospect of healing the breach between them and the mother church, they proceeded to do the proper work of a church court. At the first there were but four seceding ministers, but their number increased so rapidly that they found it necessary, in 1744, to constitute themselves into a synod, consisting of three presbyteries.

Origin of Associate and Associate Reformed Churches
A missionary spirit characterized the Associate Synod of Scotland from the very first, and one of its fields of missionary labor was the American colonies. That Synod received petition after petition from the Scotch and Scotch-Irish emigrants to America, to send them ministers. For a time nothing could be

done in answer to these petitions, on account of the scarcity of ministers at home; but in 1753 two missionaries were sent to Pennsylvania, who organized themselves into a presbytery, under the name of the Associate Presbytery of Pennsylvania. Afterwards other ministers were sent, and on May 20, 1776 the presbytery was divided into two, viz., the Associate Presbytery of Pennsylvania and the Associate Presbytery of New York. There were at this time a few ministers in the United States who belonged to the Reformed Presbyterian or Covenanter Church. A union was formed between the Associate and Reformed Presbyterian churches, June 13, 1782, and the united body was called, from the name of the churches composing it, the Associate Reformed Church. However, two ministers of the Associate Presbytery of Pennsylvania disapproved of this union and continued their old organization. This presbytery was so strengthened by other ministers, sent out by the Associate Church of Scotland, that on May 3, 1800, it formed itself into a synod, designated as the Associate Synod of North America.

This was the origin of the Associate and Associate Reformed churches in this country. The two denominations occupied the same territory, and held substantially the same doctrines. The conviction grew stronger and stronger that they should be united. Efforts were made in the direction of union, but for many years these efforts were unsuccessful. At last on May 26, 1858, the union between them was consummated in Pittsburgh, Pennsylvania, and the united body was called the United Presbyterian Church of North America.

The United Presbyterian Church is proud of its heritage and its distinctives. Before mentioning these, however, we pause to remember that our church is even prouder of her catholic faith and practice. She thinks of herself as but one small fragment of the whole church of Christ. And while she proudly wears the name Presbyterian she knows she is but one member of that great tradition.

Distinctive Features of the United Presbyterian Church

Yet like William James's crab that protested, "I am not a crustacean, I am a crab!" so the United Presbyterian Church does not desire to be lost, as yet, in the larger family but wishes to be seen also in her own individuality. There are things to which she would point and say: These mark a United Presbyterian church. Her happy balance between sound doctrine and good works is one characteristic, she claims. An educated clergy, a missionary zeal, the practice of stewardship, a great respect for the Sabbath, and the use of Psalms in worship—these and other features make her what she is.

Her ideal of sound doctrine and a charitable spirit is well expressed in her motto, "The truth of God; forbearance in love." Whether she has or has not sacrificed some truth to forbearance, she means by this formula to express thereby the time-honored Christian polity: "In essentials unity; in doubtful things liberty; and in all things charity." Her background is Scotch, her tradition includes Seceders, and Covenanter blood flows in her veins. She professes to preserve their integrity while avoiding all excessive narrowness. And whatever faults she may have, through the years she has been a peace-loving church—perhaps too peace-loving—but peace-loving she has been.

An educated clergy is another trait. This is a characteristic of which a minister likes to boast to a prospective new member. Ours is a relatively small church, but its leaders are as thoroughly trained as those of any other Christian denomination and better than many. Almost without exception a United Presbyterian minister must have had four years of college training and three years of seminary work. The church has six colleges and one theological seminary in this country alone, all of which stand well among institutions of their own type.

A Church Fired with a Missionary Passion

The United Presbyterian Church is a missionary church. A by-word has it that the denomination was founded on the banks of the Allegheny and the Nile. A great part of our foreign work is indeed concentrated in Egypt, the Sudan, and Ethiopia. The land of the five rivers, the Punjab or North India, is the other area for our world evangelistic endeavor. Of our 267,464 members it is to be noted that 68,705 or more than 25% are outside this country. We United Presbyterians believe that God has prospered our work at home to the degree He has, because we have tried not to be disobedient to the heavenly vision and have carried the Gospel to the uttermost parts of the earth. The annual missionary conference at New Wilmington, Pennsylvania is at once the enthusiastic evidence of our zeal for missions and also the source of much of it.

A trait in our church which may strike the new member who comes from certain other denominations is the absence of stress on church-sponsored commercial devices for raising funds. Bake sales and such are not unknown in the United Presbyterian Church, but for the most part they are conspicuous for their absence. The reason is that the United Presbyterian Church has tried to teach its people to be personal stewards of their means. We encourage tithing and strongly urge every individual to lay aside on the first of the week as the Lord has prospered him. Needless to say it is this fact which explains the high position the denomination has always held in per-capita contributions. Where stewardship is taught and practiced other schemes for meeting a challenging budget are not necessary.

A Psalm-Singing, Sabbath-Saying Church

And, of course, everyone knows us as the "Psalm-Singing Church"—even 20 years after we gave up the exclusive use of psalms in public worship. They still retain a deserved prominence in our services. The newcomer may encounter a strangeness about the songs in the front of our Psalter Hymnals, but if he is a discerning Christian he will note that what they lack in familiarity they make up in spiritual excellence.

When you hear the word "Sabbath" you may be reasonably certain that, if you are not in a synagogue or with the Adventists, you are in a United Presbyterian church. There is more than an inherited Scotch tenaciousness that accounts for the persistence of that word. It has the same kind of justification that "Thee" and "Thou" have. They are appropriate and distinctive words for distinguished objects of reference. Just as it is fitting that the Lord be addressed in exalted and formal language, so it seems well that His day should have a special and sacred name. A parishioner of mine, formerly of another denomination, said to me: "I am glad the United Presbyterian Church has retained the word 'Sabbath.' Our family has now adopted it because it expresses something that 'Sunday' no longer conveys."

There is more to the church than a bundle of distinctives and yet they point to where she is. She loves Christ; she loves souls; she loves righteousness and she is seeking after peace. God bless her, with all her virtues—with all her faults—we love her still.

V. A Survey of Christian Practice

We have been discussing what Christianity in its various forms, is. Now we come to the question, "What is a Christian?" We leave the spectator attitude and ask how we may become a part of what we have seen. To become a Christian we must yield to the authority of Jesus Christ in every phase of our lives: personal, family, church and world.

Personal Commitment to Christ a Primary Requisite

First of all comes one's personal commitment to Christ. As individuals, we must acknowledge our need of the Savior and trust in His atonement for our sins. There is the catch! Christianity is for sinners only. "I came," said Christ, "not to call the righteous but sinners." This is the "offense of the cross." Christ is attractive to many who never accept Him because they would have to confess their sins to do so. I have often likened God's gift of His Son to a gift of Emily Post's *Etiquette*. That book is desirable, contains things we all would like to know, is worth four or five dollars and goes well with an Oriental rug. But would you like to receive it for a birthday present?

"No!"

"Why not?"

"Because the gift of the book would imply I needed it!"

That is the catch. That is also the catch in the Gospel. It is good news, of infinite value, a sublime story of death and sacrifice. Why then do not all men believe? Because the Gospel of redemption implies that men need redemption. Let it be understood clearly that no one can be a Christian who does not acknowledge this need and confess his sins.

Once we have been born again (regeneration) and consequently see ourselves as we sinfully are (repentance) and Christ as He gloriously is (faith) we turn away from our sins (conversion) and under His leadership we begin to do more and more unto sin and live more and more unto God (sanctification). This process of sanctification, or becoming more and more like Christ, is a totalitarian effort. Our entire being must be subjugated to Him: our *bodies* must be presented as living sacrifices; our every *thought* must be captive to Him; our *actions* must be so completely under His direction that "whether we eat or whether we drink, or whatsoever we do, we do all to the glory of God"; in short, we must "love the Lord our God with all our heart, soul, mind and strength, and our neighbors as ourselves."

Surrender of Substance, as well as Self, Is Essential

Not yet is our personal discipleship complete. We must not merely present all that we *are* to Him, but also all that we *have*. All our time, all our money and all our talents must be His or we are none of His. As indications that all we have is His, He asks for token gifts. Of time, for example, He requires the Sabbath day. That is the Lord's day, to be used not for ordinary pursuits, or personal gain, and certainly not for business (except in emergency) but for the worship and praise of His name in the church and Sabbath school; for the cultivation of religion and fellowship in the home and family. Of money, He requires the tithe or tenth of our income. What more we can give for His work and charity He accepts as freewill offerings, but the tithe He requires. Of talents, He wants whatever you have in His service. If you can teach, or sing, or cook, or sew, or lead, or work, or have any gifts, they can be used.

Each Family An Epitome Of The Kingdom

In addition to surrendering ourselves to Christ, we must bring our families under His benign Lordship. His covenant is not with us only, but also with our children. Hence each family is an epitome of the kingdom of heaven. Children should be brought up in the nurture and admonition of the Lord and given all the training and worship that appropriately belong to a child of the King. Not only should grace adorn the family meal but no day should elapse without the family altar when all together worship the Lord Jesus Christ in the intimacy of the family circle. In addition to rites in the home, there should also be a general atmosphere of kindliness pervading all. Each member of the family should assume his scriptural role: the father should be head of the house, who, because he has most authority, must love most; the mother while revering her husband should exercise a benignant reign over her children in such a way as not "to provoke the children to wrath," and the children, of whom "such is the kingdom," should love God first and their parents next because they stand in the place of God.

Church Attendance and Worship are Necessary Habits

Again, if we love Christ we will love the Church for which He died. It was His custom to worship on the Sabbath day; the New Testament Christians were forbidden to forsake the assembling of themselves together as the manner of some was. Furthermore, He instituted His Church, with the authority of the keys, and it has ordained regular service for the Sabbath and at other times for the spiritual needs of its people. It is, therefore, a duty to support the church by attendance as much as by gifts.

An unfortunate habit of nonattendance, except at irregular intervals, has developed in our time. Some have even said to me that it was a Roman Catholic notion that church attendance is necessary, while the Protestant comes to church when he desires to do so. It is true that the Roman church requires attendance; but it is false that the Protestant church does not. The Protestant and Catholic church both require attendance; their difference is the reason given for attendance. The Catholic comes because the church requires it; the Protestant comes because God requires it. Let us be very clear on this—the Protestant church teaches that it is a violation of the express requirements of the Word of God for any Christian to be absent from church without physical inability. The delinquent church attender is living in sin. Absenteeism is immorality. And God will not hold him guiltless who takes His name in vain (by professing it without worshiping it).

Although church attendance is a matter of duty, the Christian who has worshiped often cannot remember anything but the delights of God's house. There may have been a time when he came because he had to come. He only knows that he could not do otherwise than praise God and be anywhere than in his pew, not because he should not, but because he would not.

Witnessing, Winning Others, First Line of Duty

With respect to the world from which the Christian came he has two lines of duty. First, to go back and win others from it to the salvation which is in Jesus Christ. He is a witness, an evangelist. In the early Christian church every member was a preacher. That is why and that is how the church conquered the world. So every Christian is responsible for his neighbor and will cultivate every opportunity, directly or indirectly, to preach Christ. No one can ever know that he is saved until he feels the impulse to try to save others through Jesus Christ.

His second line of duty to his world is to bring Christ's teachings to bear on it. This he will do by example and by precept. His life will be different now: he loves his enemies, he goes the second mile, he turns the other cheek, he forgives offenses, he fights corruption, he stands firmly for every righteous cause and, like his Master, he goes about doing good. As a result all men take notice that he has been with Jesus. He is the friend of the oppressed, the champion of the underprivileged, the foe of bigotry, the opponent of greed; he loves his neighbor as himself, is generous to the needy, is sympathetic to the poor, the companion of the sick; he rejoices with those who rejoice and weeps with those who weep. His heart in the other world, he acts as if he had no interest but this; devoted to Christ, he is obsessed with men.

That, dear friends, is your manner of life, that is your witness, and that is your simple Christian duty.

Who Is This Jesus?

We had a very interesting professor at Harvard University who used to attempt to introduce Christ to his classes. In attendance he would have, in addition to the divinity school men, a number of regular university students. The latter were often totally ignorant of Christ. This fact, far from dismaying the professor, rather pleased him; for from these students he got what he liked to call "the virgin reaction" to Jesus.

The theological students, having been acquainted with Jesus before, could only afford the philosophy of the second glance. But Dr. H. J. Cadbury, who himself had studied the texts hundreds of times, could always learn something from those who would give the fresh response of the newly introduced.

Let us attempt to put ourselves in the position of these students and try to experience the initial response to Jesus Christ.

When we read the accounts of Jesus we instinctively recognize Him as the perfect man. Matthew describes one whom we see to be the ideal Jew; Mark, the ideal Roman; John, the ideal Son of God; and Luke, the universal ideal who is every man's ideal and God's as well. Furthermore, every man who approaches Christ seems to feel the same thing—He is the ideal of that man. To the artist Christ is the One altogether lovely. To the educator He is the master teacher. To the philosopher He is the wisdom of God. To the lonely, He is a brother; to the sorrowful, a Comforter; and to the bereaved, the Resurrection and the Life. To the sinner, He is the Lamb of God that takes away the sin of the world.

The early Puritan leader Thomas Watson has said, "You are quite amazed that He is incomparably better than you could have expected. He is tender without being weak, strong without being coarse, lowly without being servile. He has conviction without intolerance, enthusiasm without fanaticism, holiness without pharisaism, passion without prejudice. This man alone never made a false step, never struck a jarring note. His life alone moved on those high levels where local limitations are transcended and the absolute law of moral beauty prevails. It was life at its highest."

The virgin reaction of the world to Jesus Christ, then, is this: He is the ideal, the perfect man; the moral paragon of the race. I do not wish to gloss over the fact that not absolutely everyone has agreed with this verdict. I know that George Bernard Shaw spoke of a time in Christ's life when, as he said, Christ was not a Christian. I know that some have thought that Socrates died more nobly than Jesus; that others believe Christ to have been surpassed. But the overwhelming testimony of the world is to the perfection, the incomparable perfection, of Jesus of Nazareth. These few exceptions could be easily shown to rest on fundamental misconceptions of certain things which Jesus said or did.

Moreover, those who take exception usually think that some imagined fault is a failure of Christ to be, as G. B. Shaw said, Christian! It is evident that they know of no higher standard by which to test Christ than that of Christ Himself.

But now we find ourselves in an extraordinary situation. If we admit, as the world does, that Christ is the perfect man, we must then admit that He is also God!

Why, you ask, if we acknowledge Christ to be the perfect man, must we then acknowledge Him to be God also? Is there not a great difference between man and God—even between perfect man and God? Why should the admission of the one require the admission of the other? Why must the perfect man be God?

For this reason: Because the perfect man *says* He is God.

And if He is not God, then neither could He be a perfect man.

Just a minute, you say, what proof do we have that Jesus Christ ever claimed that He actually is God?

We have overwhelming evidence that He entertained this high opinion of Himself. This, for example, is what He says:

"I and my Father are one" (John 10:30).

"No man cometh to the Father, but by Me" (John 14:6).

"He that hath seen Me hath seen the Father" (John 14:9).

"Before Abraham was, I am" (John 8:58).

"I adjure Thee by the living God, that Thou tell us whether Thou be the Christ, the Son of God," the high priest asked. "Thou hast said," was Christ's reply (Matthew 26:63–64).

"Baptize," He commanded, "in the name of the Father, and of the Son, and of the Holy Ghost" (Matthew 28:19).

"Whom do ye say that I am?" He asked His disciples. "Thou art the Christ, the Son of the living God," Peter replied (Matthew 16:16).

"Blessed art thou, Simon Barjona: for flesh and blood hath not revealed it unto thee, but My Father which is in heaven," He said (Matthew 16:17).

Well, you say, is this not a characteristic way for religious teachers to speak? Do not all of them make grandiose statements?

It is true that Bronson Alcott once said to a friend, "Today I feel that I could say, as Christ did, 'I and the Father are one!'"

"Yes," the other replied, "but the difference is this: Christ got the world to believe Him."

The significant thing is this: not one recognized religious leader in the history of the world has ever laid claim to being God—except Jesus.

Moses did not.

Paul was horrified when people tried to worship him.

Muhammad insisted that he was merely a prophet of Allah.

Buddha did not even believe in the existence of a personal God, and Confucius was skeptical.

Zoroaster was a worshiper, but he was not worshiped.

We repeat—of the recognized religious leaders of all time, Jesus of Nazareth—and Jesus of Nazareth alone—claimed to be eternal God.

Not only did Jesus on various occasions definitely affirm His deity but it is perhaps more telling still that He always assumed it.

Take, for example, the Sermon on the Mount. This is regarded as predominantly moral instruction. No heavy theology here, they say. This is Christ telling us what we are to do, not what we are to believe about Him.

It is true that He does not directly claim to be God in this passage. Indirectly, however, He says a great deal about Himself and lays impressive incidental claim to His divinity.

Note these six distinct pointers to His supernatural being in this one sermon on Christian morality (Matthew 5–7).

First, He says with absolute authority who shall and who shall not inherit the kingdom of God (the Beatitudes). If I, for example, said anything like that, on my own authority, you would smile pityingly or frown.

Second, He said that His disciples would be hated and suffer persecution for His sake. Suppose that I said that Martin Luther suffered for my sake, what would you think about me?

Third, "but I say unto you" is a constant refrain through this sermon, by which Christ assumes His right to speak with the authority of the Word of God on which He was commenting.

Fourth, He says that in the last judgment people will say to Him, "Lord, Lord"; but "then I will profess unto them, I never knew you: depart from Me, ye that work iniquity."

Fifth, the sermon concludes with the parable of the two houses, one built on sand and the other on a rock; one to fall and one to stand. And what is this rock? His teaching.

Finally, the people sensed the supreme dignity of this person who had taught them, for they observed that "He taught them as one having authority, and not as the scribes."

What did Jesus' contemporaries think of Him?

"Behold the man," said Pilate.

"Truly this was the Son of God," said the centurion who watched Him die.

"Never man so spake," the people said.

"Behold the Lamb of God," was the testimony of John the Baptist, whom all men recognized as a prophet.

"My Lord and my God," said doubting Thomas.

When Jesus asked His disciples who they thought He was, Peter, standing near Caesarea Philippi, a city built in honor of Caesar who was claiming divine honors, and not far from the grotto to Pan, the god of nature whom many worshiped, said: "Thou art the Christ, the Son of the living God."

John said of Him, "We beheld His glory, the glory as of the only begotten of the Father, full of grace and truth."

And Paul adored Him with a most abundant variety of expressions as his great God and Savior, Jesus Christ. For example, he uses the expression, "unsearchable riches of Christ," and other expressions concerning Christ's riches in his epistles. What does Paul mean by the "unsearchable riches of Christ"? That is the very point. It is impossible to put enough meaning into the expression to do justice to the feeling of the Apostle. Rendell Harris, attempting to translate this expression in Ephesians 3:8, threw up his hands in despair and cried: "The unexplorable wealth of Christ!"

What of the influence of Jesus Christ on the succeeding centuries? Shortly before His death, He said: "Believe Me for the very works' sake. Verily, verily, I say unto you, He that believeth in Me, the works that I do shall he do also; and greater works than these shall he do" (John 14:11-12).

These were very ordinary men to whom Christ—admittedly the most extraordinary person ever to appear in human history—said that they should do greater works than He had done. A strange prediction that was, and stranger still that it has been fulfilled. Yet even stranger still is how it has been fulfilled.

When Christ uttered this prophecy, infanticide was a common thing. Quintillian and others regarded it as a beautiful custom to abandon infants. It was the followers of Jesus, to whom Jesus had said, "Suffer the little children to come unto Me, and forbid them not," who put an end to this "beautiful custom." Clement, Origen, Tertullian, the fathers of the church, exposed the horror of infanticide. And the weakest of all creatures, the human infant, became the best protected of all, as the followers of Jesus continued to much greater lengths the emancipation of childhood.

Murder for pleasure was eradicated by the disciples of Christ. When Jesus uttered the promise about "greater works," the Romans regarded gladiatorial combats as the choicest of amusements.

Another example is cannibalism. Many a soldier in World War II subsequently told of his amazement to find himself welcomed rather than devoured in some remote island where he had been stranded. How glad were such men, who trudged wearily through the jungles with a fear of what the next clearing would reveal, when they saw Christian churches and knew that they were safe. These were the experiences which made missionaries of GI's and produced the now-famous "khaki-colored viewpoint." They found the church there, for the disciples were doing greater works than their Lord.

Time would fail us to mention all the *gesta Christi*. Suffice it here to repeat what James Russell Lowell said a century ago: "Show me a place on the face of the earth ten miles square where a man may provide for his children in decency and comfort, where infancy is protected, where age is venerated, where womanhood is honored, and where human life is held in due regard, and I will show you a place where the gospel of Christ has gone and laid the foundation."

We are fully aware that to attribute Godhood to any man is a colossal affirmation. It borders on the incredible—the impossible.

But when we consider the impression of Christ's perfect humanity, the great claims He made for Himself in the most humble way, the unrestrained adoration and worship of those who knew Him, the miracles associated with Him whose life was a "blaze of miracle," and the constant recurring of His name throughout the world, we propose that it is impossible to deny Christ's deity.

It is difficult to believe; it is impossible to doubt.

What will you do with Jesus?

The Will of Man

I notice, you notice, that we are choosers. You are here reading this because you chose to. I am addressing this topic because I choose to. If you and I had not chosen to do what we are doing, neither of us would be writing or reading. We have never met or heard of a human being who was not a chooser. William James (I think) said man is a "fighter for ends." I saw a photo recently of a baby in its mother's arms obviously reaching for a flower. It was already a fighter for its goal.

We did not choose to be born, but once conceived we choose. We have seen pictures of a fetus squirming to avoid a needle or clamps or whatever. Willing is nature; willing is human.

Definition

So man has this power of choice. We call it the will of man. Some philosophers say that willing is not a resident power of will or faculty. All we know is that man chooses.

Some even say that saying man is a chooser is going too far. These philosophers choose not to believe there is a will of man. They see only a willing man.

It is true that we only see man willing. We do not see a will of man. We cannot say that there is a residual power or will or faculty, these philosophers contend.

"What is the will of man?" we ask.

They reply, "Nothing; there is only the willing of man." We traditionalists are simply postulating a will of man because we constantly see man willing and wrongly suppose that there is this imaginary faculty—the creation of our own imaginations.

How does the traditional believer, in a faculty called the will, answer these astute critics? He first asks how can a man react to stimuli in the way of choosing without a power to do so. It is certainly man's nature to respond to stimuli positively or negatively. It is human nature to choose. So human nature acting by choosing is his nature. Is not man's natural response to stimuli a power of human nature? If it were not man's nature to respond to stimuli, he would be like the rocks which are unaffected by severe blows. It is not a rock's nature to respond to stimuli. Man always responds to stimuli. It is his nature to respond. Is that constant responding not a power which is called will?

Man responds to stimuli by thinking. He cannot be stimulated without thinking. That also is constant in all human beings. Man thinks, just as man chooses. That is the kind of being he is. When stimulated he thinks, he feels, he judges and he wills. All of these are natural responses to stimuli. Can it be denied that man has powers—faculties, for thinking, feeling, willing? Would he be a man if he did not think, freely will? He has a power to do these things naturally.

Is the critic really saying anything other than that? He admits that humans do so respond to stimuli constantly and invariably. The traditionalist agrees with this. What is the real difference here?

Is it merely a semantic difference? Both agree that this behavior is natural and invariable. The traditionalist wants to call the perennial choosing the function of a will. The critic chooses not to go beyond the functioning. It is the functioning that traditionalists and critics agree on. Why not let the matter rest there?

The traditionalist cannot leave it there because, he maintains, functioning requires power. The rock does not function voluntarily because it does not have the power to do so; nor do stars, grass and the universe in general, apart from God, angels and men, respond by willing.

The critic insists that there is no need to postulate an additional something. Most living bodies react to stimuli. If there is a need for a so-called power-base, it is the animal itself. Why postulate additional power and faculties? If they did exist, one would expect to find them as one finds muscles, nerves, ligaments, tendons and the like. Where do you find these "powers"? Who ever saw a "faculty"? All we see or know is that the animal or plant reacts this way and that.

We know that there are locatable areas of the brain which control sight, hearing, feeling, etc. When these areas are destroyed, these responses cease.

Could the area through which sight comes be called the power of sight or faculty of sight? Yes and no. Yes, it is necessary to sight. No, it does not of itself produce sight. The body is involved in this area when sight occurs. That is all that can be said or claimed.

The traditionalist insists that that is not enough. This section of the brain is more than merely the area involved in sight. It is indispensable. If it is not functioning, there is no sight. True, the critic says, we do not deny that this area is necessary for sight. It simply does not have any "power" of itself to produce sight. Why postulate more than the necessary?

I guess that the traditionalist must grant the critic's point and would lose nothing if he did. Then why must he combat the obvious or add the superfluous? He still has man the chooser, the decider, the will-er.

But does he have man with a will? Does he have man with a sense of right? Does he have a man who can know himself, others, God? Is there an area of the brain where stimuli produce the thought of God, of man, of angels, of self? And responsibility therefor? How can stimuli produce the image of the stimulated?

But what is the location of the faculty which produces this reason? And where is the will to admire, study or kill? And whence does love or despising get its existence? And whence is the power that makes us despise ourselves for doing one and not the other? Are we willing (!) to say that there must be faculties for thus responding; but if we do, where, we ask, are they? We simply agree that there are such responses and we are responsible for our responses.

It seems that all must agree on the "that." Those responses occur, but are ignorant of the "how."

So what is the definition of the "will of man"? All we can say is that there is no such "thing." It is a rather misleading way of hypothesizing the way men respond to stimuli, or, rather, that men react to stimuli.

Application of the Definition

If there is not a faculty called "will," does that end responsibility? Of course not. It is the man, the person, who is responsible. The way he responds to stimuli reveals his nature which is judged by God and His representatives.

How is the "original sin" of man thus understood? Well, original sin means that after the fall in the garden of Eden, all mankind—in Adam—died. That is, he (we) lost virtue-reaction. In its stead came a sin-reaction. As we had in Adam a response of nature, we now (prior to regeneration) have a sin response. That means that in Adam we responded to stimuli according to God's preceptive and holy will. When we fell that was replaced by responding sinfully to stimuli. That is what is called original sin—fallen man chooses to do evil when stimulated. In other words, the "will of man" means that, in his unregenerate state, he always chooses to violate rather than obey God's holy will.

Man's total being always, invariably, unchangeably chooses sin. That is, so long as he remains fallen, he will choose to do evil though warned by God and punished by man for so doing. Original sin means that response from which sin originated, and that is the way of man's total being.

Man will always choose evil because, as Christ says, "He who commits sin is the slave of sin" (John 8:34). He is a willing slave. You ask, "If by nature he is the slave of sin, where does slavery to sin come in?" We answer that the slavery is that he cannot escape the punishment of sin. He freely chooses every sin he does, but is also punished for every sin he does (now and hereafter). He likes the sin, but tries to avoid the punishment, which he cannot. He is tied to the post to which the inevitable lashes come.

Try as he will, the sinner cannot escape his punishment which is his ultimate misery. He squirms, and pulls and grasps, but what holds holds only tighter. He is the slave of his sins. There is no escaping his bonds, strive as he will.

When the Jews who had believed in Jesus heard this word that He would "free" them, they were offended by the One they had professed to believe in. They were offended by His gracious words that He would make them free. They did not need to be free, they indignantly insisted. This showed how great their bondage was. They rejected and derided their Lord in His very willingness to save them. They were free in that they chose what they wanted to choose. That was their sin. They freely chose it. If they had admitted that their abuse of their freedom was their sin, they would have been saved.

These "believing" Jews never had their sinful freedom come home to them as Paul did. "I was alive apart from the Law once, but when the commandment came, sin revived and I died" (Romans 7:9). When Paul the Jew knew and admitted that he was dead in "original sin" he came alive. "Who will set me free from the body of this death? Thanks be to God through Jesus Christ our Lord!" (7:24–25). These Jews of John 8 did not know and would not admit their death. They were "alive apart from the Law." They were the walking dead. "She who lives in pleasure is dead while she lives."

So to will pleasure is to will death. Sinners are suicides who do not know or admit it. Nevertheless, in truth they will it, for Scripture is the "Word of truth."

Free Will

What, then, of free will? The will is always free; or, more correctly, the person who wills always wills freely. That is, the free-willer is never compelled.

For example, a person never freely wills to breathe. Breathing is a natural necessity; willy-nilly. But can a person will not to breathe? So long as he is a person (at least, a person in this world) he cannot will not to breathe. If he can ever will not to breathe, he ceases to be. He may then will to be in another, in a disembodied state. But so long as he is in this world, man breathes willy-nilly. He does not will to breathe; he breathes in order to will. Or, better, he breathes as a human being and thus becomes liable to choosing, if and when stimulated. It is his given nature to choose when stimulated. And it is his given fallen nature to choose evil whenever and however stimulated.

Thus, when stimulated by an invitation to go to church he may choose to go or not to go. In this fallen nature if he chooses to go or not to go he will choose either sinfully. He will never choose to go to church virtuously because he hates God and will not worship Him. If he joins in prayer, he will have chosen to do so sinfully for God is not his soteric Father and he does not want God's will to be done or His kingdom to come.

If fallen man chooses not to accept the invitation to go to church, he will, as always, choose not to do so sinfully, especially because he has an obligation to do so as he should be seeking repentance.

So we see the cause of man's choosing or the functioning of his choices. They come from his nature, and his nature comes from his Creator. Man's Creator first made man to choose virtuously, but when, in spite of that, he chose sinfully, God took away his nature to choose virtuously and punished him with a nature to choose sinfully. His original nature was changeable, apparently by himself. His fallen nature is unchangeable by himself because it is his nature so to choose. The perplexity here is that he could once change his divinely given nature, but, subsequently, was unable to choose to change his divinely imposed nature.

What is the answer to our perplexity? Most theologians admit that there is no explanation of the perfectly good man's ability to choose to change his good nature. There is no perplexity at all about his inability to choose to change his evil nature.

The solution to the perplexity of man's ability to choose to change his good nature is usually that human nature is, by its nature, changeable. Man's nature is unlike God's nature which even God cannot change. But that is merely giving a name to the perplexity and calling it a solution to the perplexity. The perplexity remains: How could man, whose original nature was to choose virtuously and only virtuously always, suddenly reveal an ability to change? No one has ever solved that problem except with the horrible solution that is worse than the problem: God changed the otherwise unchangeable nature of righteous man and then damned him to hell for doing what he otherwise could never have done!

So we see why theologians have chosen to solve the perplexity by giving it a name and rejecting with horror the only rational solution.

Could the tempting-speaking-serpent not solve the perplexity? Satan does not have creative power. He is also not a fool seeking to undo what God Almighty had done, namely make an unchangeable nature good. We ought not to give the devil his "un-due," simply because it is easy to blame the devil and impossible to blame God.

So we humans must continue to live with our very human problem: How could we have destroyed ourselves when we were incapable of even hurting ourselves and then unable to change ourselves when our eternal life depended on it?

Living with that perplexity, we know that we now have an unchangeable (by ourselves) nature which dooms us to hell because we always and increasingly choose what is evil. Only God can save us, and that would have to be by mercy, for our sins could never merit anything but divine judgment.

Being on God's part it would have to be sovereign and arbitrary and costly to God who will by no means acquit the guilty. If it is to bestow mercy, it must be costly, because He must receive our guilt by imposing it on Someone who could endure it—His only Son, who would be willing to take human nature to Himself and shed His human blood for the remission of sins.

That sacrifice of the Son would purchase a new, willing-good nature in His chosen ones. Their "wills," of course, would be changed because wills are only natures choosing. In this case, they would be good natures choosing.

The Battle of Wills

Of course, if these new natures are placed in bodies where the old sinful nature survives, a battle royal will follow.

Manifestly, a God-given good nature versus a man's sinful nature means inevitable victory for the former.

We have so far seen the nature of the will of man; the causes of its volitional operation; the perplexity of the original human nature which nevertheless changed itself to a sinful nature, and the sinful nature which can only changed by God and become victorious over the remnants of the old, surviving sinful nature after struggle in this world and life in heaven.

Objections

Let us now consider some objections to this overall crisis of the will of man.

1. There is an objection to the first created will of man. There are those who simply cannot accept a created will, good or evil. A will, they say, cannot be created by anyone other than the man himself. So the person must be created neutral to choose what is right or not choose what is wrong for a stipulated period of time, and then, when he chooses, be given a good or bad nature accordingly. This way man becomes sinner or saint as he chooses. Punishment and reward shall be according to what he does for a second stipulated period. So it is man, the chooser, all the way. That, they say, is right and so man can complain if condemned and punished, or blush if approved and rewarded.

What do we say to objection number one? For one thing, this has a creature without the ability to choose, choosing to gain the power of choosing. This is a manifest contradiction. If the first person (if you can call him that), was made without the "power" to choose, how could he choose to eat the forbidden fruit, or not? How could he choose the power to choose without the power to choose the power to choose? Adam had to be able to have the natural ability, and according to Scripture, he was created with the moral ability (only) to choose virtuously. As I said above, how a perfectly good person such as Adam could have chosen sinfully is the greatest perplexity in the Christian theology. And now along comes objection number one with an even greater perplexity, how a person could choose without the ability to choose.

Our objector will object again at that last remark. He will say that he does not maintain that Adam did not have the ability to choose. He maintains only that Adam could not have been created with a fixed disposition to choose righteously. Our response is that if Adam had any ability to respond volitionally to stimuli, that would have to be toward what is good or evil. If he had neither it would be like the rock's resistance without will or purpose.

So God, if He created human beings, would have to create them with an ability to respond virtuously or viciously and be culpable or rewardable therefor. But, being God, He can do no evil. So He cannot create humans with an ability to sin for which they would be culpable. God must have created man with an ability to respond virtuously and only virtuously. Yet the man God created to choose virtuously, chose viciously. This is, as admitted, our perplexity but it is not relief, but only hopeless aggravation to teach that God created man with no ability at all.

When the Arminians say that humans were created with the ability to respond virtuously or viciously, they attribute authorship of evil to God. God cannot create a person evil, nor with an ability to do evil though opposed by an ability to do good. God would still be the author of the ability to do evil in an innocent, who would still be damned for exerting his God-given ability.

The Arminians reply to Calvinists that man is now, since the Fall, created by God with an ability to do evil continually.

The Calvinists deny that God is the author of evil. They reply that God, in that case, is not the author of evil, but sin followed by God's judgment of it brings God's creation into that condition. In any case, that would not relieve Arminians of their making God the author of evil (and that without justification).

So, admitting the Calvinist's perplexity (or weakness, error, if you insist) Arminians cannot defend their attack which is, first, preposterous, because it has humans choosing without the power of choice; or, second, making God the author of evil by creating a man with a prevailing power of choosing evil and sending him to hell for so choosing.

2. A second objection to the Reformed view of the will of man is in God's making a perfect man with a perfect will which is nevertheless opposed to the perfect will of God. Jesus Christ wanted the will of God to drink His cup of wrath to be removed, He sweated blood in His effort to have it changed. "Not My will, but Thine be done." So, they charge, we have Christ's perfect will fighting mightily against the perfect will of God. Indeed, Christ only found peace when He gave up His will for the will of God.

First, before we respond to this criticism, let us see how Arminians, who accept the perfection of Christ who still sweated blood struggling with the will of God, handle this apparent contradiction. They will not admit that Christ sinned against the will of God. They seem to solve the problem by thinking that Christ was only trying to avoid the terrible impending suffering. Christ's will was not against God's will, but against the suffering of Calvary. Granted, Calvinists reply, but it was the will of God that Christ undergo that dreadful suffering. So the Arminian is not addressing the problem, but simply locating its cause.

Now let us address ourselves to the Arminian critique of Calvinism here. First, the determined will of Christ was not against the determined will of God: "Not My will, but Thine be done." It was not Christ's will to oppose God's will: "*Not* My will, but Thine." Christ says that it was not His will to deny, but to affirm the will of God. Christ had to shed blood in concurring with the awful will of God. But concur Christ did. What could be plainer? "Not *My* will, but Thy will."

The Arminian critic will say that Christ's saying "not My will" meant the renouncing of His will. We say no; it was not Christ's will, never was Christ's will, and He is saying it never will be other than God's will even though that cost Christ dearly. Renouncing is not of something present, but of it never being present however horrible the cost of doing God's will may be. So far from implying that Christ's will was ever opposed to God's will, it was affirming that it never ever would be. Probably nothing can show more clearly the unchangeable will of Christ in harmony with the will of God than the episode in the Garden of Gethsemane. The elect's salvation hung on Christ's perseverance in the will of God in the garden. We know that even the cross of Calvary could not keep Jesus Christ from doing the will of God. "Having loved His people, He loved (chose to love) them to the end."

So the Arminian charge that the Calvinist doctrine of the will of man was destroyed in Gethsemane is the exact opposite of the truth.

3. A third objection to the Reformed view of the will of man is Paul's saying that he could have been rejected from the will of God by losing his salvation (1 Corinthians 9: 27).

The Calvinistic error here is alleged to be that Calvinists teach that true faith and willingness to trust Christ in this world and the next can never by lost by man. Here Paul is saying that he, a true believer, could become a castaway, which Calvinists deny. So it is Calvin versus inspired Paul.

Calvinists admit that if their doctrine ever opposes the inspired testimony of the Apostle Paul, they are wrong—fatally wrong. To deny Paul is to deny God. To deny God is to perish.

But Calvinists plead innocent to the charge of opposing the teaching of the inspired Apostle. Let me cite his words again so that the reader may see whether he does say that, true believer that he is, he yet may fall.

"I buffet my body and make it my slave, lest after I have preached to others, I myself should be a castaway" (1 Corinthians 9:27). What Paul says is that if he ever stops beating his body, he will fall from his present state of grace. He does not say that he may or can ever so cease beating his body. It is no doubt tempting to Paul to cease because beating (disciplining) one's body is not easy. Paul indicates here that it is difficult. It is a fight—a fight to the finish. Paul feels many of the blows. If he is ever knocked out he is knocked out of the kingdom of God. Paul is determined never to be knocked out. He'll win the decision at the end of his life and then the battle is over forever.

At the end of his life, he said: "I have fought the good fight, I have finished the course, I have kept the faith; in the future there is laid up for me the crown of righteousness" (2 Timothy 4:7–8).

Moreover he said before the end of his life that he was persuaded! "For I am convinced that neither death, nor life, nor angels, nor principalities, nor things present, nor things to come, nor powers, nor height, nor depth, nor any other created thing, shall be able to separate us from the love of God, which is in Christ Jesus our Lord" (Romans 8:38–39).

We would find it blasphemous almost to say that Jesus Christ could ever lie. It would be blasphemous to say that the Son of God could ever, conceivably, lie. Neither did Christ say that. But He did say: "If I say I do not know Him, I shall be a liar like you" (John 8:55).

Of course, if the Son of God could say that, Paul would not

dare say otherwise of himself. And if Christ and Paul could declare the great *if*, what Christian can say otherwise?

If any professed believer did actually give himself over to
lying or yielding to sin, even that would not be a fall from grace.
It would, rather, prove that he never was in grace. "If you have
it you never lose it. If you "lose" it, you never had "it."

But didn't Demas forsake the Apostle, "having loved this
present world"? Yes, and thereby proved that he had never followed him. The appearance was real, but the following was appearance only. Even that was lost when Demas' love for this
world, which had been hidden, was revealed by his giving up
even the pretense.

But could Paul, who could never be a Demas, feel he may
have been a Demas? I think Paul could have (needlessly) feared
that he could fall though he taught and knew that true saints
never fall. So he could have erroneously feared that he was not a
true saint, on some occasion or occasions. That does not
contradict his inspired teaching that God will continue His
work in true saints till the day of judgment and forever
(Philippians 1:6).

As long as Paul was imperfect he could imperfectly believe
that he was not a true saint. He may have had to fight with that
doubt and even be uncertain about the outcome so long as he
remained an imperfect saint.

One thing was absolutely certain: if he ever ceased to fight,
he would be a castaway. Christ being perfect never doubted.
However, that did not prevent Him from saying what was
true, that if He ever became a liar, even He would be lost forever! He knew He could never become a liar, but He also knew
that if He did He would be a sinner lost forever.

So we hope it is clear to Arminians that fighting against sin
and staying in the middle of the battle, even when down for the
count of nine, where if ever one hears the count of ten he is out

forever, does not imply that one will ever hear the count of ten.

4. A fourth objection to the Reformed biblical view of the will of man is this: free will implies the possibility of the saint's losing his good will. As a free person he can always choose the evil as well as the good. If he ever becomes unable to choose the good or the evil he ceases to have free will. He, though good, can choose the evil and perish forever. If Calvinists make redeemed man unable to will the evil habitually, they have destroyed his manhood.

This was the prevailing view of the will in the eighteenth century that Jonathan Edward's masterful *Freedom of the Will* demolished classically. But the Arminians seem never to have read their obituary, or, at least, to have understood it. They keep reiterating the arguments. Jonathan Edwards put it to rest over two centuries ago. That being the sad case, let me state here the mere essence of that classic answer.

Since the Arminian view of free will is that the will spontaneously, without cause, chooses, one can see that their view is rationally absurd and soteriologically non-moral. They claim the opposite in both areas.

First, the Arminian view of free will is rationally absurd. It is absurd because it presents the will as choosing without cause or stimulus. If there is no reason for choosing, why would one choose? If there were no reason, why would the will choose? It would be choosing non-rationally. It would be making endless choices irrationally. Man's nature, since the will is but a manifestation of that, would be an irrational entity. It would be a loose cannon, occurring here, there and everywhere without cause.

Man as a chooser would be meaningless, insane. If asked why he chose this or that, this from that, his answer would be, "I had no reason." But even if he answered at all that would mean that the question caused him to answer it, unless, having no answer, he would be perpetually silent if not irrelevant or crazy. If having no cause, the person would not respond to the question and anything he said would have no relation to the question unless accidental. Nor would the questioner have any reason for this question which would emerge as an answer but could be "the moon is made of blue cheese"—though there could be no reason for saying even that. The hearer of the imagined listener would not be listening for he would have had no reason for doing so. If the notion of a free will acting freely in the Arminian way is not absurd, we cannot imagine what is (though even that charge could not arise since absurd sentences could not cause me to judge critically).

Now Arminians, not being crazy, but rational persons (in spite of their free will doctrine), cannot choose to accept this charge of absurdity. So they, invariably, charge this charge of absurdity with absurdity, while denying that the original charge of absurdity produced any deliberate response cause; they would resist, insisting that they were as sane as any.

All I am saying here in a caustic journalistic style, Jonathan Edwards spells out pedantically and oh so tediously. He even spells out the meaning of cause, so methodically that one would assume that even an Arminian would see its significance.

A second reason (as if a second were necessary) for rejecting the Arminian view of the will of man is its non-morality or immorality. It is because of its assumed morality that Arminians advocate the rationally absurd.

For the Arminian, a caused choice is a compelled choice, and a compelled choice is not a free choice of a free will. Evangelical Arminians feel this in the depth of their souls. If a choice is caused by motives, freedom is destroyed and access to the saving Gospel of Jesus Christ is destroyed with it. This is the reason above all reasons that makes evangelical Arminians the defenders of immoral irrationality. Calvinists, in their view, are

determinists, fatalists, opponents of free will, and thereby destroyers of the Gospel which they profess to love. Calvinists
destroy free will and the possibility of salvation.

Why this frightful opposition to Calvinism? It is all because
evangelical Arminians see Calvinists as destroyers of free will.
The intensely tragic thing is that Calvinists are destroyers of
free will as understood by Arminians. In their own mind,
Calvinists are thereby serving Christianity which they see
Arminians destroying. Free will is the heart of this age-long
controversy within Christianity.

Because of this I call Jonathan Edwards's *Freedom of the Will*
a gospel tract. Heavy as the book is, the author says it is a
necessary refutation of rising Arminianism with its threat to all
the doctrines of the Bible.

This indictment was not only because of the absurdity of
Arminianism, but even more because of its non-evangelical,
immoral implications. Wherein is its immorality? Christ says,
"If you love Me, keep My commandments" (John 14:15).
Arminians cannot be morally compelled by those words. If
they obeyed Christ because He commanded them to do so,
they would not be freely obeying Him. True obedience would
be destroyed if Christ's words caused followers to obey Him.
Even love could not influence them. If they chose to obey because Christ first loved them, that would be unfree, compelled,
not real faith in Christ. One cannot be moral and caused to
choose such because of Christ's love, authority, exhortation or
command.

To be moral one must choose freely; that is, without cause.
One must have no reason for coming to Jesus Christ. Coming
must not be motivated by His love, for that would be immoral
compulsion. Yet to come to Christ for no cause is immoral because the Word says: "We love, because He first loved us"
(I John 4:19).

So the very zeal of the Arminians for free will is a determined (!) opposition to the Gospel of Jesus Christ. All
Arminian acts of faith have no reason and their profession of it
is hypocritical. I do not say this of all who call themselves
Arminians, many of whom do not truly understand what they
profess. But a person who believes something for no reason or
cause is not accepting Christ's invitation. If he were responding
to Christ's invitation, he could not (according to Arminianism)
be responding to Christ's invitation. That which would appear
virtuous would, *a la* Arminianism, be truly wicked.

5. Finally, let us address a fifth objection to the Reformed
view of the will of man. There are those who argue that caused
choice of the will is a compelled choice and therefore no free and
virtuous choice. In simple words, they believe that teaching a
caused will is fatalistic. If God or circumstances cause a person
to choose, that is a determined, non-free, non-virtuous choice.
It is fatalism versus Christianity. This objection is part of the
Arminian repertoire, but it is independently maintained by
many non-Arminians.

Specifically, if God has eternally predestined these responses of men, man's choosing is not his choice, but God's
choice. Man could not choose otherwise. Man is not free to
choose as he wills, but only as God has willed. Man had no
other choice. He could not choose otherwise.

Our answer to this objection is very simple: It is mere dog-
matism. The critic asserts, on his own authority alone, that because God preordained man cannot freely choose what God has
foreordained. No argument is given. Mere assertion is no argument.

We ask, why can man not freely choose what God has foreordained? What is to prevent it? What can God not foreordain in
such a way as to do no violence to the will of man?

The critic says that if God has foreordained, man cannot

choose otherwise. Who says that man may choose to choose, no otherwise that God has chosen? I know that I am now choosing what you will later read. Knowing that God has chosen eternally that I would choose as I am now choosing does not take away my consciousness that it is my choice that pushed my pencil across the page, or sometimes punches my word-programmer, or activates my recorder. I assure my reader that no invisible force is forcing me. Interesting that I would be a plagiarist if I were only copying what someone had written an eternity before. I guarantee the reader that I am the sole author of this essay. Incidentally, its many faults show that God was not the ghost-writer. If God had pushed my pencil this would be truly inspired, which you and I know certainly is not the case. I am asking God with every line I write that He will forgive me all my faults herein and overcome them to the blessing of my readers. Any virtue in these pages I do ascribe to the influence of God on my mind and heart, and only indirectly and partly to my thinking and articulation. Praise the Lord from whom all mini-blessings flow unforced.

The critic says that I couldn't write differently if I wanted to write differently. Well, I write only what I will to write. True, I never will want to write differently than God has decreed. But His decree does not force me not to write otherwise. I simply have no desire to write otherwise. In fact, I never write or want to write differently than I am thinking at the moment. I almost wish I could blame some of my many faults on God! God does all things well, absolute proof that He never forces me to write!

Am I inferring that God did force the writers of Scripture who did write infallibly? There is something more like force in their writing. They were certainly not left to their own natural thinking alone, as I am. Nevertheless, though they were "carried along by the Holy Spirit" (2 Peter 1:21, NIV), that divine influence did not force their pens but supernaturally illumined their minds and inflamed their hearts that they themselves wrote what they saw and felt, "for no prophecy was ever made by act of the human will, but men moved by the Spirit spoke from God" (2 Peter 1:21, NASB).

I think and hope that I have answered the main, if not all the objections to this view of the will of man. I have never found any sound criticism of the will of man as the responding of the human mind according to the stimuli it receives. This is the way the will of man functions in heaven, earth and hell. Wicked wills will always find every stimulus a goad to evil willing. A saint having both a will to evil and to good will always be stimulated to a mixed response. A perfectly holy person in heaven will always find stimulations a goad to virtue.

Christians and Boycotting

I understand boycotting to mean doing no business with some essentially legitimate business because it is doing some new illegitimate business. Thus, a fast food restaurant, considered essentially legitimate, is not to be patronized while it engages in pornographic advertising, and a legitimate motel chain not patronized because it makes filthy movies available in its rooms. Further examples are not needed to elucidate the point.

Places boycotted for some new evil they introduce usually practice old evils (such as selling alcoholic beverages, cigarettes, Sunday newspapers, being open for ordinary unnecessary business on the Sabbath, advertising various synagogues of Satan for worship, not adequately opposing occupancy of its rooms by unmarried couples, having bars, and so on).

The first thing that meets the eye when Christians boycott this way is their inconsistency, which everyone (Christians included) admits is evil. That is, if a Christian boycotts a legitimate business because of *some* evil in which it engages, why does he not boycot for any and all evil in which it engages? He cannot be boycotting for some evils done when he does not boycott for other evils done. Scripture teaches us to abstain from *all* evil; but this Christian only opposes *some* evil—as if one can practice selective morality.

So it is apparently not God by His Word who controls that boycotter's life, but something else. This bears a false witness both to God and the religion the Christian believes that God has revealed.

What would the principle be, since it is not obedience to God? Clout? To show the world that organized Christianity has clout? That we can bring great companies to their knees before *us*? (It is not God, remember.)

If my definition of the "boycotting" we are discussing is sound, I cannot see how this criticism can be avoided. And if this criticism is sound, it would seem that such boycotting is a sin because it deflects the glory that belongs to God onto His servants. No servant of the Lord, whose sole goal in life is to glorify God our Savior, will *knowingly and deliberately* engage in any activity which draws glory from the One to whom it belongs to the one to whom it does *not* belong. Holding prayer meetings with mixed or pure multitudes would aggravate the situation rather than ameliorate it.

I consulted my Oxford dictionary, and found "boycott" defined as "refuse to hold relations with." How does the Christian faith apply *that* definition? First, Christians are to "refuse to hold relations with" non-believers in religion, in marriage, and in their immoral activities (2 Corinthians 6:14f). Second, they are not to "refuse to hold relations with" unbelievers in their normal, outwardly-moral activities, or we would have to go out of the world! Third, this implies that we may eat at a fast food restaurant, a given motel, etc., as long as we do not condone, approve, or support *any* immoral activies. In other words, we do not buy their cigarettes, Sunday newspapers, alcohol, or view their filthy movies on special or regular television. Fourth, this kind of boycotting would go on all the time *as an essential of being a Christian!* If all true pastors constantly reminded their people of God (who ought not to need reminding, not to mention organizing), a really effective boycott would be automatic and understood as an act of obedience to God. God's "clout" through His people would be so well understood by the wicked that they would not even be tempted to their gross evil—doing evil for sordid profit that would not be forthcoming. Through their pocketbooks they would inevitably think of the true God and, if God pleases, may be delivered out of darkness into the Kingdom of God's dear Son.

I strongly favor true, biblical boycotting of all evil all the time.